Liquidity Lost

Liquidity Lost

The Governance of the Global Financial Crisis

Paul Langley

OXFORD
UNIVERSITY PRESS

Great Clarendon Street, Oxford, OX2 6DP,
United Kingdom

Oxford University Press is a department of the University of Oxford.
It furthers the University's objective of excellence in research, scholarship,
and education by publishing worldwide. Oxford is a registered trade mark of
Oxford University Press in the UK and in certain other countries

© Paul Langley 2015

The moral rights of the author have been asserted

First published 2015
First published in paperback 2016

Published in the United States of America by Oxford University Press
198 Madison Avenue, New York, NY 10016, United States of America

British Library Cataloguing in Publication Data
Data available

Library of Congress Cataloging in Publication Data
Data available

ISBN 978–0–19–968378–9 (Hbk.)
ISBN 978–0–19–877888–2 (Pbk.)

For Grace and Tom

Preface

Sparked by the first months of the contemporary global financial crisis, the project that became this book began over six years ago. The initial focus for the project was upon the performativity of crisis management; that is, how re-iteratively naming and acting on the crisis as one of 'liquidity' served to affirm and keep in place the prevailing organization of global financial markets. I was interested in how the rendering of the crisis as a technical matter of money market liquidity enabled governance that treated the crisis as a temporary blip, as a momentary pause in three decades or so of global financial innovation centred on Wall Street and the City of London.

In early 2008, I applied for a Visiting Fellowship to study liquidity at Durham University's Institute of Advanced Study (IAS), with a view to con-tributing to the IAS 2009–10 research theme of 'Water'. I was very fortunate that my application for an IAS Fellowship was successful. The Institute pro-vided a wonderful research environment during the winter months of 2010. However, much had changed in between times. The crisis entered a period of such intensity in the autumn of 2008 that the edifice of global finance genuinely appeared to be on the brink of collapse. From the point of view of my project, the spiralling crisis produced a sprawling array of crisis governance initiatives that went far beyond the so-called 'liquidity injections' of the central banks. By June 2009, for instance, the Bank of England calculated that the cost of the complex and multiple public commitments made in the course of crisis management in the United States, United Kingdom, and Eurozone already ran to US$14 trillion, equivalent to around half of the combined annual gross domestic product (GDP) of these economies.

Given that crises of banking and finance are typically defined in economic theory and market practice as liquidity crises, it was especially revealing that the contemporary crisis could not be contained through the terms and tech-niques of liquidity. The loss of liquidity proved to be much more than merely an abrupt and momentary halt to global financial circulations that was amen-able to the long-established last resort lending facilities of the central banks. When liquidity was lost in the contemporary crisis, that which made the flows of global finance possible—narratives, confidences, business models, monet-ary policies, regulatory policies, and so on—also unravelled and ruptured. As it transpired, then, the Visiting Fellowship at Durham's IAS provided an opportunity for me to pause and reconsider the parameters of my project, and to do so amid the ongoing struggle to control the crisis. I would like to thank Susan J. Smith for encouraging my application to the Water theme, and the IAS Directors and the other Visiting Fellows of 2009–10—especially Ash Amin, Colin Bain, Stefan Helmreich, and Marilyn Strathern—for our conversations.

The completion of *Liquidity Lost* is the result of the support I have subsequently received from a large number of people. Most recently, since October 2011, I have benefitted greatly from the rich intellectual environment provided by my colleagues and students at the Department of Geography, Durham University, and a period of research leave from teaching and administrative duties within which to complete the book. Thanks are also due my previous colleagues at the University of York and Northumbria University. Jacquie Best, Donncha Marron, and three anonymous advisers provided very helpful feedback on my initial attempts to write an introductory chapter, and to frame the book's enduring contribution. David Musson from Oxford University Press again showed great faith in my work, and Clare Kennedy ensured that the book passed through the final stages.

The fieldwork that contributed towards this book included a total of twenty-two research interviews. Representatives of HM Treasury, the Financial Services Authority, and the commercial banking and investment management industries provided interviews in London during September 2011. Representatives of the Federal Deposit and Insurance Corporation, Federal Reserve Bank of New York, *New York Times*, Securities and Exchange Commission, and the banking, fund management, and securitization industries provided interviews in New York and Washington, DC, during March 2012. Confidentiality prevents me from thanking the individuals concerned. I hope this book does justice to the understandings and sharp insights that they were kind enough to share with me.

Many draft papers, individual chapters, and less formal presentations upon which this book is based have been delivered in various settings since 2008. These have included: Association of American Geographers annual conferences in 2009, 2012, and 2013; the 2008 CRESC Annual Conference, and the CRESC conference on 'Finance in Crisis/Finance in Question' in 2010; conferences of the Critical Finance Studies network, hosted by University of Amsterdam (2010) and Stockholm Business School (2013); a number of workshops and seminars hosted by the Department of Politics and International Studies, Warwick University, most notably, 'Political Economy of the Sub-Prime Crisis' (2008) and 'Financial Resilience in the Wake of the Crisis' (2013); 'Political Economy, Financialization, and Discourse Theory', Cardiff University Business School, 2009; the Social Studies of Finance Association Conference held in Paris in 2010; the Royal Dutch Academy of Science

Interdisciplinary Summer Course of 2010, organized by Ewald Engelen of the University of Amsterdam; the School of Geography Seminar Series, Nottingham University, 2011; 'Economization of Uncertainty', University of Helsinki, 2011; 'Understanding Crisis in Europe Workshop', University of Bristol and University of the West of England, 2012; 'Methodologies of Everyday Life and International Political Economy', University of Copenhagen, 2012; 'Temporalities of Debt and Guilt', COST Action ISO902 Workshop, University of Hamburg, 2012; and 'Regulation, Law Enforcement and the Financial Crisis', Max Planck Institute for Foreign and International Criminal Law, 2012. I would particularly like to thank the following people for their invitations to speak, supportive comments, questions, provocations, and private correspondence: Ben Anderson, Thomas Bay, Nina Boy, James Brassett, Chris Clarke, Stephen Collier, Adam Dixon, Ismail Erturk, Shaun French, Daniela Gabor, Csaba Gyoery, Marieke de Goede, Joyce Goggin, Sarah Hall, Eric Helleiner, Laura Horn, Mark Kear, Turo-Kimmo Lehtonen, Martijn Konings, Andrew Leyshon, Bill Maurer, Randy Martin, Liz McFall, John Morris, Ben Rosamond, and Hugh Willmott.

Earlier versions of some of the material contained in the book has also been published previously: 'The performance of liquidity in the sub-prime mortgage crisis', *New Political Economy*, 15, 1: 71–98 (doi:10.1080/13563460903553624); 'Toxic assets, turbulence, and biopolitical security: Governing the crisis of global financial circulation', *Security Dialogue*, 44, 2: 111–26 (doi:10.1177/0967010613479425); and 'Anticipating uncertainty, reviving risk? On the stress testing of finance in crisis', *Economy and Society*, 42, 1: 51–73 (doi:10.1080/03085147.2012.686719). In all cases, the journal editors and anonymous reviewers who commented on my submissions pushed me to tighten up my arguments in the course of publication, so I would like to express my gratitude to them. The author would also like to thank Taylor & Francis and Sage for permission to reproduce copyright material.

My final words of thanks must go to my family: Lou, Grace, and Tom. This book has benefitted immeasurably from Lou's knowledge of social theory and burgeoning book collection, as well as her unwavering love and support. She also knows a thing or two about the logic of the derivative. Grace has moved into double-digits during the time that it has taken to complete this book. She is kind, wise, and, thankfully, very patient. My enduring memory of the 2008 high point of the global financial crisis will always be of watching it unfold on late-night television news, accompanied only by our newborn son Tom. He has since had to ask, on far too many occasions, 'have you finished your book yet, Dad?'

PL

Contents

List of Abbreviations

ABS	asset-backed securities
AIG	American International Group
A-IRB	Advanced-Internal Ratings-Based
AMLF	Asset-Backed Commercial Paper Money Market Mutual Fund Liquidity Facility
APF	Asset Purchase Facility
BCBS	Basel Committee on Banking Supervision
BHC	bank holding company
BIS	Bank for International Settlements BRF Bank Recapitalization Fund
BRF	Bank Recapitalization Fund
CAP	Capital Assistance Program
CBO	Congressional Budget Office
CCAR	Comprehensive Capital Analysis and Review
CDOs	collateralized debt obligations
CDS	credit default swaps
CEBS	Committee of European Bank Supervisors
CFTC	Commodity Futures Trading Commission
CMBS	commercial mortgage-backed securities
COLR	capital of last resort
CPFF	Commercial Paper Funding Facility
CPP	Capital Purchase Program
DMO	Debt Management Office
EBA	European Banking Authority
ECB	European Central Bank
EU	European Union
FCIC	Financial Crisis Inquiry Commission
FDIC	Federal Deposit Insurance Corporation
FPC	Financial Policy Committee
FRB	Federal Reserve Board

FSA	Financial Services Authority
FSOC	Financial Stability Oversight Counsel
FSB	Financial Stability Board
G-7	Group of 7
G-20	Group of 20
G-30	Group of 30
GDP	gross domestic product
GMAC	General Motors Acceptance Corporation
HBOS	Halifax Bank of Scotland
IASB	International Accounting Standards Board
ICB	Independent Commission on Banking
IMF	International Monetary Fund
LCR	liquidity coverage ratio
LIBOR	London Interbank Offered Rate
LOLR	lender of last resort
MBS	mortgage-backed securities
MMIFF	Money Market Investor Funding Facility
MMLR	market maker of last resort
MPC	Monetary Policy Committee
NAO	National Audit Office
OBR	Office for Budget Responsibility
OCC	Office of the Comptroller of the Currency
OECD	Organization for Economic Cooperation and Development
OIS	overnight index swaps
OMO	open market operation
OTS	Office of Thrift Supervision
OWS	Occupy Wall Street
PDCF	Primary Dealer Credit Facility
PERAB	President's Economic Recovery Advisory Board
P-PIP	Public-Private Investment Program
PRA	Prudential Regulation Authority
QE	quantitative easing
RBS	Royal Bank of Scotland
RTC	Resolution Trust Corporation
SCAP	Supervisory Capital Assessment Program
SEC	Securities Exchange Commission

List of Abbreviations

SIV	structured investment vehicle
SLS	Special Liquidity Scheme
SNB	Swiss National Bank
SSF	social studies of finance
STS	science and technology studies
TAF	Term Auction Facility
TALF	Term Asset-Backed Securities Loan Facility
TARP	Troubled Assets Relief Program
T-bills	Treasury bills
T-bonds	Treasury bonds
TSLF	Term Securities Lending Facility
UK	United Kingdom
US	United States of America
VaR	value-at-risk
VAT	value-added tax
VIX	Chicago Board Options Exchange Volatility Index

1

Introduction

Present across official, popular, and critical academic imaginations, a consensus prevails in understandings of the governance of the contemporary global financial crisis. While debates rage over the causes and consequences of the crisis that began in the summer of 2007, the means and ends of the initiatives which sought to manage the crisis have been consistently explained in essentially the same terms. The governance of the global financial crisis appears to be a set of emergency and historically unprecedented actions undertaken by sovereign state institutions, especially the central banks, treasuries, and regulatory institutions in the United States of America (US) and United Kingdom (UK). The purpose of these interventions would also seem apparent: to rescue the markets, the banks, and finance capital. In short, the consensus holds that the governance of the contemporary global financial crisis was a matter of the state saving capitalist markets from themselves, and of the public socialization of private losses.

This book provides an alternative account of the how the global financial crisis was governed from 2007 through to 2011. It shares with the prevailing perception a focus upon the management of the crisis in the US and the UK: not only was the crisis 'made in America', but the global dominance of the US dollar and the global reach of Wall Street and the City of London is such that, in effect and in the first instance, Anglo-American crisis governance was global crisis governance. The book's remit thus does not extend to the ways in which the crisis was governed as the eye of the storm travelled latterly to the Euro currency area. It also does not look elsewhere—to interstate groupings (e.g. the Group of 20, G-20), international organizations (e.g. the Bank for International Settlements, BIS), and private transnational associations (e.g. the Group of 30, G-30)—in order to explore the principal mechanisms through which the crisis was managed (Germain 2010; Helleiner et al. 2010; McKeen-Edwards and Porter 2013; Porter 2014). Rather, the book offers an analysis that will make Anglo-American global crisis management intelligible in a different way. It will show that the consensus, which casts sovereign state institutions as salvaging markets, serves to conceal a great deal more than it reveals about how the global financial crisis was governed. And, although one of the results of crisis management has indeed been that its costs are now being unequally and unevenly socialized on both sides of the Atlantic, the book will show that to understand crisis governance in these terms is to confuse its consequences with the contingent processes and practices through which it was enacted.

The book's challenge to the consensus over the governance of the crisis of global finance is also a challenge to the deeply engrained frameworks of thought upon which that consensus is founded. Economics and political economy feature fundamental disagreements over whether stabilizing actions in times of crisis can and should be avoided, or whether they are indeed inherent to capitalist finance. Yet, these otherwise sharply contending fields contain significant shared assumptions about financial crisis management that, whether explicitly acknowledged or not, lead to startlingly similar accounts of the governance of the contemporary crisis. As Chapter 2 will outline, for both economics and political economy, it is the sovereign institutions of the state which are the agents that engineer crisis management, and the perennial aim in moments of rupture is to restore the circulations of the markets, banking, and finance capital. As will be encountered across Chapters 3 to 8, moreover, this consensus tends to frame explanations of the specific interventions that were made in an attempt to control the contemporary crisis, from the so-called 'liquidity injections' of central banks as monetary sovereigns, to the austerity programmes of treasuries as fiscal sovereigns.

The book's analysis of the governance of the global financial crisis is grounded not in economics and political economy, then, but in the field of cultural economy. Cultural economy is an interdisciplinary academic venture which primarily covers sociology, human geography, anthropology, and business and organizational studies (Amin and Thrift 2004; Bennett et al. 2008; du Gay and Pryke 2002). Gaining momentum over the last decade or so, it is the outcome of diverse responses to the implications of the 'cultural turn' in social theory for understandings of economy. It features, but is certainly not limited to, an interest in the efficacy of the theories and methods of science and technology studies (STS) for the study of economy (e.g. Callon 1998; Pinch and Swedberg 2008; Woolgar et al. 2009). Cultural economy has also achieved particular traction through research into financial markets that, reflecting the strong imprint of STS, is often labelled as 'the social studies of finance' (SSF) (Kalthoff 2005; Knorr Cetina and Preda 2005, 2012; MacKenzie 2009). Cultural economy and SSF do not provide, however, a ready-made and established set of conceptual tools for thinking anew about the governance of the global financial crisis. The book's analytical motivations are thus intertwined with a further purpose: to develop the conceptual means by which the management of financial crises can be understood in the terms of SSF and cultural economy.

The severe turbulence of the contemporary crisis caught SSF somewhat off-guard. SSF consolidated during a period of financialized economic growth. Intensifying across three decades or so, and propelled by compounding asset bubbles which centred on stock markets and latterly on real estate and debt markets, these processes came to an abrupt halt in the crisis. While finance was booming, there was little to question the preoccupation of SSF with the socio-technical processes through which markets are made, and with what Calişkan and Callon (2009, 2010) define as the research agenda of 'economization' and 'marketization'. Government programmes and regulatory authorities did occasionally feature in SSF accounts of these processes in new markets, but tended to remain an unopened 'black box' while the seemingly self-regulating financial markets being studied were forging ahead (MacKenzie 2005). Explanations of regulatory change, and the politics therein, were largely left to political economists, although not all in that field were satisfied with such a division of labour (e.g. Konings 2010). As a consequence, and despite being in a position to provide insightful and distinctive accounts of the unravelling of markets once the crisis hit (e.g. Langley 2008a; MacKenzie 2011; Poon 2009), SSF developed something of an analytical blind-spot to the kinds of governance interventions which held finance together as boom turned to bust.

The actions of crisis management can be conceived of, however, in the terms favoured by SSF. There was, for example, no blueprint for controlling the crisis; governance was typically tentative and incremental, and often featured the kind of *in vivo* experiments that are also present in processes of marketization (Beuneza et al. 2006; Muniesa and Callon 2007). Crisis management also brought together fragments of old and new ideas, techniques from the past, and long forgotten and freshly minted institutional and legislative provisions; in other words, like marketized actions, governance actions had to be assembled (Hardie and MacKenzie 2007), and were put together in a process akin to the *bricolage* of financial market innovation (Engelen et al. 2011). Attempts to control the crisis were also marked by the materiality and power of 'market devices' (Muniesa et al. 2007)—such as, for instance, bank balance sheets—that actively calculated and literally figured the crisis; again, similar to marketization processes, governance was thoroughly socio-technical (MacKenzie 2009; Preda 2009). Therefore, it is by broadening the vision of the SSF, and by reaching out to what Michael Pryke and Paul du Gay (2007) call a 'cultural economy of finance' to enable this task, that the book develops an alternative account of the management of the global financial crisis.

As it targets the consensus view on crisis governance, the book's analytical and conceptual motivations also fold into a political purpose. For the philosopher Jacques Rancière, 'the essence of consensus...does not consist in peaceful discussion and reasonable disagreement, as opposed to conflict and violence' (2010: 42). Instead, as he continues, at the core of consensus is 'the distribution of the sensible' and 'the annulment of dissensus'; that is, limits are placed on what is thinkable, sayable, and doable by dominant perceptions which serve to close down political space for dissent. Thus, the consensus on crisis governance certainly did not prevent debate in the course of the crisis, and neither does it prevent ongoing deliberations. As will be shown throughout Chapters 3 to 8, how best to govern the problems of the crisis was the subject of considerable uncertainty and dispute among economists, media analysts, bureaucrats, and politicians. And, at the time of writing in early 2014, the consensus continues to create scope for disagreement: on either side of the Atlantic, politics now centres on how the state can best be configured in response to a vast array of post-crisis problems, whether monetary, fiscal, or regulatory. Consider, for example, present debates over curtailing the so-called 'quantitative easing' (QE) of 'unconventional' monetary policy, the effectiveness and consequences of fiscal austerity, and achieving the right balance between regulatory capital requirements and the supply of credit in banking.

Nonetheless, by separating out hierarchical domains of practice and functions in such a way that crisis governance is taken to be, by definition, the sovereign institutions of the state acting upon malfunctioning markets, the consensus produced (and continues to produce) a closure of the space for political dissent. What this boiled down to was 'the assertion that there is a specific place for politics' that 'can be nothing but the place of the state' (Rancière 2010: 43). 'Conflicts' over how the crisis should be governed were reduced to technical and liberal pluralist questions over the 'problems to be resolved by learned expertise and the negotiated adjustment of interests' (2010: 71). Revealing, in this respect, is the bewilderment and frustration that was typically provoked by the most significant expression of dissent that emerged to contest Anglo-American global crisis governance: the Occupy Wall Street (OWS) movement.

Media coverage struggled to explain the OWS encampment at Zuccotti Park from mid-September to mid-November 2011, largely because it did not articulate a clear set of demands and interests that could be translated into specific policy actions, or reconciled through the political processes of the state (see Catapano 2011). Some academic supporters of the claims that OWS made on behalf of 'the people' and 'the ninety-nine per cent' also cast doubt on the efficacy of the movement because it spurned leadership hierarchies and a strategic agenda for future action (e.g. Žižek 2011). However, in the terms of

Rancière (2011: 13), 'the framing of a future happens in the wake of political invention rather than being its condition of possibility'. Emancipatory politics is a matter of opening up new possibilities and the prospects for the creation of political subjectivities, and not the designing of a new order to come. Indeed, as a range of academic analyses suggest, what was radical and significant about OWS was precisely that it interrupted and disturbed the precepts and practices of crisis governance (e.g. Douzinas 2013; Harcourt 2013). As a contribution to this dissensus, the book is clearly modest. Yet, when offering a creative, analytical, and conceptual contribution that unsettles how the governance of the global financial crisis might be understood, the book also seeks to be an inventive, political contribution towards the redistribution of the sensible in the post-crisis organization of global finance.

By way of an overview of what follows, Chapter 2 begins by elaborating upon the methodological and conceptual tools that are employed throughout. Underpinning the book's research and analysis is Michel Foucault's (2003a) method of problems and problematization. Emerging in his later work, this is a method that extends the archaeological and genealogical approaches that Foucault (1972) previously developed, after Nietzsche, in order to interrogate power-knowledge relations and discursive formations. It is a method that explicitly directs inquiry to consider the ways in which problem-objects are abstracted, such that they can be acted on through apparent solutions. Putting the method to work here, crisis governance is not explored as a set of institutional interventions taken in the face of materially evident crisis circumstances. Rather, researching how the crisis was rendered governable requires careful attention to the contingent manner in which it was made up and managed, as a number of relatively discrete technical problems that each required their own dedicated response and which delimited and depoliticized crisis governance.

Chapter 2 also begins to develop the conceptual anchor point for the book's analysis of financial crisis governance; that is, the concern with agency and action which intersects a variety of approaches to cultural economy (McFall 2008; Pryke and du Gay 2007). For cultural economists, what is typically thought of as 'agency', 'as the capacity to act and to give meaning to action' (Callon 2005: 4), is not centred upon and possessed by institutions and persons, such as firms, managers, banks, financial market traders, and consumers. Instead, cultural economy research employs a variety of categories that are broadly united in conceiving of agency as decentred and distributed, relational and compounded. Agency is thus a processual hybrid that requires connections between 'human beings (bodies) as well as material, technical and textual devices', all of which are 'mobilized' and 'take part in the action' (Calişkan and Callon 2010: 9). As extant research in SSF attests, cultural economy conceptions of agency have significant implications for the analysis of marketized actions. As the book will show, these implications extend to understanding crisis governance actions which apparently centre on the agency of sovereign state officials and institutions.

Across Chapters 3 to 8, the book is structured to make visible an overarching argument: the global financial crisis was not governed as a given development, as a crisis of markets, banking, or finance capital. Rather, the crisis was abstracted as a range of provisionally figured and relatively discrete problems; namely, and primarily, as technical problems of liquidity, toxicity, solvency, risk, regulation, and debt. As Table 1 summarizes, the book's main chapters will analyse how, from summer 2007, the crisis of global finance was turned into six specific problems, each with dedicated solutions to be ostensibly

Table 1 The problems and solutions of crisis governance

Problem	Solution	Principal actions
Liquidity (money and capital markets)	Liquidity from central banks ('liquidity injections' and 'liquidity facilities')	Open market operations (OMOs) and discount window lending; programmatic interventions in money and capital markets; and quantitative easing (QE) (Federal Reserve and Bank of England, from 08/07)
Toxicity (sub-prime assets)	Temporarily remove toxic assets from circulation ('bad banks')	Maiden Lane LLC I, II, III (Federal Reserve, 03/08 and 11/08); and Troubled Assets Relief Program (TARP) (US Treasury, 10/08)
Solvency (banking)	Recapitalization of banks ('bank bailouts')	Bank Recapitalization Fund and allied actions (HM Treasury and Bank of England, 10/08); Capital Purchase Program and allied actions (US Treasury and Federal Reserve, 10/08); and ad hoc bailouts of individual institutions in both US and UK
Risk (probabilistic risk management)	Anticipatory techniques ('stress testing')	Supervisory Capital Assessment Program (Federal Reserve, Federal Deposit Insurance Corporation, Office of the Comptroller of the Currency, 02/09)
Regulation (banks and depository institutions)	Structural regulatory reform ('Glass–Steagall lite' and separation of retail from 'casino banking')	'Volcker rule' (President's Economic Recovery Advisory Board (01/10), Dodd–Frank Wall Street Reform and Consumer Protection Act, 07/10); and 'Vickers' ring-fence' (Independent Commission on Banking, 09/11, Banking Reform Act, 12/13)
Debt (sovereign debt)	Fiscal deficit reductions ('austerity')	'Emergency budget' (HM Treasury, 06/10); 2011 Budget and National Commission on Fiscal Responsibility and Reform (02/10); and Budget Control Act (08/11).

enacted by the state. Chapter 3 begins at the beginning, so to speak, by analysing how the crisis was rendered and governed as a seizure of liquidity in money and capital markets. Financial crises are typically understood—by definition, and by economists of various hues—as liquidity crises. That the crisis could not be controlled as a liquidity problem, even when it was acted on in ways that broke the mould of the established last resort lending practices of central banks, was thus especially telling as to its depth and magnitude. The loss of liquidity was not merely an abrupt halt in the circulations of global finance that authorities sought to repair. It was also a moment when that which made those circulations possible—narratives, confidences, calculations, business models, monetary policies, regulatory policies, and so on—also unravelled and ruptured.

Although Chapters 4 to 8 address the ensuing struggle to forge and manage the crisis in other ways and once liquidity had been lost, this series is only chronological in broad terms. It is certainly not the intention of the book, as is the case in some official and academic accounts (e.g. BIS 2008, 2009, 2010; Thompson 2012), to present the crisis as a number of identifiable phases to which authorities marshalled their corresponding responses. The diagnosis and treatment of the crisis as problems of liquidity and toxic assets did indeed largely precede the puzzle of bank solvency, for instance, and the crisis has settled-out most recently as a problem of sovereign debt which apparently requires fiscal austerity measures by way of obligatory solution. However, and alongside the problems of liquidity, toxicity, and solvency, the attempts to govern the crisis as problems of both risk and regulation that eventually gained traction during 2009 had been largely ongoing from the end of 2007.

To underline the contribution of the book in another way, it does not seek to be an exhaustive empirical survey of financial crisis management, as enacted in its Anglo-American heartland between 2007 and 2011. Not only would this arguably be beyond the scope of any single book, it is also not my motivation here. Neither does the book offer technical assessments of the success, or otherwise, of this or that intervention in achieving a resolution to the crisis. This is not a book that is concerned with making an academic contribution to lesson learning about how future crises might be managed more effectively (cf. Davies and Green 2010; Goodhart 2009; Griffith-Jones et al. 2010; Turner et al. 2010; Wolf 2008a). Instead, as it works towards a cultural economy account of how the crisis was governed as a series of problems, the book develops a line of inquiry set out by Peter Miller and Nikolas Rose in their agenda for the study of 'governing economic life'. As they understand it, given the tendencies for the liberal governing of economic life to be 'eternally optimistic' and 'a congenitally failing operation', 'The "will to govern" needs to be understood less in terms of its success than in terms of the difficulties of operationalizing it' (1990: 10–11). Thus, and as Chapter 9 underscores by way of conclusion, what is of interest here is how crisis governance emerged as an achievement in and of itself, and not whether it can be said to have functioned successfully or to have achieved its stated ends.

What the book will show is that the governance of the global financial crisis was enacted with great difficulty through relatively distinct, problem-orientated apparatuses of governance. As provisional and multiple attempts to prevent the unravelling of global finance, these apparatuses were strategic but distributed and relational forms of agency. They clearly featured sovereign state institutions, but were certainly not reducible to them. As they framed and acted upon the crisis, each governance apparatus mobilized and assembled a number of specific elements in relation. Chapters 3 to 8 will draw out these specificities: what did it take, for example, for an apparatus to come together which rendered the crisis governable as a technical problem of liquidity? Across these chapters, moreover, the book will also argue that the discrete apparatuses of crisis governance had certain tendencies which they shared to a greater or lesser degree. That which the consensus on sovereign states salvaging markets conceals is, therefore, not merely the contingent and fragmented ways in which the crisis was governed as a series of problems. It also obscures the very character and content of crisis governance; that is, the proclivities that were typically present as each apparatus of governance was assembled, and the ordering preferences that were largely common across them.

As state institutions were mobilized in crisis governance apparatuses, what was especially notable was how sovereign monetary, fiscal, and regulatory techniques were reconfigured. The prevailing perception of crisis management imagines dormant sovereign powers—'sent to the oblivion of history by the apologists of market fundamentalism' prior to the crisis, according to Castells et al. (2012: 3)—being wielded on an unprecedented scale by state institutions. The crisis thus appears to usher in a 'return of the state' (Eppler 2009; Grewal 2010; Plender 2008), and to produce a welcome shift in the 'balance' between state and market, or public and private authority, in favour of the former (e.g. Germain 2012). As the then President of France, Nicolas Sarkozy, put it in a speech made at the height of the crisis in September 2008, 'Self-regulation is finished. *Laissez faire* is finished. The all-powerful market that is always right is finished' (in Thornhill 2008). What this dichotomous thinking obscures, however, is not only the 'permanent activity, vigilance and intervention' of the state during the preceding boom years (Foucault 2008: 246), but how sovereign monetary, fiscal, and regulatory techniques were dynamically transformed in order that they could be put to work in the governance of the bust.

The apparatuses of crisis management also did not stand apart from and govern over the economy of markets and banks, but actually enrolled the discourses and devices of economy. The crisis was certainly a moment of disaster for economic science as a discipline that, over the last forty years in particular, perfected theories that made powerful explanatory claims about the financial markets (e.g. *Economist* 2009b; Fine and Milonakis 2011). But, the same cannot be said for economics that, in its original and ancient formulation of *oikonomia*, is a practical and managerial disposition for administering order (Agamben 2011; Mitchell 2008). The knowledges, terms, and techniques of economics were immanent to the administration of the crisis. This is not to argue, however, that crisis governance should be understood simply as the imposition of a consistent economic theory, ideology, and political programme. It is in these instrumental terms that, following a roughly twelve-month period of 'Keynesian schadenfreude' at the peak of the tumult (Elliott 2009; Stiglitz 2008a), the persistence of neo-liberal economic policies tends to be explained by much critical academic commentary on the crisis (e.g. Crouch 2011; Gamble 2009; Hall 2011; Harvey 2010; Mirowski 2013, Peck 2013a). Crisis management was broadly neo-liberal in orientation, to be sure: when extensively mustering sovereign techniques, it held firm ordering preferences not only for the market exchange of classical liberalism, but for the competitive and entrepreneurial market society of neo-liberalism (Foucault 2008: 145–7). However, crisis governance revealed more about the power of economics as a means of administration than it did about the grip of neo-liberalism as a coherent body of economic thought. The specific economic discourses that were activated, as governmental apparatuses both framed problems and proffered solutions, were multiple, fragmented, and, at times, contradictory. And, significantly, crisis management also mobilized a diverse array of calculative devices of economy that were already at large within the financial markets when crisis came, not least because they provided quantitative, material indicators of the extent and nature of the problems at hand.

While the management of the crisis was replete with all manner of measures and metrics, what also characterized the relatively discrete governance apparatuses was that they sought to elicit an affective atmosphere of confidence. The contemporary crisis certainly gave impetus to academic explanations that seek to bring emotions and collective affective energies to front and centre in the study of financial markets, typically as a corrective to orthodox economic assumptions about the rationality of market agents. For instance, behavioural economics, which stressed tendencies to 'irrational exuberance' in the 'new economy' stock market bubble at the turn of the millennium (Shiller 2001), again had ample grist for its mill when the crisis hit (Heukelom and Sent 2010; Shiller 2008). Longer-standing Keynesian insights into the 'animal spirits' that move markets were also given a new lease of life and scientific sheen when combined with the psychological methods of behaviouralism (Akerlof and

Shiller 2009). The crisis also rejuvenated the interests of sociologists in market emotions (Berezin 2009; Pixley 2012; Swedberg 2012). And, calls have been made for SSF to address the field's neglect of the affective forces that, in conjunction with the calculations of market devices, make market action possible (Callon 2012; Zaloom 2008). What this book will show, however, is that such calls for the study of financial markets to pay greater attention to emotional and/or affective dynamics largely miss the point: inciting an atmosphere of confidence in order to reanimate finance was a crucial concern in crisis governance. Without drawing on a clear body of economic thought to specify what 'confidence' is, or why conditions of confidence are crucial for financial flows, governance apparatuses often attempted to work on and through its generative energies.

Moreover, apparatuses did not govern the crisis as a dislocation of market, banking, or financial capital circulations per se, but as posing a fundamental threat to the financialized security of the population in which those uncertain circulations are deeply implicated. The governance of the crisis as a security dilemma in Anglo-America was a matter of restarting, and keeping in motion, the vital and turbulent flows of global finance because of the opportunities that they apparently afford for the wealth and well-being of society. Crisis governance operated, in short, at the interstices of 'finance/security' (de Goede 2010, 2012; also Aitken 2007; Amoore 2011; Boy et al. 2011; Lobo-Guerrero 2011; Martin 2007). What was to be secured was not merely the markets, the banks, and the financing of the productive economy that they are said to provide for, but the continuation of three decades or so of popular stock market investment and privatized pensions, on the one hand, and the expanded and widespread availability of mortgage loans and consumer credit, on the other (Langley 2008b). The governance of the crisis was, in short, a range of ordering interventions that attempted to ensure the persistence of the global circulations of a particular, valued form of Anglo-American, neo-liberal life.

Although the legacies of crisis management continue to play out, it is clear at present that new means of modulating the intensities of global financial circulations and of preparing for the eventualities of the next financial crisis did emerge from the apparatuses of crisis governance. Viewed in the round, the heat of crisis management did not produce a consistent vision of emboldened state institutions ruling out or reigning in the uncertain circulations of global finance, or an associated return to precautionary techniques for addressing the future threats of another financial crisis. There has been no coherent or explicit attempt to crisis-proof finance. Instead, and alongside the consolidation of certain supposed crisis-relieving actions into longer-term agendas for monetary and fiscal policymaking (i.e. QE, austerity), crisis governance heralded change in the mechanisms designed to 'modulate'

(Deleuze 1992) and to 'mitigate' (Collier 2008) the destructive forces of uncertain global financial circulations. Previously nascent or marginal techniques were brought to the fore and became mainstream in global finance, broadly paralleling developments witnessed across a range of other domains over the course of the last decade or so (Amoore 2013; Anderson 2010; Walters 2006).

As Chapters 5, 6, and 7 will show, rendering the crisis governable as problems of solvency, risk, and regulation provided, in particular, a significant spur to the development of techniques that govern through, as opposed to against, uncertainty. These are the techniques which have been corralled into governmental programmes designed to advance the 'resilience' of banks and banking systems, and to offer a 'macro-prudential' approach to financial stability and regulation. To date, and in sum, the bequest of crisis governance has been a will to put in place new technical fixes capable of reconciling the vicissitudes of global financial circulations with the prospects that they seemingly hold for wealth creation and popular security.

2

Financial Crisis Governance

Introduction: 'central bank and government interventions' to 'normalize credit'

> Increasing pressures on the financial system have prompted wide-ranging central bank and government interventions. While the ultimate goal of these interventions has been to help normalize credit conditions and thereby the resumption of sustainable economic growth, their immediate aim was to restore confidence in the financial system.
>
> International Monetary Fund, *Global Financial Stability Report: Navigating the Financial Challenges Ahead*, October 2009: 117

When looking back across the very costly, multiple, and complex crisis management measures of the preceding two years, the International Monetary Fund (IMF) provides a particularly succinct and illustrative example of the consensus on the governance of the contemporary global financial crisis. It is in terms such as those expressed by the IMF (2009) that, both during the tumult and subsequently, crisis governance has been perceived in official circles, the popular imagination, and critical academic analyses alike. For the IMF, the means of crisis governance were 'wide-ranging central bank and government interventions'. Similarly, the popular perception is of politicians and bureaucrats undertaking a public bailout of the banks, funded by the printing of money and the burdening of taxpayers. Critical academic accounts largely concur, as they stress and interrogate the often historically unprecedented actions of sovereign monetary and fiscal authorities, alongside the seemingly limited regulatory response to the crisis. The ends of crisis governance, meanwhile, were to 'restore confidence in the financial system' and thus to 'normalize credit conditions', according to the IMF. Likewise, the popular view is of actions that served to restart the markets and maintain a status quo dominated by Wall Street and the City of London. And, in critical academic studies, the purpose of crisis management appears to be the resuscitation of the circulations of global banking and financial markets, largely in their pre-crisis, neo-liberal capitalist form.

In contrast with the consensus, this opening chapter will make three initial steps towards the book's alternative analysis of how the contemporary global financial crisis was governed. The first section below will show how customary perceptions of crisis management rest, explicitly or otherwise, on deep-seated assumptions that are shared by economics and political economy. Official and mainstream explanations and expressly critical academic interventions thus essentially converge upon a largely singular framing, as the sovereign institutions of the state are positioned as the agents of crisis management which serves to restore the circulations of finance. The second and third sections mark out the broad contours of a cultural economy approach, and thereby provide foundations for an analysis of financial crisis governance that does not begin from the assumptions shared by economics and political economy. The focus for the second section is upon the method of problems and problematization, a feature of the later work of Michel Foucault (2003a). Rather than taking crisis governance for granted as a set of sovereign institutional interventions made in the face of materially evident crisis circumstances, the method calls for attention to the ways in which the crisis could be made amenable to particular solutions only once it was transformed into a series of problems. The final section of the chapter builds on debates in cultural economy that conceive of agency and the capacity for action as not simply possessed by persons and institutions, but as a strategic and relational assemblage. It shows how such a conception of agency can inform an analysis of the problem-centred governance of the global financial crisis, an analysis in which the crisis is understood to be rendered governable through distinct *dispositif* (apparatuses). It also draws out a range of insights from these and allied debates in order to begin to identify certain tendencies that, present across each of the apparatuses of crisis governance to a greater or lesser degree, will be further explored and elaborated in subsequent chapters.

The Economics and Political Economy of Financial Crisis Governance

In real-time media reports and subsequent book-length treatments by journalists, commentators, and insiders, the actions which attempted to govern the global financial crisis in Anglo-America appear to be decisions taken by key politicians and bureaucrats, often in negotiation with leading figures from Wall Street and the City of London. Such popular accounts of the crisis represent a particular genre of writing practice that, as John O'Brien (2011: 291) notes, entails 'narrative conventions' that 'elide the distinction between persons and things, making the operations of finance into acts of personal imaginative engagement'. Newspaper and magazine cartoons during the crisis, for example, consistently pictured state officials as emergency workers of one kind or another, or what Vincent Reinhart (2011: 72) calls 'a sort of Corps of Financial Engineers': fire-fighters wielding hoses spraying out water or dollars; embattled lifeboat crews heading out across choppy seas; and surgeons operating on near-death and Frankenstein-like financial bodies. Similarly, books by insiders and journalists tend to begin by listing their cast of characters (e.g. Barofsky 2012; Lowenstein 2010; Sorkin 2010). Portrayed variously as heroic, corrupted, and as possessing or lacking the insight necessary to their task, these are the individual agents who feature in blow-by-blow descriptions of the crisis and its management.

Official speeches, press releases, and reports made during the course of the crisis, along with mainstream and critical academic analyses, do not concentrate upon the persons and personalities of crisis management. Through a focus on institutional actions, they nonetheless reinforce the state-centred portrayal of crisis governance present in insider and journalist accounts. Images of state officials as emergency workers are replaced by 'the state' as 'emergency responder' (Berlant 2011). Foundational in official and academic accounts is the notion of the 'lender of last resort' (LOLR). The term lender of last resort can be traced to Sir Francis Baring's 1797 book, *Observations on the Establishment of the Bank of England* (Humphrey and Keleher 2002: 79). Here Baring refers to the Bank as 'the dernier resort', an adaptation 'from the French *dernier ressort*, the legal jurisdiction beyond which it is impossible to take an appeal' (Kindleberger 1996: 146). Shortly thereafter, in 1802, Henry Thornton (2002) provided the first explicit attempt to articulate the idea of the LOLR. In doing so, however, Thornton was actually arguing for limits to be placed on the monetary and financial practices of the Bank of England, and not for their extension (Knafo 2013: 128–33). In the context of the suspension of gold convertibility and war with Napoleonic France, the Bank was at the forefront of a rapid expansion of banknote issuance which Thornton, an advocate of the gold standard, wished to see curtailed. Unlike most of his bullionist contemporaries, Thornton also wanted the Bank to utilize the powers granted to it by the sovereign in a quite different way.

It is Walter Bagehot's (2008) *Lombard Street* of 1873, however, that is widely acknowledged as making the most influential arguments in favour of central bank action in the face of financial crises (King 2010). The Bank of England of which Bagehot wrote was a private bank that enjoyed the privileges of its monopoly position. His arguments centred on the public role that it should play, in the context of a burgeoning banking sector at home and the growing global role of the City of London. As Samuel Knafo (2013: 157–8) summarizes, while the notion of LOLR 'had been used in earlier debates', in often negative terms, 'as a way to describe the financial system and its reliance on the Bank', by the latter half of the nineteenth century it 'took on an increasingly programmatic aspect as financiers campaigned to extend the responsibilities of the Bank of England towards the rest of the financial community'. Exercising those responsibilities fully would turn on the key techniques of central banking that the Bank was to fitfully develop amid the tight strictures of the international gold standard, including, most notably, those of the discount window and open market operations (OMOs) (2013: 159–64; see Chapter 3). Nonetheless, what *Lombard Street* most clearly articulated were a set of ideas that have subsequently come to be widely known as the 'Bagehot principle' or 'dictum' which guides the action of the central bank as LOLR: lend feely and promptly, at a penalty rate and against good collateral, to solvent but illiquid banks.

Nearly a century-and-a-half on from *Lombard Street*, Bagehot's principle continues to provide the touchstone for theoretical debates over the LOLR function among academic economists (e.g. Goodhart and Illing 2002). And, while it refers in its narrow and most widely accepted definition to the emergency liquidity operations of central banks, the LOLR idea also tends to provide a pivot for state-centric explanations of crisis governance more broadly. Consider, for example, the reflections on contemporary crisis governance offered by Paul Tucker, Deputy Governor of the Bank of England, in a conference speech delivered at the Bank of Japan in 2009. What Tucker calls 'the repertoire of official sector interventions' in the crisis is held to have been three-fold. First, it included last resort lending, 'as Bagehot would have recognized it' (2009: 2). This was accompanied, second, by the 'new territory' of the role of 'market-maker of last resort' (MMLR) (2009: 14). Also termed 'dealer of last resort' or 'investor of last resort' (Cooley et al. 2011; Mehrling 2011), central banks and treasuries as MMLR purchased all manner of 'illiquid' or 'toxic' assets in order to prevent a further collapse in their prices (see Chapters 3 and 4). Third, Tucker identifies the importance of those interventions undertaken by treasury institutions to recapitalize seemingly insolvent banks—or, more colloquially, to 'bailout' banks that were 'under water'—and labels these acts of crisis governance 'capital of last resort' (COLR) (2009: 17; see Chapter 5). While the notion of LOLR may provide scope, then, to consider and debate changing forms of crisis management, it nonetheless firmly centres the agency of crisis governance upon the institutions of the state.

A second and more recently coined idea—'moral hazard'—also features strongly as practitioners and orthodox economists cast crisis management as the preserve of the state. Providing a shorthand for doubts about the efficacy of last resort lending which have been expressed since the time of Thornton's writings (Humphrey and Keleher 2002: 82–3), moral hazard is a mutable concept. It travelled to wholesale finance from earlier applications in insurance, and came into common usage during the Mexican and Asian financial crises of the mid-to-late 1990s (Ericson et al. 2000; Leaver 2012). As the then

Chairman of the Federal Reserve, Alan Greenspan (1997), defines it, moral hazard is 'a distortion of incentives that occurs when the party that determines the level of risk receives the gains from, but does not bear the full costs of, the risks taken'. It follows from the idea of moral hazard that, as Greenspan continues, last resort lending 'should be reserved for only the rarest of disasters'. Grounded in wider and historic controversies about 'free banking' and the role of the sovereign state in the production and reproduction of monetary relations (Dowd and Timberlake 1997), moral hazard is thus cited as a warning about the management of financial crises by the state. The ever-present possibility that the state will act as LOLR in a future crisis is said to interrupt the otherwise rational risk/reward calculations and discipline of the market in the present.

During the contemporary crisis, the supposed distorting effect on market rationality of previous crisis management was found to have contributed to the excessive leverage and risk taking that fuelled the boom, and to have spurred the growth of market institutions which proved 'too big to fail' in the bust (e.g. Dowd and Hutchinson 2010). Moral hazard was also invoked by economists who argued against LOLR interventions made during the crisis by the Federal Reserve and US Treasury, for instance (Taylor 2009). It featured, moreover, when state officials explained and justified their approach to crisis management. Consider, by way of illustration, the words of Federal Reserve Chair, Ben Bernanke (2008a), taken from a testimony he gave to the US Senate Committee on Banking, Housing, and Urban Affairs in September 2008:

> The Federal Reserve believes that, whenever possible...difficulties should be addressed through private-sector arrangements—for example, by raising new equity capital, by negotiations leading to a merger or acquisition, or by an orderly wind-down. Government assistance should be given with the greatest of reluctance and only when the stability of the financial system, and, consequently, the health of the broader economy, is at risk.

The notion of moral hazard—which positions the state as key to crisis governance at the same time as it critiques that role by asserting that the market is best left to its own devices—was thus very much present in the governance of the turmoil.

Bernanke's testimony is also revealing as to the way in which the ends of ostensibly state-centred governance were explained during the crisis, especially in official circles and by economic thinking. That which action was said to be seeking to avoid included 'systemic distress' (Tucker 2009), and 'an unnecessary loss of confidence in the system as a whole' (King 2008). Indeed, for Mervyn King (2008), 'so-called systemic risk...is why central banks have sometimes acted as "lender of last resort"' in the past, and why they did so in the contemporary crisis. The purpose of crisis governance thus appeared to be the maintenance of a natural system or circuit of flows, movements, and circulations in financial markets and banking which are deemed to be of essential importance to 'the health of the broader economy' (Bernanke 2008a). Textbook economic definitions of the intermediary functions of finance—allocating investment capital and providing credit to the 'real' economy—were often drawn together with metaphorical and figurative imaginaries. In the course of the crisis, for instance, the system of financial circulations was imbued with a vitality that appeared as the water that irrigates the land (Chapter 3), and as the blood that sustains and nourishes the economic body (Chapter 4).

Critical academic analyses of crisis governance tend to leave aside debates about moral hazard. Instead, they offer accounts of why the role of the state as LOLR is necessary and unavoidable in maintaining financial and economic circulations, and how the sovereignty of the state makes the role of LOLR possible. This is the case for the two most prominent framings—post-Keynesian economics and Marxist political economy—which are widely understood to provide the 'common foundation' for the critical analysis of financial crises (Epstein and Wolfson 2013: 2). In the Keynesian tradition, crises and thus crisis management are endemic to finance because of the uncertainty which arises from the intersubjective nature of markets. Markets, for Keynes (1964: 156), operate in 'the third degree where we devote our intelligences to anticipating what average opinion expects the average opinion to be'. 'Animal spirits' are always present in these interpretive processes, and valuation is based upon collective expectations which are likely to be self-fulfilling and fragile (Akerlof and Shiller 2009). Keynesian economic policies are therefore dedicated to managing and manipulating expectations of the future, encouraging 'real' investment flows in support of the goal of full employment (Skidelsky 2011). From this viewpoint, financial crisis management is a confrontation with a particularly acute instance of the endemic problems of markets.

Post-Keynesian accounts of the contemporary crisis typically found form with reference to the 'financial instability hypothesis' of Hyman Minsky (1982, 1986). Indeed, some went as far as to proclaim the crisis as 'the Minsky moment' (Cassidy 2008; *Economist* 2009a; Lahart 2007). Also informing Charles P. Kindleberger's (1996) classic comparative economic history—which itself provided a touchstone for state officials during the crisis (e.g. Tarullo 2009a)—Minsky's analysis emphasizes the ways in which a financial market mania is necessarily debt-fuelled. Intersubjective and speculative positions are leveraged positions, leading to 'progressive illiquidity' as debt obligations cannot be met once panic sets in (Nesvetailova 2007). In Minsky's (1982: 26) terms, 'Stability is destabilizing'. However, given the significance of finance to productive investment and real economic growth, the state, for Minsky, has little choice but to intervene to prevent complete collapse in a crisis. It should also work more broadly to minimize and control waves of speculation (Borio 2010; Nesvetailova 2010; Mehrling 2011). As such, failures of state agency in exercising the LOLR function—most notably by US authorities in the years immediately following the Wall Street Crash of 1929 (Kindleberger 1986)—are said to have highly detrimental economic, social, and political consequences.

When viewing the LOLR function as inherent to crisis-prone finance, post-Keynesian economics also highlights how such emergency lending capacities arise from sovereign power. It is only through the monopoly privileges institutionalized in central banks in particular—as the sovereign authorities charged with the issue, control, and validity of national money of account—that the LOLR function is said to be possible (e.g. Amato and Fantacci 2012; Ingham 2004).[1] In the course of the historically contingent processes that have come to bind nation states and money (Gilbert and Helleiner 1999), the private credit monies (i.e. debts) issued by banks and markets become denominated in the public money of account, and the central bank is thus positioned atop the institutional hierarchy of monetary governance by dint of its authority over the issue of 'base money'.[2] The result is said to be something of an implicit contract between private finance and the state, and recent decades have increasingly witnessed the former benefitting from the guarantees of the latter (Allesandri and Haldane 2009). From this perspective, in Geoffrey Ingham's terms, contemporary crisis management was a continuation of a prevailing trend in which 'Vast profits from increased risk taking are privatized and the losses and insurance costs are socialized' (2011: 252), as 'states created and distributed massive amounts of new money which eventually resolved the immediate acute phase of the crisis' (2011: 231).

That the last resort lending capacities of the state are a result of monetary sovereignty is similarly stressed by Marxist political economy. Here, however, the endemic crisis tendencies to which the state responds are said to be found in the nature of capitalism, rather than in the nature of markets and money. By way of a necessarily brief illustration, consider the hugely influential work of David Harvey.[3] As Harvey (2011: 6) reminds us, 'Capital, Marx insisted, is a process of circulation, not a thing. It is fundamentally about putting money into circulation to make more money'. Continuity of flow in the circulation of capital is thus essential to capitalism, and, for Harvey, a rupture in financial circulation is a particularly significant moment. This is because of the ability of finance capital to switch investments and thereby generate 'spatial fixes'— such as, for example, real estate speculation—which help to alleviate and move around the tendencies to overaccumulation in commodity production and the circuit of capital more broadly (Harvey 2001). The speculative circulations of finance capital can only temporarily overcome the contradictions of capital, however, and will also independently precipitate crises. Consequently, for Harvey (2010: 115–16):

capitalism has to create external power in order to save itself from its own internal contradictions. It needs to re-create the equivalent of the external feudal or non-capitalist gold reserve that it has historically fed upon. This it does by locating the power of infinite money creation within a neofeudal institution like the Federal Reserve.

Central banks are said to be at the 'commanding heights' of 'the hierarchy of monetary institutions' for Harvey (1982: 247), as they seek to 'guarantee the creditworthiness and quality of private bank moneys'. This includes providing a means of balancing the accounts of private banks on a daily basis, and extends to crisis management: 'the central bank becomes the supreme regulatory power' (1982: 281) and the state, as 'the core of the strategic control centre' (1982: 324) perpetually manages 'the underlying contradictions that plague the circulation of interest-bearing capital' (1982: 323). So, at the apparent height of the contemporary crisis in autumn 2008, the 'extraordinary lengths' that 'political power went to' were of little surprise to Harvey (2011: 7), as 'It was a matter of life or death for capital, as everyone in power recognized'. And, as he has it (Harvey 2010: 10), 'the policy was: privatize profits and socialize the risks; save the banks and put the screws on the people'.

Post-Keynesian and Marxist contributions to the prevailing understanding of the governance of the global financial crisis draw critical attention, then, to the structural significance of state sovereignty. It is only because of sovereignty that the endemic crisis tendencies of finance do not realize the ultimate collapse of money, markets, and capitalism. What is more striking, however, is how official, mainstream, and critical explanations of crisis governance converge to produce consensus and what Rancière (2010) terms the 'distribution of the sensible'. Despite sharp disagreement over whether interventions are necessary or unavoidable, both economics and political economy contribute to the consensus view on how crisis management is enacted, and on the purpose of crisis management. Sharing assumptions about last resort lending, both hold that it is only the sovereign institutions of the state which have the capacity to act in a crisis, and the state is positioned accordingly as the agent of crisis management. Sharing assumptions about (but not understandings of) the circulations of economy, both regard keeping financial flows in motion as the immediate aim of crisis governance.

Mapping Financial Crisis Governance

In an interview he gave shortly before his death in 1984, Michel Foucault (2003a: 23) responded to a query as to why phrases such as 'history of problematics' had become prominent in his recent work. He explained that this is a methodological move to analyse 'thought' about 'a domain of action' that 'establishes it as an object' and is 'provoked' by 'a certain number of difficulties around it'. This move is, he suggests, quite different from a methodological concern with 'representations' and 'an analysis in terms of deconstruction' (2003a: 23–4). It can also be read as an extension of his previous treatment of discourse, not merely as language and signs, but as 'practices that systematically form the objects of which they speak' (Foucault 1972: 49; Foucault 2003b). As Rabinow and Rose (2003: xviii) underscore, the 'thought' which Foucault views as producing problems includes the operations and outputs of material and scientific technologies of knowledge. In this respect, Foucault's later method has much in common with 'the study of power' in STS, which Michel Callon (1986) calls 'the sociology of translation'. Here scientific and expert definitions of a problem are said to establish 'obligatory passage points' that enrol human and non-human actors in the process of working towards solutions. Similarly, and to draw a parallel with the work of Bruno Latour (2005: 6), Foucault's later method sets out to interrogate and question the power relations which lead to 'making things public' as an 'object of concern'.

The method of this book is to follow the 'development of a given into a question' and, in doing so, to detail the 'transformation of a group of obstacles and difficulties into problems to which diverse solutions . . . attempt to produce a response' (Foucault 2003a: 24). The result is 'a map' rather than 'a tracing', in the terms of Deleuze and Guattari (1987: 5, 13), an analysis that does not merely chronicle and reproduce the consensus on how financial crisis governance was performed. In mapping financial crisis governance, the research process for the book has been 'topological' (Collier 2009). It has followed the associations between a diverse array of official documents (e.g. policy statements, press releases, speeches), media reports, and authoritative academic commentaries which, in real-time, served to stabilize the given of the crisis as a series of problem-objects. Each set of associations tended to converge around a broadly agreed set of devices and indicators which provided an anchor point for calculating the scale and extent of the problem. There was, however, no common trajectory to the stabilization of each of the problems of crisis governance. This was particularly the case as the initial and relatively unequivocal rendering of the crisis as one of liquidity became complemented and contested by a number of additional and alternative courses of action. The research process therefore also considered official reports and insider accounts that reflected on attempts to govern the crisis after the event, so to speak, such as those offered by international organizations, state agencies, and former state officials. It also entailed historical research into the governance of previous financial crises, most notably when the problems and solutions of contemporary governance were themselves rendered with explicit reference to, or by analogy with, crisis management initiatives in the past. The initial documentary mapping of associations for each problem-object was also supplemented by two rounds of in-depth, face-to-face semi-structured elite interviews, which were conducted with representatives of relevant institutions in London, New York, and Washington, DC.

Also crucial to the book's mapping of the will to govern the crisis, to return to Foucault, was to tease out what the series of problems that were stabilized and acted upon shared 'as a work of thought'; that is, 'a point of problematization' (2003a: 24). The transformation of the crisis into a range of more-or-less discrete problems had common conditions of possibility, relations of power that had no single source, centre, or origin, but which effectively placed limits on what could be thought and done. As will be outlined in the following section and developed in subsequent chapters, this common point of problematization ensured that relatively discrete crisis governance actions shared, to a greater or lesser extent, a certain character and content. When following the contingent formation of diverse and multiple crisis governance initiatives, then, the method of problems and problematization deployed by this book also entails a commitment to draw out the tendencies which were present across and between them.

Conceptualizing Financial Crisis Governance

The transdisciplinary field of cultural economy provides the conceptual foundations for this book's challenge to the consensus on the governance of the global financial crisis. As noted in Chapter 1, questions of agency and action provide a key point of intersection for diverse approaches to cultural economy. The broad unity with which cultural economy researches the distributed and relational qualities of agency is also marked, however, by conceptual debates that are of particular significance to conceiving of crisis governance anew. For leading cultural economists Michel Callon (2008) and Donald MacKenzie (2009), action and agency are understood through the conceptual category of 'socio-technical *agencement*'. As Callon (2008: 38) acknowledges, this category is developed from Gilles Deleuze's pragmatist philosophy. Specifically, the category is rooted in Deleuze's (2006) short essay which asks 'What is a *dispositif*?', and his later work with Felix Guattari on 'machinic assemblages' (Deleuze and Guattari 1987).[4] What is especially notable for a cultural economy account of financial crisis management, however, are the differences between the Deleuzean *dispositif* and the original formulation of this category by Michel Foucault.

According to Rabinow and Rose (2003: xv–xvi), Foucault first used the concept of *dispositif* to refer 'in its ordinary French usage' to 'tools and devices', thereafter developing it 'to mean a device orientated to produce something—a machinic contraption whose purpose in this case is control and management'. Such apparatuses gather together, in Foucault's (1980: 194) own terms:

> a resolutely heterogeneous grouping composing discourses, institutions, architectural arrangements, policy decisions, laws, administrative measures, scientific statements, philosophic, moral and philanthropic propositions; in sum, the said and the not-said, these are the elements of the apparatus. The apparatus itself is the system of relations that can be established between these elements.

Deleuze (2006: 338) similarly stresses the heterogeneity of the elements or 'lines of different natures' that, in relation, 'compose ... and pass through' a *dispositif* as 'a multilinear whole'. And, for Deleuze, this is crucial to the provisional and emergent properties of assemblages, to the fluidity and fragility of agency and action which he does not locate in a larger socio-spatial order (Law 2009). In contrast, for Foucault (1980: 196), the distributed agency of a *dispositif* is 'always inscribed in a play of power'.[5] A *dispositif* is 'essentially of a *strategic* nature' (1980: 196, *original emphasis*), a particular configuration that 'has as its major function at a given historical moment that of responding to an urgent need' (1980: 194–15). In sum, as Rabinow and Rose (2003: xvi) have it, Foucauldian *dispositif* are 'strategic assemblages ... initially formed as responses to crises, problems, or perceived challenges'.

Paired with the method of problems and problematization, the category of *dispositif* (apparatus) holds a particular efficacy for a cultural economy analysis of the provisional, distributed, and relational agency of financial crisis governance. The analytical value of the Foucauldian *dispositif* is multiplied, moreover, once we consider the ways in which it is developed in the context of his later work on security and liberal government (Foucault 1991, 2003c, 2007, 2008). Conceived of as 'apparatuses of security' that feature but exceed the institutions of the state (Foucault 2007), the discrete interventions that rendered and acted on the problems of contemporary financial crisis governance can be seen to have taken contingent, processual, and lively forms. For each apparatus that governed the crisis, how state institutions came together in dynamic relations with other heterogeneous elements was, as such, a specific and historical question. At the same time, the apparatuses that were forged in the course of crisis governance also had common conditions of possibility. In Foucault's (2007: 10–11) terms, 'the general economy of power in our societies is becoming a domain of security', such that apparatuses of security have certain 'general features'. It follows that the apparatuses that governed the contemporary crisis had certain tendencies which they shared to a greater or lesser degree. By placing the concept of security apparatuses in the context of Foucault's later work and the debates that it has engendered, the common tendencies which gave financial crisis governance apparatuses their character and content can begin to be identified.

Modes of Power and Sovereign Techniques

Foucault's (2007) analysis of apparatuses of security is part of a trajectory of research in which he gradually establishes the contours of three different modalities of power relations. These are forms of power/knowledge that emerge in, and are productive of, the ordering of Western Europe since the seventeenth century. Sovereign power, in Foucault's analysis, is a juridical, territorializing, and centralizing mode of power (Foucault 2003c: 27–8, 2007: 5), a political rationality and panoply of techniques and practices that make possible the right to rule of the sovereign and their institutions. The 'logic', 'grid of intelligibility', or 'grammar' of sovereign power is thus that which tends to occupy Foucauldian research into the exercise of sovereignty (Connolly 2004; Dillon 2004; Edkins and Pin-Fat 2004). This is a logic which establishes, and to some extent is defined by, the sovereign's right to punish and to take life in line with the doctrine of *raison d'État* and the security of the state. It is also a rationality that is challenged and transformed by its co-presence with other modalities of power. For Foucault, sovereign power has become adjoined and scrambled by two further modes of power and their associated rationalities, programmes, and techniques. What unites these further modes of power is their common object referent, the administration of the population.

Disciplinary, police, and surveillant power relations came to the fore from the eighteenth century to the early-to-mid-twentieth century, as demographic expansion, capitalist industrialization, and urbanization took hold (Foucault 1977). Disciplinary power seeks to synchronize and standardize individual bodies through rule-bound enclosures (factories, schools, hospitals, prisons, and so forth). Especially when correlated with sovereign power, however, the rationalities of discipline serve to work on individual bodies 'from the point of view of the state's strength' (Foucault 2008: 318). Meanwhile, the 'contemporary system' of 'biopolitics' and 'governmentality' that slowly developed from the mid-eighteenth century with the rise of liberalism, has come to pre-eminence as disciplinary societies have waned (Foucault 2007: 6–8; Deleuze 1992). In contrast with sovereign and disciplinary power, the knowledges and techniques of the biopolitical rationality seek to secure life itself (not the state), and to do so 'at a distance' through the apparently natural and uncertain processes that are 'immanent to the population' (Foucault 1991: 100).[6] A 'free' society becomes the 'condition and final end' of government (Foucault 2008: 319), where 'freedom' is less a choice and more an obligation to secure oneself. For contemporary, neo-liberal government, the art of administration is thus to create the conditions in which the entrepreneurial opportunities for wealth, well-being, and security, seemingly afforded by the vital and uncertain processes of population, can be realized.

For a cultural economy analysis of how financial crisis governance was contingently assembled and enacted, two crucial insights follow from the place that the concept of apparatuses of security occupies in Foucault's account of power and its modalities. First, while state institutions were of undoubted significance to the apparatuses of crisis governance, what made the mobilization of central banks, treasuries, and regulators possible was not simply the sovereign rationality of power. To be sure, it was through state building that the monopoly rights of sovereigns were founded, including the right to tax their population, to regulate their markets, and to control and manage the money that circulates as legal tender within their territory. Central banks, for instance, were typically established under law in order to finance the war efforts of sovereigns (Carruthers 1996). Later, they came to oversee matters of 'sound money', and to attain to the status of the monopoly issuers of national currencies in order to guarantee the collection of taxes and accumulation of sovereign revenues (Knafo 2013). The contemporary, biopolitical rationality of power is characterized, however, by the continual questioning of political sovereignty (Collier 2011), such that the securing of life is seen as endangered by 'governing too much' (Foucault 2008: 17). In the interventions of contemporary financial crisis governance, then, the strategic mobilization of state institutions cannot be solely understood in terms of the reason of state, and the related capacity of the sovereign to declare an emergency and 'state of exception' (cf. Agamben 2005; Best 2007; Brassett and Vaughan-Williams 2012).

Second, situating the concept of security *dispositif* within the 'triangle' of 'sovereignty-discipline-biopolitics' (Foucault 1991: 102) enables an account of how sovereign techniques were reconfigured and redeployed in discrete crisis governance apparatuses. It is indeed the case that, as Dillon and Lobo-Guerrero (2008: 266) neatly put it, 'there is no biopolitics which is not simultaneously also a security apparatus'. However, this should not obscure the ways in which the meaning and practice of extant sovereign techniques were, in effect, reworked in the 'problem space' of each crisis governance apparatus and amid the play of multiple modalities of power (Collier 2009: 80). Not only were strategic questions of the role of the state 'more acute than ever' in the governance of the crisis (Foucault 1991: 101), but the 'necessary modifications' of dynamic sovereign techniques were only realized in relation to the various heterogeneous elements which were also enrolled in each of the crisis governance apparatuses (Deleuze 1992: 7). Put differently, and to take terms from Muniesa et al. (2007: 2), the monetary, fiscal, and regulatory techniques of the state were not 'already "agenced"' in crisis governance. While central bank techniques of last resort lending have a long history that stretches back over two centuries, for instance, the specific form taken by those techniques were typically quite distinct in contemporary crisis governance apparatuses (see Chapter 3).

Economy and Economics At Large

The power of economics is not ideological in the sense that it 'cognitively captures' state and society alike (Epstein and Wolfson 2013: 3), but is a question of expertise and scientific claims to know which authenticate and authorize actions (Foucault 1991; Miller and Rose 1990). Understanding economics in these terms recovers the ancient formulation of *oikonomia*—meaning a practical and managerial disposition for the functional order of good housekeeping—while recognizing that the nature of economic knowledges and their contribution to rationalities of power and rule have changed over time (Mitchell 2008). It is in these terms, for example, that Agamben (2011) interrogates how the divine rule of Christian theology operated in the practicalities of *oikonomia* through to the seventeenth century. The flowering of economic science thereafter can thus be seen as crucial to the biopolitical modality of power discussed above, as statistical and probabilistic demography emerged 'in correlation with the birth of economic thought' (Foucault 2007: 366; Porter 1986). It was through economics, moreover, that 'naturalness' was written into population as a society of living beings, not as a matter of 'nature itself' but as 'processes of a naturalness specific to relations between men', including 'what happens spontaneously when they ... exchange, work, and produce' (Foucault 2007: 349). Thus, while liberal government is marked by juridical limits on sovereign power and legal guarantees of the rights of individuals, a second and further set of ontological limits are present in liberal government that are produced by economics as 'bioeconomic processes' (Terranova 2009: 239); that is, as the natural laws and logics of the market.

The broad suggestion, then, is that 'economy' is not that which is governed over in the course of contemporary financial crisis management, but is itself a crucial means through which the crisis is administered. Three specific implications follow for the analysis of the economic elements of the apparatuses of crisis governance. First, as the crisis was made up and managed as a number of relatively discrete problems, the mobilization of expert economic discourses was especially significant to envisaging an end point at which the ostensibly natural processes of the financial markets would be restored. How these processes were understood was not necessarily and always clear, however. As Mark C. Taylor (2004) has shown, the conception of the domain of the financial market as a physical, mechanical, and self-organizing system that tends towards equilibrium is constant across economic theory from the eighteenth century to the present. From such orthodox economic conceptions of finance, it followed that what was 'most important of all' in contemporary crisis governance was achieving 'an equilibrium' (Foucault 2003c: 246). However, as governance apparatuses forged and grappled with questions that were typically conflated under the rubric of a return to 'financial stability', this appeal to normalcy did not always and necessarily imply that the crisis was regarded as something of a blip in the otherwise natural and equilibrating tendencies of markets. The vital processes of financial markets were to be restored, for sure, but this was also premised with economic conceptions of finance that pointed to the need for further actions in order to harness and stabilize those processes in the future.

Second, and related, apparatuses of crisis governance did not mobilize a coherent and singular economic theory. Rather, the *dispositif* of crisis governance were typically 'apparatuses of resonance' for multiple economic theorizations of finance (Deleuze and Guattari 1987: 211). The mid-twentieth-century body of thought that Foucault (2008) refers to as 'American neo-liberalism' was certainly present.[7] So too was the long-running thread of liberal thought that is recovered, as Pat O'Malley (2000, 2009) suggests, when the neo-liberal logic of the optimization of life stresses the entrepreneurial opportunities for wealth and well-being afforded by the uncertain future. At the same time, crisis governance apparatuses featured the enrolment of a multiple and somewhat fragmented array of heterodox economic ideas. These included, for instance: the rules of thumb for central banking advocated by Walter Bagehot; Keynesian and post-Keynesian conceptions of finance which posit endogenous tendencies to speculative credit bubbles; and complex adaptive systems theorizations that regard financial ecosystems as non-linear and prone to 'tipping points' rather than tendencies to equilibrium. In crisis management apparatuses, what mattered was not the intellectual consistency between economic theories and concepts, but their confluence in the strategic pursuit of 'financial stability' and the restoration of uncertain financial circulations.

Third, the enactment of crisis governance through economy featured the mobilization of certain market devices of economics 'at large' and 'in the wild' (Callon 2007). The pragmatic calculations of models and tools are always already present in the socio-technical assemblage of markets, especially those devices that make pricing, exchange, and circulation possible (Callon and Muniesa 2005). With the onset of the crisis, market devices did not merely calculate the extent of the crisis as, for example, a liquidity crisis evidenced by a steep rise in the cost of interbank borrowing. Gathered together in relation with other elements in crisis governance apparatuses, the devices of economics at large were actually crucial to bringing into being the 'material givens' of the problems to be acted on (Foucault 2007: 19). It was through these devices that both the scale and the nature of the problems of crisis governance came to be known.

Affect and an Atmosphere of Confidence

The global financial crisis was animated by a whole host of emotions and collective, affective energies—shock, fear, anxiety, panic, anger, and shame, for instance.[8] Accordingly, the crisis provoked a range of calls for greater credence to be given to the role of emotions and shifting sentiments in academic explanations of financial markets, calls that were common to economics (Akerlof and Shiller 2009; Heukelom and Sent 2010; Shiller 2008), sociology (Berezin 2009; Pixley 2012; Swedberg 2012), political economy (Widmaier 2010), and, indeed, cultural economy (Callon 2012). A return to the roots of cultural economy conceptions of economic action and agency holds significant promise in this regard. As Deleuze and Guattari (1987: 399) put it, when writing of 'desire':

> Desire has nothing to do with a natural or spontaneous determination; there is no desire but assembling, assembled, desire. The rationality, the efficiency, of an assemblage does not exist without the passions the assemblage brings into play, without the drives that constitute it as much as it constitutes them.

From the vantage point provided by Deleuze, then, distributed and relational forms of assembled agency necessarily enrol 'the passions', an insight that has certainly not gone unnoticed in cultural economy accounts of market *agencements* (e.g. Deville 2012; McFall 2009). Yet, Foucault's (2007) albeit more limited writings on 'desire' suggest something more. What Deleuze and Guattari (1987: 166) term 'plugging into' and 'effectively taking charge of desire' is, for Foucault, a notable feature of a biopolitical rationality that seeks to secure life through the apparently natural processes which are imminent to the population (Massumi 2005). Once 'desire' comes to be viewed, from the eighteenth century onwards, as the 'one and only one mainspring of action' across 'the population taken as a whole', then it 'becomes accessible to governmental technique' (Foucault 2007: 72–3). Such technique, as Foucault continues, seeks to work on 'how to say yes to this desire', and is concerned with 'everything that stimulates and encourages ... this desire, so that it can produce its necessary beneficial effects'.

It follows that the apparatuses that governed the crisis sought to 'say yes' to desire in the financial markets, and to once again prompt the entrepreneurial embrace of opportunities that are seemingly afforded by the uncertain financial future. Moreover, as Ben Anderson's (2009, 2012) research suggests, stimulating and encouraging such desire required that governance apparatuses deployed techniques that worked on the affective conditions present within markets, conditions that are most usefully conceived of as an 'affective atmosphere'. Much like the light, air, and heat that sustains life, it was an affective atmosphere or 'climate of confidence' that appeared to be vital to nurturing the domain of finance and making the markets viable once again (Callon 2012). Three implications follow for an analysis of the ways in which crisis governance apparatuses targeted and sought to elicit an affective atmosphere of confidence.

First, despite consistently attempting to plug into the affective atmosphere of market confidence, 'confidence' itself was a loosely defined 'epistemic object' in crisis governance (Knorr Cetina and Breugger 2000: 149; McCormack 2012). Reflecting the absence of any sustained theoretical or empirical treatment of confidence across the field as a whole (Swedberg 2012), the economic thinking on confidence which was immanent to crisis governance contained no clear and common intellectual point of reference. Confidence certainly occupies an important analytical place in the aforementioned work of Bagehot and Keynes, and occasionally these thinkers were indeed invoked as an atmosphere of confidence was pursued across crisis governance apparatuses. More often than not, however, confidence was simply reiterated as being essential to sustaining the uncertain claims and obligations of financial circulation, statements that were intermittently accompanied by a reminder that 'credit', from the Latin 'credo' and 'credere', means 'to believe' or 'to trust'.

Second, whether or not the condition of confidence could be restored to financial markets was explicitly recognized to hinge upon how crisis governance action itself was received. Cajoling confidence was a not a 'disciplinary technique', a matter of working on the psychology of individual market bodies to make them happier, less anxious, or more optimistic, for instance (Ahmed 2010: 8). It also went beyond the 'economy of words' that Holmes (2009: 382) identifies as the 'distinctive communicative dynamic' of 'the practices of central banking', or what Abolafia (2012) similarly calls the 'interpretive techniques' utilized by central banks to justify and shape the meanings of their technical and expert judgements. Rather, restoring confidence in crisis governance was more akin to the marketing, merchandizing, and packaging techniques deployed in consumer markets (e.g. Lury 2009; Thrift 2008). To paraphrase from Franck Cochoy's (2007) account of the 'captation' of consumers, crisis management apparatuses did not seek to control confidence, but to lure, attach, and enrol market publics to their confidence-restoring measures.

Third, while devices of economics at large provided calculations of the material givens of crisis governance, they also produced proxy indicators that were treated as barometers which made visible the 'perpetually forming and deforming, appearing and disappearing' atmosphere of confidence in markets (Anderson 2009: 79). This duality was possible because, as Zaloom (2008: 257) notes, emergent calculations of prices and other aggregate market measures may be made up of individual practices, but 'Collectively, the shifts in price and therefore in mood can seem like the vagaries of a sentient being'. Acting upon the material givens of the crisis was thus often and simultaneously an attempt to know and to govern affective givens, to extend terms from Foucault (2007: 19). What was especially notable, moreover, was the way in which certain barometers of confidence became pragmatic points of reference through which the success or otherwise of a governance action was assessed, both in real time and subsequently. As Brian Massumi (2005: 2) observes of neo-liberal governance more broadly, 'The outcome is read in the indicators. Correctness is not deduced from first principle, it is diagnosed'. Improvements in barometers of the affective atmosphere of confidence were taken, in effect, to be a measure of the degree to which market publics had become attached to a governance apparatus, and of the extent to which confidence had been mobilized.

Uncertain Circulations and Financialized Security

The complex and lively processes and 'interactions' of the population are, for Foucault (2007: 352), 'circular effects'. Apparatuses of security therefore have a particular spatial and temporal orientation, one that seeks to reproduce the uncertain circulations which appear as vital to life itself: 'the circulation of people, merchandise, and air, etcetera' (2007: 29). Uncertain market circulations specifically come to be known to pose possible dangers to the population, such as, for example, periodic scarcity in the supply of grain to urban areas (2007: 30–42). The response of neo-liberal government to such security threats to the future of life is not a matter of preventing circulation in the present, however. This is because it is upon the contingencies and indeterminacies of circulation that the dynamic and entrepreneurial production of wealth and well-being apparently rests (Foucault 2008; see Dillon 2007; O'Malley 2009).

The circulations of money and finance are of particular import when 'liberty is the condition of security' (Gordon 1991: 19). As Georg Simmel stresses in *The Philosophy of Money*, money as a pure instrument of valuation is reliant upon its exchangeability and constant circulation: 'when money stands still, it is no longer money according to its specific value and significance' (2004: 571). For Simmel, the 'significance' of monetary valuation and circulation extends to the symbolic imaginings and associations of money that, becoming present in modern metropolitan life, accompany its movements (Allen and Pryke 1999).[9] It is in these terms, then, that Simmel probes the associations between money in circulation and the 'individual freedom' of liberal modernity. By 'uniting people while excluding everything personal and specific' (Simmel 2004: 347), money appears to loosen social bonds and flatten hierarchies as it makes all things and desires available at a price. Yet 'money', in the first instance, is a means of measuring and sustaining the uncertain promises to pay and power relations of credit-debt, and not an enabler of exchange (Graeber 2012; Ingham 2004; Lazzarato 2012). The claims and obligations of credit-debt become transferable, and can be represented as financial instruments circulating in markets, once they are denominated in a shared money of account. The associations between monetary circulation and freedom identified by Simmel are thus always and already associations between finance, freedom, and security.

Over roughly three decades or so prior to the contemporary crisis, moreover, uncertain financial market circulations explicitly came to appear as crucial to wealth and well-being in Anglo-America. This was not merely a matter of the growing contribution of financial accumulation to economic growth (Christophers 2013), or of the role of capital investment and credit in nourishing the productive economy and employment. Under a set of processes that French and Kneale (2012; Marazzi 2010: 66) usefully label 'biofinancialization', close interrelations also developed between the saving and borrowing of everyday life on the one hand, and the circulations of global financial markets on the other (Langley 2008b). The rise of mutual fund stock market investment displaced retail deposit account saving and collective retirement insurance. Security thus came to turn to a lesser extent upon thrifty provision for the future and the calculation, pooling, and spreading of uncertainties as 'risks'. It was now much more a matter of the entrepreneurial 'embrace' of risk and uncertainty (Baker and Simon 2002), accompanied by the depoliticization of the unequal distribution of rewards (McNay 2009). At the same time, growing and unprecedented levels of mortgage and consumer credit came to be seen to play a positive role in facilitating the prosperity of all (Smith 2008; Marron 2009). While outstanding debt obligations from everyday life were repackaged and capitalized as wholesale investment opportunities on global markets (Langley 2006; Leyshon and Thrift 2007), they also became an object for management and manipulation by individuals and households themselves (Langley 2014). And, as Lazzarato (2012: 94) argues, it is this entrepreneurial engagement with debt that—alongside the management of precarious employability, falls in real wages, and the shrinking availability of public services—came to characterize the lived experience of (in)security for the majority.

A crucial feature of contemporary crisis governance apparatuses thus comes into view. Severe dislocations in financial circulation were not regarded as strictly monetary, market, and banking issues with implications that threatened to spill over into the 'real economy' of production. How to keep the wheels of finance turning was also prefigured by a wider predicament, a dilemma of financialized security. Especially as the crisis deepened from the summer of 2008, it was expressly governed as a security question. To that end, and no matter how different apparatuses made up and managed the crisis, governance was characterized by 'maximizing the positive elements, for which one provides the best possible circulation', and 'minimizing what is risky and inconvenient' (Foucault 2007: 19). There was to be no 'radical realignment of security and freedom in the socio-economic register of security' (O'Malley 2009: 37). Uncertain financial circulations had to be relatively free flowing and very much open for business because their supposedly productive capacities were now deeply implicated in the securing of life itself.

Mechanisms of Modulation and Mitigation

During the middle 40 years or so of the twentieth century, the challenge posed to Western liberal freedoms by economic crisis, communism, and fascism produced an intensification of state programmes and interventions designed to defend and guarantee those freedoms. Warfare, welfare, and the Cold War thus went hand in hand. That disciplinary forms of 'control' proliferated and came to be regarded as the 'mainspring' in the production of a standardized population of free individuals from the 1930s is, for Foucault (2008: 67–70), a key example of how 'crises of liberalism' can be 'linked to crises of the capitalist economy'. The mid-century intensification of disciplinary programmes and techniques extended, moreover, to the reorganization of global financial markets (see Chapter 7). Given that the severe dislocations of the Great Depression were traceable to the Wall Street Crash of 1929 and the Austrian and German financial crisis of 1931, future financial crises were held to be a threat to freedom and were to be prevented through precautionary means. Financial market circulations were thus gradually positioned as 'the servant' in Eric Helleiner's (1993) terms, enclosed in national economies through capital controls, tightly regulated and placed in the service of 'real' economy of production, and made subservient to state policies of Keynesian macroeconomic planning and the Bretton Woods system of fixed exchange rates (Best 2005; Blyth 2002; Germain 1997; Helleiner 1994; Langley 2002).

The 1970s was another moment when a 'crisis of the general apparatus of governmentality' took hold amid an economic crisis (Foucault 2008: 70). This crisis became manifest, in the realm of finance, in the removal of capital controls, the deregulation of stock markets and banking, and the abandonment of the system of fixed exchange rates that, together, opened the way for 'casino capitalism' (Strange 1986). What also gradually crystallized, moreover, were certain technical means of addressing the destructive forces of newly unleashed and uncertain financial circulations, and the future security threats that they posed. Monetary policy was slowly transformed (Krippner 2007), and interest rates eventually became the crucial tool for tempering macroeconomic and price volatilities (Davies and Green 2010: 23–51). To take terms from Deleuze (1992), monetary policy now sought to 'modulate' the intensities of macroeconomic movements and flows, and was widely celebrated for having produced the so-called 'Great Moderation' (Bernanke 2004).[10] From the late 1980s, 'mechanisms of mitigation' (Collier 2008: 226) also developed that turned on the probabilistic calculation, capitalization, and distribution of the future uncertainties of credit-debt as risks (Kalthoff 2005; Mikes 2011; Millo and MacKenzie 2009; Power 2007). The prospect of 'systemic risk' arising from any future financial crisis was therefore seemingly pre-empted in the present by risk management and risk trading, hedging risks in derivative markets, and so on (see Chapter 6).

Placing contemporary crisis governance in these comparative historical terms has significant implications for the book's cultural economy analysis. At the time of writing, in early 2014, the contemporary global financial crisis does not appear to have produced a generalized crisis of neo-liberal government (Cooper 2010; Hall 2011; Mirowski 2013, Peck 2013a).[11] Rather, and emerging from the apparatuses that governed the crisis, certain supposed crisis-relieving actions have consolidated into longer-term agendas for monetary and fiscal policymaking (see Chapters 3 and 8). New technical means for modulating the intensities of global financial circulations, and for preparing for the eventualities of future crises, have also developed out of crisis governance programmes. The apparatuses that rendered the crisis as problems of solvency, risk, and regulation were important, in particular, in providing 'intermediary diagrams' of how the dangers of global finance should be tackled once the immediate tumult had passed (Deleuze 1999: 30). That these new techniques and outlines for action have been subsequently corralled into two overlapping governmental programmes—one proffering a 'macro-prudential' regulatory approach (Baker 2013; Datz 2013), the other designed to advance the 'resilience' of banking (BCBS 2010; BIS 2013: 52–65)—would seem to underline their significance.

Uncertain global financial circulations are not presently being subjected to sovereign and disciplinary limits, constrains, and restrictions of the kind that developed from the 1930s. The orientation of contemporary crisis governance, as noted above, was 'above all and essentially' a matter of 'guaranteeing' and 'ensuring circulations' (Foucault 2007: 29). However, emerging from crisis governance, uncertain financial circulations are also no longer simply considered to be governable through the generalized macroeconomic modulations of monetary policy that focus primarily on price stability (Davies and Green 2010). Rather, the constantly shifting intensities of financial flows are singled out for special 'macro-prudential' attention that seeks to temper and counter the peaks, troughs, and cycles of their 'variable geometry' in the aggregate and systemically (Deleuze 1992: 4). Consider, for example, the recently minted Financial Policy Committee (FPC) of the Bank of England which, according to the Deputy Governor for Financial Stability, Paul Tucker (Tucker et al. 2013: 192), has a 'primary role ... to identify, monitor, and take action to remove or reduce risks that threaten the resilience of the UK financial system as a whole'.

Also emerging from crisis governance is change in the mechanisms which are routinely deployed in the present in order to mitigate future threats arising from the uncertainties of global finance. There is no return to the precautionary mechanisms of the mid-twentieth century, and pre-crisis faith in probabilistic risk and the associated pre-emptive logic of the derivative have waned considerably (Amoore 2011). To draw on Anderson's (2010: 791) useful schematic of the different 'logics' for governing the future of life in the present, what unites 'precaution' and 'pre-emption' is that they 'aim to stop the occurrence of a future'. For a precautionary logic, this is a matter of 'stopping a process before it reaches a point of irreversibility', while for a pre-emptive logic it is a case of 'initiating a new process' such as the creation of derivative contracts. Assuming that future financial crises cannot be 'stopped', what is sought under the rubric of resilience is the 'preparedness' of banking for the eventualities of the next crisis. Measures to, for example, continue to recapitalize banking, revise risk management, and introduce liquidity and leverage ratios aim 'to stop the effects of an event disrupting the circulations and interdependencies that make up a valued life' (2010: 791). The residues of crisis governance are, to date and in sum, new technical fixes seemingly able to square the circle of governing through uncertainty in order to provide for financialized security.

Conclusions

This opening chapter began by exploring the consensus on the governance of the contemporary global financial crisis, a consensus that positions the sovereign state as acting to rescue the circulations of banking, the markets, and finance capital. It focused, in particular, on how the consensus is rooted in certain assumptions that are shared by economics and political economy. Although each of these fields offer a range of sharply contending knowledge claims about finance, they were nonetheless shown to provide an essentially singular account of how crises of finance are managed. The chapter then moved on to set out the considerations and parameters of an alternative, cultural economy analysis of the governance of the contemporary crisis. In terms of method, the chapter developed the potential of Foucault's concern with problems and problematization. A cultural economy approach was thus held to research how the contemporary crisis was rendered governable by mapping the contingent associations that served to stabilize it as a series of problem-objects. Such a method was paired with a conception of agency and action in financial crisis governance that, rooted in the thinking of Foucault and Deleuze in particular, is understood to be distributed, relational, and strategic. When setting the stage for an analysis of each of the discrete security apparatuses that governed the contemporary crisis in the chapters that follow, also highlighted here were a number of tendencies that are more-or-less present across each of those apparatuses. In what follows, then, I will explore the multiple, problem-orientated apparatuses that sought to govern the global financial crisis. I will also further elaborate upon that which was broadly common to the governance assemblages, most notably: the reconfiguration of sovereign techniques; the mobilization of discourses and devices of economy; the eliciting of an affective atmosphere of confidence; the restarting of uncertain circulations to secure a financialized way of life; and the emergence of new means of modulating and mitigating the future threats posed by uncertain circulations.

Notes

1. This insight is gleaned from Keynes himself, and more broadly from the 'Chartalist school' of monetary theory and research in historical sociology, in which Keynes and the likes of Harold Innes, Georg Friedrich Knapp, and Max Weber are regarded as the founding thinkers (Carruthers 1996; Hobson 1997; Ingham 2004). Here monetary sovereignty is inextricably linked to fiscal sovereignty because, in the first instance, the state enforces legal tender within a territorial space in order to guarantee the quality of the taxes it collects.
2. 'Base money' or 'high powered money' is currency in circulation plus the reserves held on deposit by banks at the central bank.
3. There is, of course, a significant debate between Marxist political economists over financial crises and their management, and not all contributors to those debates would share the views of Harvey (e.g. Duménil and Levy 2011; Lapavitsas 2009; for a useful discussion, see Callinicos 2012).
4. When underscoring the relevance of the category of *agencement* to questions of economic and market agency, Callon, MacKenzie, and their collaborators clearly seek to update the actor-network theory of STS (Law and Hassard 1999). In doing so, they contribute to a much wider body of 'assemblage theory' that, provoked primarily by the pragmatist philosophy of Deleuze, extends to a number of disciplines and fields (e.g. Anderson and McFarlane 2011; de Goede 2012; Ong and Collier 2004).
5. Agamben (2009) offers a similar, Foucauldian reading of the category of *dispositif*. But, for Agamben, apparatuses are necessarily concrete manifestations of the sovereign mode of power.

6. 'Population' in this sense does not refer to a mass of individuals, but to an abstracted and aggregated 'set of living beings' (Foucault 2008: 317). From the mid-eighteenth and especially nineteenth century, the population comes to be known in terms of 'its own regularities, its own rate of death, of diseases, its cycles of scarcity, etc.' (Foucault 1991: 99).

7. What Foucault (2008) demarcates as 'American neo-liberal' economic theories break with classical liberalism's emphasis on the 'abstract logic' of market exchange among equals, and instead advance the 'ideal logic' of entrepreneurial competition between interests across all domains of social life (Terranova 2009).

8. 'Affect' is understood here as impersonal and transpersonal intensities, energies, and passions which circulate between bodies (Massumi 2002).

9. As Allen and Pryke (1999) note, this aspect of Simmel's distinctive contribution to the social theory of money tends to be overlooked. Instead, his work is usually positioned alongside Marx and Weber, due to the emphasis that it places upon the way in which money makes commensurate a diverse array of objects, relations, services, and so on. I would argue that the insights Simmel provides for thinking through money in liberal society stand, despite the way in which he advances an evolutionary understanding of 'modern money' that does not pay sufficient attention to the material practices and pragmatics that constitute diverse forms of money across space and time (Gilbert 2005; Maurer 2006).

10. As David Savat (2009: 51–7), after Deleuze (1992), expands on what he calls 'mechanisms of modulation', 'modulation attempts, by way of calculation, to anticipate the emergence of patterns of flow or energy within a turbulent system'. It is concerned not with creating an end product as such, but with ensuring the continuous, imminent, and 'pure functionality' of the system of flows itself.

11. What comparative historical inquiry would seem to suggest is that, should a crisis of liberal government consolidate in the wake of the contemporary global financial crisis, then it is likely to take a decade or so to crystalize (Blyth 2002; Hay 2011; Helleiner 2014).

3

Liquidity

Introduction: 'When the music stops...'

> When the music stops, in terms of liquidity, things will be complicated. But as long as the music is playing, you've got to get up and dance. We're still dancing.
>
> Chuck Prince, Chairman and CEO Citigroup, 9 June 2007

Chuck Prince's frivolous and now famous description of the continued 'dancing' of Citigroup reflected, with hindsight, the serious concern that the 'music' of liquidity in global financial markets was about to fall silent.[1] Within two weeks of Prince's remarks, Wall Street's fifth largest investment bank, Bear Stearns, pledged $3.2 billion worth of loans to support one of its hedge funds. The fund's collapse in early August 2007—along with a second operated by Bear, and three similar funds run by BNP Paribas who cited 'a complete evaporation of liquidity' (Lowenstein 2010: 96)—hailed the beginning of what was to become the global financial crisis. Citigroup, Bear, BNP, and all manner of institutions across the globe had built up huge portfolios of assets related to and derived from the repayments of sub-prime mortgagors in the US: mortgage-backed securities (MBS) and, especially, collateralized debt obligations (CDOs), and credit default swaps (CDS). Much of this speculative investment was funded by a massive volume of often very short-term debt, which was regularly 'rolled over' and renewed in money markets. However, as doubts over the value of sub-prime assets took hold, new issues stalled, prices plunged, and secondary trading ground to a halt. Unable to unwind their positions and racking up major losses in capital markets, investors were also unable to access fresh debt or renew their existing obligations in money markets.

Stark illustrations of how this situation posed a threat to global finance were not long in coming. IKB Deutsche Industriebank revealed large losses on sub-prime assets in late August, and was saved from collapse by the German government and a consortium of major German banks. Northern Rock—a former building society that financed a growing share of the UK mortgage market, lending via short-term borrowing and securitization techniques—was granted emergency loans by the Bank of England on 14 September 2007 (NAO 2009a; Shin 2010: 132–51). Once news of the Bank's support for Northern Rock broke in the mainstream media, retail depositors began to withdraw their cash. In the first 'run' on a UK bank since Overend Gurney on 'Black Friday' in 1866, £4.6 billion was removed from Northern Rock accounts between 14 and 17 September alone, equivalent to twenty per cent of the bank's deposits. Television images of crowds queuing outside Northern Rock's high-street branches featured on twenty-four-hour rolling news channels across the world. Meanwhile, back on Wall Street, Citigroup announced $6.5 billion worth of losses in mid-October 2007, rising to between $8 billion and $11 billion by 4 November, then the largest known quarterly loss by a US financial institution. Chuck Prince hung up his dancing shoes and resigned.

The focus for this chapter is upon the actions of crisis governance that, broadly sharing Chuck Prince's diagnosis of the problem, sought to keep the continuous and looping soundtrack of liquidity playing in global money and capital markets. I want to ask how the crisis was abstracted as a relatively discrete problem of liquidity and made amenable to interventions by the Federal Reserve and the Bank of England. From the second week of August 2007, the central banks began an array of interventions that sought to ensure that more institutions would not confront fates of the kind that befell IKB and Northern Rock. Indeed, for the best part of the next twelve months, the crisis continued to be made legible largely as a problem of liquidity (*Financial Times* 2008). It was 'illiquidity'—often referred to as an 'evaporation of liquidity' from money and capital markets that were said to have 'dried up', 'seized up', or 'frozen over'—which was to be acted on in the first instance. A range of interventions were undertaken that were typically represented as the 'pumping' or 'injecting' of liquidity. Such interventions certainly did not exhaust the involvement of the Fed and the Bank in the apparatuses of crisis governance, as will be shown in subsequent chapters. What is of principal interest here is how the central banks were mobilized in an apparatus that forged and worked on the issue of liquidity, and especially how the techniques of last resort lending, which have featured in the governance of financial crises since the nineteenth century, were revised in unprecedented ways (Mehrling 2011). The targeting of money market liquidity was broadly consistent with established last resort lending techniques, but pumping liquidity directly into capital markets through programmes of QE broke new ground.[2] Indeed, activist QE programmes to purchase extensive amounts of government debt and supply huge volumes of liquidity have provoked some to suggest that the crisis heralded the onset of 'central bank-led capitalism' (Bowman et al. 2013; Thompson 2013).

The chapter moves through three main parts. I begin by introducing the key liquidity injections of the Fed and the Bank during the crisis, and place them in the context of the principal sovereign techniques of last resort lending; namely, OMOs and discount window lending. I show how both techniques were reworked such that the Fed, in particular, could 'open the spigot' (Irwin 2013: 6), and inject liquidity on a massive scale and in ways that redefined last resort lending. The second part of the chapter shows how the liquidity problem came to be taken as given through the relational coming together of certain discursive, material, and affective elements in a discrete governance apparatus. The third part of the chapter moves on to address directly the Federal Reserve and Bank of England, conceived of as the main institutional elements of the apparatus. The liquidity injections of the central banks turned on the minting of 'base money' in the form of bank reserves, and this served to keep in circulation many of the transferable debt claims that were stacked up during the boom years. While this was made possible by the rationality of monetary sovereignty institutionalized in central banks, action is shown to have nonetheless entailed the distributed and relational agency of a contingently arranged apparatus in which sovereign last resort lending techniques were rearticulated.

Liquidity Injections

On 9 and 10 August 2007, the Federal Reserve, European Central Bank (ECB), and the central banks of Japan, Canada, and Australia made up to US$320 billion worth of emergency reserves available to banks at interest rates below those prevailing in global money markets. The ECB took further action on the following Monday. Beneath a headline stating that 'The Federal Reserve is providing liquidity to facilitate the orderly functioning of financial markets', the Fed's accompanying press release of August 10 stated that:

> The Federal Reserve will provide reserves as necessary through open market operations to promote trading in the federal funds market at rates close to the Federal Open Market Committee's target rate of 5–1/4 per cent. In current circumstances, depository institutions may experience unusual funding needs because of dislocations in money and credit markets. As always, the discount window is available as a source of funding.[3]

The immediate problem at this time was that 'depository institutions' were only providing short-term debt to each other at highly inflated rates of interest. They were retaining cash to meet their own obligations and were fearful of so-called 'counterparty risks', unsure precisely which of their number were struggling to deal with the souring of investments in assets related to and derived from sub-prime mortgages. Highly leveraged non-depository institutions and conduits, also heavily reliant upon the circulations of commercial paper and 'repos' in the money markets in order to make their investments, were experiencing particular difficulties renewing their existing short-term debt, let alone accessing new funds.[4] These institutions included the Wall Street investment banks, and the hedge funds, private equity funds, and structured investment vehicles (SIVs) of the so-called 'shadow banking' sector.

OMOs were one of the two channels through which central banks attempted, from August 2007, to inject liquidity and address 'dislocations in money and credit markets'. OMOs, and the second channel, the standing loan facilities of the discount window, each arise from the routine sovereign techniques of central banking; that is, respectively, the monopoly over the issue and management of money as legal tender on the one hand, and the clearing and payments procedures of 'the bankers' bank' on the other.[5] Put simply, OMOs are a monetary technique that is crucial to making effective throughout the economy the decisions on interest rate targets for overnight reserve loans which constitute the principal 'lever' or 'thermostat' of contemporary monetary policy (BIS 2008: 68; Krippner 2007: 484; Mann 2010a: 610). However, central bank's OMOs also provide the most widely used and routine mechanism for addressing aggregate liquidity problems in money markets (Humphrey and Keleher 2002). This is because, in order to make good on their calculations about the supply and demand for reserves and their broader interest rate policy decisions, central banks intervene in markets by trading government securities, acting as counterparties in repo transactions, and lending out their holdings of government securities such that they can be used as collateral in repo transactions (Freixas et al. 2002: 35–6; Mehrling 2011: 26–7).[6] The OMOs that heralded the onset of crisis governance were, in short, a commitment to significantly scale up central bank money market actions that were already ongoing and open-ended.

OMOs were crucial to the implementation of a monetary policy of aggressive interest rate reductions that, while seeking to broadly stimulate economic activity and ward off deflation in the 'real' economy, operated through the 'transmission mechanism' of money market liquidity in the first instance (Bowman et al. 2013: 463–4). The Federal Reserve led the way on interest rate cuts. Between September 2007 and December 2008, the Federal Open Market Committee lowered the target rate on ten occasions, taking it from 5.25 per cent to 0.00–0.25 per cent (FRB Markets Group 2008, 2009). The result was 'the lowest target for overnight fed funds trading in U.S. history' (FRB Markets Group 2009: 4). Meanwhile, the Bank of England was initially more reticent to cut interest rates. Like the majority of central banks in the

Global North, the Bank had increased interest rates in mid-2007 in response to global commodity price increases, and the onset of the crisis did not produce a uniform monetary policy response (BIS 2008: 56–65). The Bank's early caution on interest rates gave way, however, and it largely came to follow the unprecedented policy trajectory set by the Fed. The Bank's Monetary Policy Committee (MPC) made nine cuts that, from December 2007 to March 2009, took the Bank base rate from 5.75 per cent to 0.50 per cent.

Despite the unparalleled and occasionally globally coordinated interest rate cuts that were made in response to the crisis, 'the dysfunctional state of the financial system severely blunted the impact of lower interest rates. Major central banks therefore took additional measures' (BIS 2009: 91). Such 'additional measures'—sometimes referred to as 'balance sheet policies' because they involved 'the use of the central banks' balance sheet to alter private sector balance sheets through modifications of collateral, maturity and counterparty terms on monetary operations' (Bowman et al. 2013: 466)—included changes to the conduct of OMOs. Broadly speaking, instruments other than government securities were much more readily accepted as collateral to cover repo lending by the Bank and the Fed, and the terms that applied to repo lending were also lengthened (BIS 2008: 70–1). The minimum fee rates at which primary dealers could bid at auction to borrow securities from the Fed's Trading Desk were also significantly reduced on a number of occasions, and limits on the scale of securities lending to individual institutions were raised (FRB Markets Group 2008: 5, 2009: 19).[7]

Securities lending was also the focus for programmatic interventions by both the Fed and the Bank, wherein relatively liquid government securities were lent out against relatively illiquid collateral on a massive scale. Announced largely in response to the problems of Wall Street's investment banks in March 2008, for instance, the Fed's Term Securities Lending Facility (TSLF) was 'intended to promote liquidity in the financing markets for Treasury and other collateral and thus to foster the functioning of financial markets more generally'.[8] Similarly, the Special Liquidity Scheme (SLS) of April 2008, which permitted banks to swap mortgage-related and other assets with the Bank of England for specially issued UK Treasury bills, was 'designed to improve the liquidity position of the banking system and raise confidence in financial markets'.[9] The total value of the securities borrowed through the SLS was expected to be in the region of £50 billion but, after it was extended in October 2008, the scheme ultimately lent out £185 billion worth of UK Treasury bills and came to provide the diagram for the development of a permanent, off-balance sheet securities lending facility at the Bank (Fisher 2012).

In addition to OMOs, and from the very outset of crisis governance in August 2007, the discount window provided an important channel for liquidity injections made by the Federal Reserve in particular. Indeed, during 2008, as money market dislocations became more intense, OMOs continued but became relatively less significant to the Fed's overall effort to pump liquidity. This can be seen, for example, in the figures for average daily borrowing at the Federal Reserve's discount window, called the Primary Credit Facility. Here average daily borrowing rose from $59 million (2006) to $552 million (2007) and, following a slight increase in the first months of 2008, jumped sharply to $13,701 million between 17 March and 15 September, and then again to $85,814 million between 15 September and the end of the year (FRB Markets Group 2009: 18). These huge increases in discount window borrowing from the Fed were, in part, a consequence of the so-called 'widening' of the window that took place from mid-August 2007.[10] Incrementally, the terms available on the credit that the Fed routinely offers to banks through the Primary Credit Facility were extended from overnight to ninety days, and the 'discount rate' applied to that credit fell from 100 to twenty five basis points over the target rate. Crucial to the step-wise increases in the scale of discount window lending at the Fed during the spring and autumn of 2008, however, was the enactment of specific programmes that were in addition to the routine operations of the Primary Credit Facility. Across these so-called 'liquidity facilities', three sets of interventions stand out.

First, the Fed responded to what were, in effect, blockages on discount window borrowing by depository institutions by changing the mechanisms through which liquidity was made available. In Ben Bernanke's (2008b) terms, 'the efficacy of the discount window' was limited by the 'stigma' that arose 'primarily from banks' concerns that market participants will draw adverse inferences about their financial condition if their borrowing from the Federal Reserve were to become known'. So, jointly announced in conjunction with liquidity injections by other central banks in mid-December 2007, the Fed's Term Auction Facility (TAF) made available predetermined aggregate amounts of twenty eight-day discount window credit at secret, bi-weekly auctions.[11] The scale of credit made available through each of the TAF auctions increased as money market problems worsened during 2008 (FRB Markets Group 2009: 8), rising from $20 billion at the start of the year to $75 billion at mid-year, and then more than doubling again in the autumn and through to the end of the year.

Second, not only were the lending mechanisms at the Fed's discount window modified, but eligibility for discount window borrowing was broadened to include non-depository institutions. The Primary Dealer Credit Facility (PDCF) of March 2008 was a critical intervention in this regard.[12] Prior to the PDCF and the targeted support that the Fed simultaneously provided for the investment bank Bear Stearns (see Chapter 4), the only time that the 'unusual and exigent circumstances' of Section 13(3) of the Federal Reserve Act had been invoked, such that it could lend to non-depository institutions, was during the 1930s. However, Section 13(3) was invoked again in September and October 2008, in response to 'the broadening liquidity panic' in money markets (Madigan 2009). The Asset-Backed Commercial Paper Money Market Mutual Fund Liquidity Facility (AMLF) and Money Market Investor Funding Facility (MMIFF) sought, in different ways, to buttress the important role played by money market mutual funds in the US money markets.[13] The Commercial Paper Funding Facility (CPFF) of October 2008, meanwhile, was a 'liquidity backstop' that enabled purchases by the Fed, via primary dealers, of unsecured and asset-backed commercial paper from eligible issuers.[14] Eligible issuers included banks and non-banks, to be sure, but they also included non-financial corporations.

The third significant revision to established discount window techniques also centred on the type of institutions that were the beneficiaries of the Fed's 'liquidity facilities'. Originally announced alongside the TAF in December 2007, the Federal Reserve established 'temporary reciprocal currency arrange-ments (swap lines)' with the Bank of England, ECB, Bank of Canada, and Swiss National Bank (SNB).[15] Similar arrangements were subsequently created, from mid-2008, which added ten further central banks to the swaps network. What the swap lines created was a mechanism through which the dollar-denominated liquidity made available by the Fed could be extended, indirectly and via the existing last resort lending channels of the other central banks, to non-US banks and financial market institutions. The operations of global banks, espe-cially those domiciled in Europe, had become increasingly reliant upon rela-tively cheap dollar-denominated money market debt prior to the crisis (Allen and Moessner 2010), but 'dislocation' had taken hold not only in US money markets but also in the Eurodollar and foreign exchange swap markets (BIS 2008: 71). So, while the US subsidiaries of European-based banks also secretly received billions of dollars via what was called the 'Euro-TAF' by the few who were in the know (Irwin 2013: 131–2, 154), it was through swap lines that the Fed officially, and in effect, performed the role of 'sovereign international last-resort lender' (McDowell 2012). As the crisis worsened and the number of central banks involved in the Fed's swap lines increased, the scale of this action grew considerably (FRB Markets Group 2009: 25). This largess was not, however, an act of benevolence on the part of the Fed. As the BIS (2009: 99) has it, 'addressing the US dollar shortage of foreign banks helped the Federal Reserve to enhance its control over the rates paid for US dollar funding in money markets and reduced the risk of "fire sales" of dollar-denominated assets'. It was February 2010 before the swap lines, linking the Fed to fourteen other central banks, were permitted to expire.

The liquidity injections of the Bank of England and, especially, the Federal Reserve—including the dedicated programmes of last resort lending to non-depository institutions and foreign banks that they entailed—did not stop at the shores of the money markets. From late 2008, both central banks put in place additional and targeted programmes that directly extended the provision of liquidity to capital markets. In November 2008, for example, the Fed introduced the Term Asset-Backed Securities Loan Facility (TALF). A total of $200 billion worth of loans, with terms of up to five years, were made available to holders of eligible asset-backed securities (ABS), including ABS backed by credit card receivables, student loans, and car loans.[16] During the first half of 2009, the cumulative value of loans available under the TALF was extended to $1 trillion, and the eligible ABS were broadened to include commercial mortgage-backed securities (CMBS). From December 2008, moreover, and following the failure to implement the US Treasury's Troubled Asset Relief Program (TARP; see Chapter 3), the Federal Reserve's liquidity support for the capital markets was extended yet further. As part of what was later to become known as 'QE1' ('quantitative easing 1'), the Fed began a programme of 'Large-Scale Asset Purchases' that focused on MBS issued by government-sponsored mortgage giants Fannie Mae and Freddie Mac. By the summer of 2010, the Fed owned $1.1 trillion worth of such 'agency securities' (Irwin 2013: 263), a stake in the secondary mortgage market which it subsequently continued to grow. Similarly, but operating to improve market liquidity on a much smaller scale, the Bank of England's Asset Purchase Facility (APF) of January 2009 initially focused on buying up corporate credit instruments, including bonds and commercial paper (King 2009).

The final set of direct liquidity interventions in the capital markets made by the Bank of England and the Federal Reserve focused on the government debt of their respective treasuries. While QE had begun, in effect, at the Fed, with the purchase of the quasi-public MBS of Freddie and Fannie, it was the Bank that, in March 2009, announced a new direction in the implementation of 'unconventional monetary policy' that reorientated the APF towards the purchase of UK government debt instruments ('gilts').[17] This was also a further and significant revision to techniques of last resort lending, a very public acknowledgement that the unprecedented interest rate cuts and injections into money and capital markets previously undertaken had not generated sufficient liquidity. Gilts were to be purchased primarily from pension funds and insurance companies who, armed with the Bank's cash, would 'rebalance' their portfolios through capital market investments in corporate bonds and securities. This increase in capital market liquidity was expected, in turn, to feed into higher asset prices and lower borrowing costs (Joyce et al. 2011), although the precise impacts have been hotly debated (Bank of England 2012a). Between March and November 2009, the MPC authorized the purchase of £200 billion worth of gilts. Further rounds of purchases were announced in October 2011, February 2012, and July 2013, taking the total gilts held by the APF to £375 billion.

Over at the Federal Reserve, meanwhile, US Treasury bills and bonds (T-bills, T-bonds) became the object of the $600 billion second round of quantitative easing ('QE2'), announced in November 2010.[18] Bernanke had famously used the metaphor of a 'helicopter drop' of money when speaking, in 2002, about the QE pioneered by the Bank of Japan during the 1990s in order to stimulate the Japanese economy (Irwin 2013: 87–91). The QE2 practices of 'Helicopter Ben' that were undertaken through the Fed's open market trading desk were slightly different to those of the Bank of Japan, as they purchased government debt of longer-term maturities. These purchases came on top of the roughly £300 billion worth of Treasuries that the Fed had added to its balance sheet, via standard OMOs, between March and October 2009. Following QE2, the Fed's holdings of Treasuries stabilized at around $1.5 trillion (Federal Reserve Bank of New York 2013), but the subsequent and ongoing Maturity Extension Program (known as 'Operation Twist') has witnessed the Fed selling its holdings of shorter-term instruments in order to fund the purchase of those of longer-term maturity.

The Discourses, Devices, and Desires of Liquidity

As is clear from the forgoing, the governance of the global financial crisis featured a wide range of actions that, by breaking the boundaries of the previously established parameters of last resort lending (cf. Madigan 2009), sought to address a burgeoning problem of money and capital market liquidity. How was the crisis diagnosed as a liquidity problem, such that it was made amenable to 'liquidity injections' and 'liquidity facilities' by way of apparent solution? If the problem of liquidity was not given and materially obvious, then how did it come to be regarded as such? In this section, I want to draw attention to those elements of the discrete governance apparatus that, in relation, rendered the crisis as a liquidity dilemma: specific discourses and material devices of economics that turned on, and provided measures of, the liquidity of markets; and attempts to plug into the affective confidences of liquidity.

The term 'liquidity' (referring to a state of being liquid) dates to the seventeenth century, but was first used to refer to the flows of finance during the late nineteenth century. It is an example of 'a certain oddity about the realm of finance and economics', as this 'apparently precise, technical, strict, rational and calculative' domain 'operates with concepts that are better described as metaphors rather than as a coherent conceptual grounding or set of definitions' (Nesvetailova 2010: 4).[19] Present within and beyond the realms of economics and finance, the liquidity metaphor itself contributes to a vital and circulatory envisioning of monetary and financial economies that has been in place since the eighteenth century. As Brad Pasanek and Simone Polillo (2011: 232–3) put it, 'The metaphor of liquidity borrows from the seemingly continuous flow of commodities', but that which 'seems primarily to flow is money itself, lending flows of currency and credit the appearance of a natural and automatic process'. As such, 'the metaphor of liquidity reinforces laissez-faire models of equilibrium and circulation, rather than models which recognize and recommend more interventionist principles of economic organization' (2011: 233). In symbolic terms, the watery metaphor of liquidity thus conjures up the circulation of money and finance in a particular way: markets appear as 'hydraulic systems' (Mayhew 2011), and as functioning to provide the natural and essential flows necessary to the irrigation of the 'real' economic landscape (Clark 2005).

More narrowly, and in relation to finance specifically, the liquidity metaphor tends to refer to certain qualities and quantities (Nesvetailova 2010). The qualities of liquidity are typically attributed to an asset, an investment portfolio, or a market, and become 'a way to conceive of, and to structure, financial relations' (Amato and Fantacci 2012: 75). An asset or portfolio is likely to be described as displaying the qualities of liquidity, for instance, if it can be sold relatively easily, and turned into cash and liquefied. Money in the form of currency is thus regarded as the most liquid of all assets, the safest store of value precisely because it also provides the readily accepted means of exchange in general circulation. The returns from, or interest rates payable on, financial assets are therefore sometimes described as 'a liquidity premium', 'a compensation for loss of liquidity incurred by whoever gives money in exchange for securities' (Amato and Fantacci 2012: 20). A market that is said to be liquid, meanwhile, is a market continuously populated by willing buyers and sellers, wherein transactions do not produce significant price disruptions and can be easily reversed with little cost. However, the liquidity metaphor also often refers to certain quantities in finance, 'most often associated with the pool of money or credit available in a system at any given time' (Nesvetailova 2010: 6). Liquidity, in this sense, appears to be a readily available material resource and essential substance—as in the description of a market 'awash with liquidity'—and as a measureable flow. 'Global liquidity', for example, has a single and widely recognized measure: the amount of international reserves held by national central banks.

Often it is far from clear, however, which of the qualitative or quantitative dynamics invoked by the liquidity metaphor are in play in a specific discourse. Take, for instance, the way in which markets described as liquid are also typically referred to as 'deep', where depth implies both the presence of relatively large numbers of buyers and sellers, and a ready supply of money or credit. Much to the frustration of some commentators, such multiple and conflated meanings of liquidity were indeed in circulation as the contemporary crisis was rendered as a liquidity problem. A *Financial Times* article from August 2007 asked, for instance, how crisis management could expect to achieve its ends in the absence of a clear and agreed understanding of what 'liquidity' actually meant (Lex Column 2007). What was needed, according to the article, was a focus not on the provision of quantities of 'funding liquidity', but on the 'narrow' and 'technically solid definition' of 'market liquidity' offered by mainstream economics (also, Borio 2010; Brunnermeier 2008). The point of the liquidity facilities of central banks would thus be to return markets to their liquid norm, restoring the continuous and uninterrupted exchanges and circulations which ostensibly take place as banks and financial markets function smoothly to produce and allocate credit.

In high finance in the years immediately preceding the crisis, advances in financial economics and allied market innovations were supposed to have 'perfected the markets' and, therefore, to have made liquidity crises a thing of the past (Cooper 2014). An apparent abundance of liquidity prior to the crisis symbolized the contemporary triumph of what were reified as 'the markets' (Pasanek and Polillo 2011). Liquidity was seemingly guaranteed by highly efficient markets, wherein more-or-less perfect information flows enabled the calculation, pricing, hedging, and, above all, circulation and distribution of the future uncertainties of credit-debt relations as 'risks'. In short, 'if the portfolios of economic agents include more tradable securities, sales of these securities can substitute for external funding . . . a market-based financial system could be expected to be less vulnerable to liquidity crises' (Borio 2010: 75). Financial innovation had apparently created capacities not only to calculate the probabilistic risks of uncertain credit-debt relations, but also to 'slice and dice' those risks as investment opportunities to be distributed in markets which had also become highly proficient at mitigating the downside of this or that position.

In contrast, when viewed from a heterodox economics perspective, a sudden demand for funding liquidity is an ever-present possibility that, when it materializes, actually signals and defines the crises that punctuate the history of modern finance (see Allen et al. 2011). Whether finding form as a 'run' by depositors on a fractional reserve bank, for instance, or a rupture in money and capital markets, it is a 'liquidity squeeze' or 'dash for cash' (Blinder 2013: 93) that is held to be the essential and defining feature of a financial crisis. Acknowledged in the theory and practice of central banking since the nineteenth century, for instance, and given particular credence after Keynes left his indelible imprint on economics from the middle of the twentieth century, liquidity is known to have labile, capricious, and volatile qualities. The claims to creditworthiness and confidences which liquidity entails are susceptible to contagious excesses on the one hand, and doubts and panics on the other. For Keynes (1964), moreover, tendencies to illiquidity are not merely a problem that rears its head every now and again in financial markets, as if detached from the normal run of things, but *the problem* that structurally locks capitalist financial markets into a perpetual series of crises (Amato and Fantacci 2012: 26). What Keynes termed 'the fetish of liquidity'—the belief that the 'liquidity preferences' of each and every individual investor can be served by the market—is unrealizable because all attempts to liquidate assets cannot, by definition, take place at the same time.

For post-Keynesian economists, most notably Hyman Minsky (1986), it is thus the paradoxical and illusionary character of liquidity that lies at the very heart of financial crises (Kindleberger 1996; Nesvetailova 2007, 2010; Mehrling 2011). As Amato and Fantacci (2012: 19, emphasis in original) have it, 'liquidity *does not exist* from the outset... it can only *exist* as long as... people believe in the fetish'. For them, writing in a book originally published in Italian at the height of the crisis, it follows that:

> the present situation is not simply a particularly intense and prolonged *liquidity crisis*, but also a *crisis of liquidity* as the principle governing the organization of the credit system in the form of the financial market (2012: 25, emphasis in original).

Such post-Keynesian explanations were certainly at work beyond academic circles, as the crisis was rendered as a liquidity dilemma. Recall from Chapter 2, for instance, the way in which the crisis was declared in the media to be 'the Minsky moment'. As Nesvetailova (2007: 149–55) details, moreover, economists at the ECB and especially BIS had developed a post-Keynesian explanation of the 'dark side of liquidity' during the decade that preceded the crisis. In the face of the apparent perfection of the markets, however, this did not substantively inform the pre-crisis governance of global finance. Revealingly, while the 2004 'Basel II' international standards on capital adequacy for banks authored by the Basel Committee on Banking Supervision (BCBS) at the BIS addressed a whole host of credit-debt uncertainties calculated as 'risks' (see Chapters 5 and 6), 'liquidity risk' was not considered to be a significant issue and was notable only by its absence (Jenkinson 2008; Turner 2009a). However, for Claudio Borio (2010: 70) of the BIS, what the contemporary crisis 'once more hammered home' was 'the message that the evaporation of liquidity plays a key role in the dynamics of financial distress'. Accordingly, once the crisis had taken hold, the BCBS (2008) began to integrate concerns with liquidity risk into the revision of the Basel II standards, publishing its *Principles for Sound Liquidity Risk Management and Supervision* at the height of the crisis in September 2008. This process was formally written into the 'Basel III' codes in January 2013, when the BCBS (2013) unveiled the 'liquidity coverage ratio' (LCR).[20]

The economic discourse that rendered the crisis as a problem of liquidity was not exclusively Keynesian and post-Keynesian, however. Indeed, the kernel of Keynes' critical message on the fallibilities of liquidity itself largely evaporated away in official circles and amid the broader liquidity discourse. Rather than questioning liquidity in principle, the extensive 'injecting' and 'pumping' of liquidity by central banks and the subsequent development of codes of practice on liquidity risk actually reinforced the hold of the idea of liquidity as 'the prerequisite for the very possibility of credit' (Amato and Fantacci 2012: 24). If the markets could not provide liquidity, and thereby keep transferable and derivative claims on outstanding debts in circulation, then the central banks seemingly had little choice but to provide the 'public good' of liquidity (Bryan and Rafferty 2013). If that required major new 'liquidity facilities' and modifications to the sovereign techniques of last resort lending, then this appeared to be a case of central banking practice merely catching up with the recent structural innovations of high finance which had made it more reliant upon wholesale sources of funding liquidity (Bernanke 2008b; Madigan 2009).

Chief among these innovations was the emergence of the so-called 'originate-and-distribute' model of commercial banking that, in the run up to the crisis, was roundly endorsed for increasing the circulation of credit while simultaneously advancing systemic stability (e.g. Bank of England 2006). Under this model, exemplified by many non-bank and sub-prime mortgage lenders (Langley 2006, 2008b), securitization and related techniques were used to bundle up newly minted assets and move them into off-balance sheet entities. Capitalizing on the future income streams of these assets, the entities issued bonds which were 'distributed' as risk instruments to investors (Leyshon and Thrift 2007; Partnoy 2004). At the same time, banks themselves joined the community of investors. Here asset portfolios were typically held off-balance sheet in wholly or partly owned subsidiaries, with the funding of so-called 'shadow banking' vehicles such as hedge funds, private equity funds, and SIVs coming via 'liquidity leverage' and interest rate arbitrage between short-term debt and longer-term investments (*Economist* 2008a: 4). As the Winters (2012) review later put it, then, when explaining the Bank of England's procedures for the provision of liquidity that developed during crisis management, 'It appears that markets and the role of banks in markets may have changed structurally ... so these operations should not be regarded as extraordinary'.

Of particular significance to the initial rendering of the crisis was that the liquidity metaphor—replete with the multiple meanings discussed above—provided the crucial touchstone for both mainstream and heterodox economics. From the summer of 2007, the elasticity of the liquidity metaphor contributed to the folding, blending, and partial resolution of otherwise competing economic knowledges of finance, or what, turning to Deleuze and Guattari (1987; Connolly 2008: 39–40), we might think of as a 'resonance' between divergent imaginings of the crisis. The differences between orthodox and heterodox economic perspectives on liquidity came to matter little as the crisis was repetitively and reiteratively figured as a problem of liquidity. The liquidity metaphor provided a common set of epistemological coordinates for rendering the crisis (Cooper 2014), regardless of disagreements over precisely what it takes for markets to be liquid or for funding liquidity to be available. Illiquidity was, at once, both a 'chimera' that was 'aberrant' and not 'a natural reality' of recently perfected markets (Foucault 2007: 40–1), and a repeat of the unfortunate and historically recurring reality of financial market circulations.

Consider, for example, the seemingly paradoxical position of the Federal Reserve. In the press releases that accompanied each of the liquidity injections made by Fed, the purpose of action was described, in orthodox economic terms and almost without fail, as restoring 'the orderly functioning of financial markets'. Pumping liquidity would thus restore the liquidity norm, and the tendency of the market to equilibrium. At the same time, however, and in conjunction with the close-knit global central banking community, the Federal Reserve Chairman and key staff consistently turned to Walter Bagehot's (2008) *Lombard Street* (Irwin 2013). At the Fed, it was Bagehot's heterodox economics that provided much of the intellectual undergirding for the extensive liquidity facilities which ensured that the relative inaction of the Great Depression of the 1930s was not repeated (e.g. Bernanke 2008b, 2009, 2012; Madigan 2009).[21] The firm adoption of Bagehot's principle of how a central bank should respond to a crisis—by 'lending freely' in response to 'panic'—translated, for Bernanke (2008b), into 'liquidity measures' by way of 'response to the financial turmoil'. That the contemporary context was a 'market crisis'—and not the kind of 'banking crisis' common in Bagehot's day and before deposit insurance schemes (see Diamond and Dybvig 2002)—only served, for Bernanke (2008b), as further evidence that supported a truism stressed by heterodox economics: 'liquidity risks are always present for institutions . . . that finance illiquid assets with short-term liabilities'.

The orthodox and heterodox discursive elements of the governance apparatus were also set alongside market devices that calculated the extent or otherwise of the liquidity problem. Such measures established the material givens of liquidity in money markets in particular, providing quantified gauges of the extensity and intensity of the circulations that interventions sought to address. By doing so, these calculations did not merely record the extent or otherwise of liquidity, but themselves contributed to the abstraction of the crisis as one of liquidity. The devices in question were interest rate spreads, that is, measures of the difference between the variable costs of two debt instruments regarded to entail differing degrees of risk. Across recent decades, the key interest rate spread for dollar-denominated short-term debt was the so-called 'TED spread', a calculation of the difference between the interest payable on ostensibly risk-free three-month US Treasury bills on the one hand, and on riskier three-month unsecured interbank loans in the offshore Eurodollar markets on the other (Cecchetti 2009: 58). The latter price is expressed as the London Interbank Offered Rate (LIBOR), a global benchmark for interest rates (MacKenzie 2009: 1–2). As Brunnermeier (2009: 85) explains:

> In times of uncertainty, banks charge higher interest for unsecured loans, which increases the LIBOR rate. Further, banks want to get first-rate collateral, which makes holding Treasury bonds more attractive and pushes down the Treasury bond rate. For both reasons, the TED spread widens in times of crises.

A widening of the TED spread from the very outset of the crisis was thus taken as a pragmatic indicator of the 'draining of liquidity' from interbank money markets, especially given the narrowing of the spread during the preceding years of more than ample and affordable short-term debt.

Chief among the devices that calculated and constituted the liquidity problem, however, was a second measure of interest rate spreads: the LIBOR–OIS spread. Consistently referred to in official and media accounts during the first year or so of the crisis (e.g. Bank of England 2008; BIS 2008; FRB Markets Group 2008), the LIBOR–OIS spread sets three-month LIBOR, on the one hand, against rates for overnight index swaps (i.e. the cost of an interest rate swap between variable and fixed rates), on the other (Sengupta and Tam 2008). While payment on the entire principal of a LIBOR loan is made up-front, OIS contracts are settled on a net basis at the point of maturity. What the LIBOR–OIS spread quantifies, in short, is the willingness of banks to lend to each other compared to the cost of holding a variable rate relative to a fixed rate. The higher this number is, the harder and more expensive it is for banks to borrow from each other. In the run up to the crisis, the three-month LIBOR–OIS spread averaged around ten basis points. But, with 'the "illiquidity waves" that severely impaired money markets', the spread was particularly volatile, reaching eighty three basis points in mid-March 2008, and then jumping again to 365 basis points in mid-October (Sengupta and Tam 2008). It was mid-to-late 2009 before the LIBOR–OIS spread narrowed back towards the levels that were the norm prior to the outbreak of the crisis.

As the tumult became rendered as a problem of liquidity, a further, affective element was also present in the governance apparatus. For the most part, the contribution of an affective atmosphere of confidence to animating financial markets is typically bracketed-out by economics, cast either as unimportant to explanation, or as belonging to the field of psychology. Significantly, however, confidence is a vital force in the heterodox explanations of financial markets offered by the two economists who have also had the most enduring impact on the theory and practice of liquidity; namely, Keynes and Bagehot

(Swedberg 2012). As Amato and Fantacci (2012: 16) give voice to the Keynesian take on the intractable nature of liquidity and confidence, for instance: 'the confidence that makes the markets liquid and the liquidity that makes the markets confident' seems to rest on 'nothing other than their simple and indefinitely repeatable reference to each other'. So, for Bernanke (2008b), approvingly quoting Bagehot, in a speech of early summer 2008:

> the basis of a successful credit system is confidence. In one passage, he [Bagehot] writes, '"Credit means that a certain confidence is given, and a certain trust reposed. Is that trust justified? and is that confidence wise? These are the cardinal questions"'.

Once confidence was placed at the heart of credit-debt relations—more *a la* Bagehot than *a la* Keynes—it followed that, as the BIS (2008: 103) described the opening months of the crisis, for instance, the 'surge in liquidity demand' was necessarily 'a loss of confidence in the creditworthiness of counterparties'. Movements in interest rate spreads were regarded, moreover, as material and affective signals. As Bernanke (2012: 76) later described them, for instance, what the 'spikes' in LIBOR–OIS spreads of spring and autumn 2008 'indicated' was 'that suddenly there was no trust whatsoever even between the largest financial institutions because nobody knew who was going to be next, who was going to fail, who was going to come under funding pressure'.

The facilities and programmes that 'pumped liquidity', and seemingly provided the quantities of liquidity that had 'dried up' from money and capital markets, were thus also envisaged as efforts to restore an atmosphere of confidence to those markets. They 'acted like "injections of optimism", like administrations of antidepressant drugs' (Amato and Fantacci 2012: 83). Moreover, the governance apparatus featured explicit attempts to achieve the obverse: to cajole the conditions of confidence in order to restore liquidity. In general terms, and as a variation on what former Bank of England chief economist Charles Goodhart dubbed the 'open mouth operations' of monetary policy (Krippner 2007: 503), it was held to be the case that, for the central banks, 'communications can be more beneficial than actually providing funds if they serve to increase market participants' confidence that the situation is under control' (BIS 2008: 66). The communication of a willingness to act was, in particular, described as having a 'signalling effect':

> the announcement that the central bank is prepared to engage in operations involving illiquid assets may in itself boost investor confidence in those assets, thereby reducing liquidity premia and stimulating trading activity (2008: 95).

Similarly, and with reference to the Fed's last resort lending facilities, for instance, 'the existence of the option to borrow through the discount window, even if not exercised', was said during the first nine months or so of the crisis to have 'improved confidence by assuring depository institutions that backstop liquidity will be available should they need it' (Bernanke 2008b). What such attempts to cajole confidence also carried, however, was 'a "negative signalling" risk' (BIS 2008: 67), something that was seemingly evidenced by the immediate reaction to the Fed's TSLF of March 2008, for instance. The TSLF permitted investment banks to swap mortgage-related instruments for Treasury bonds. To avoid the kind of 'stigma' associated with discount window lending in the preceding months, it was announced that this programme of securities lending would be conducted in secret. Initially, however, this secrecy was taken on Wall Street to imply that the Fed was aware of the troubles of a particular investment bank (Brunnermeier 2009: 88). Suspicion fell on Bear Stearns, which was widely known to have a huge exposure to assets related to and derived from mortgages (see Chapter 4). Rather than provoking confidence by attaching a market public to it, the TSLF initially produced the opposite effect and arguably hastened the collapse of Bear.

Base Money and Balance Sheets

While the relational mobilization of specific elements was necessary to the rendering of the crisis as a problem of liquidity, acting on that problem required that the discrete governance apparatus also arranged additional elements. For example, the legal-cum-economic category of 'collateral'—'a technical little sideline item, something on the margins, tangential...a technical matter of arcane property law...something of an afterthought in market practice' (Riles 2011: 1)—was an important element as liquidity was made available through an array of interventions (Gabor 2012). The collateral conditions on the repo lending and discount window loans of the central banks were eased in various ways, for instance, and generous discounts were applied to dubious collateral. Securities lending programmes such as the TSLF and SLS explicitly sought to target and massage the illiquid collateral held by institutions that were struggling to access collateralized money market debt. The TALF, meanwhile, made loans directly available to capital market institutions, as long as they held specific and eligible forms of collateral. The 'posting' of the assignable and transferable guarantees of collateral in order to secure funds thus went far beyond the simple 'putting up' of 'good collateral' by solvent but illiquid banks, as was called for by Bagehot's principle of last resort lending.

There were, of course, institutional elements that had to be mobilized such that the apparatus could respond to the apparent liquidity problem: the central banks. The gathering together of this element was crucial to pumping liquidity because, as a consequence of the rationality of monetary sovereignty that is institutionalized in the Fed and the Bank, they hold a legal monopoly on the production of 'base' or 'high-powered money' within their respective territories. In the terms of Deleuze and Guattari (1983: 229), there is a constant, relational, and hierarchical 'dualism' in money and finance, 'the dualism between the formation of means of payment and the structure of financing, between the management of money and the financing of capitalist accumulation, between exchange money and credit money'. What the rationality of monetary sovereignty institutionalizes in the central bank is a monopoly over the money of exchange and account in which debt obligations have to be met, a legally defined sovereign right to designate and manufacture the base money through which the 'dematerialized' relations of 'credit money' become materialized and settled. It is this routine dualism in money and finance that lies at the root of OMOs and discount window techniques, and their extension in the form of last resort lending. In the governance of the contemporary crisis, and continuing to take terms from Deleuze and Guattari, 'the state' became not only the 'regulator' that ensures 'a principle of convertibility' of credit-debt relations, but the 'guarantor' of the transferrable debts in circulation. What the actions of injecting liquidity ultimately entailed was the minting of base money, in the form of bank reserves, in order that the commodified debts which were circulating as assets in the global financial markets did not have to be liquidated.

In the post-Bretton Woods era of 'fiat money', moreover—where legal tender is no longer backed by gold or other precious metals, and instead 'promises nothing but an identical copy of itself' (Rotman 1987: 5)—the creation of base money reserves by the central banks in response to the liquidity problem, and by the Federal Reserve in particular, was potentially limitless, save for worries about inflation, monetary soundness, and its impact upon sovereign credit ratings (Buiter 2008: 7–10; Irwin 2013: 279–80; Thompson 2013). As Perry Mehrling (2011: 29) explains through historical comparison with the position of the Bank of England as LOLR during the era of the nineteenth-century international gold standard, the contemporary Fed 'faces no reserve constraint in terms of gold'. Practically, and by way of apparent solution to the liquidity problem, the Fed was able to cut its target interest rate to almost zero without fear of depleting its gold reserves, and was able to create base money reserves without putting pressure on the convertibility of the dollar into gold. With the minting of fiat base money, sovereign techniques of last resort lending were thus redeployed in radical ways. It was sovereign techniques that were literally 'making' the money and capital markets of an apparently transformed financial system that had become structurally reliant upon the circulations of liquidity.

That acting on the liquidity problem was made possible by monetary sovereignty should not be taken to imply, however, that such power was simply possessed and wielded by the Fed and the Bank. While shedding critical light on the significance of the creation of base money to liquidity injections, post-Keynesian and political economy analyses tend to offer this kind of centralized and instrumental understanding of the actions of the central banks. For example, Amato and Fantacci (2012: xi, emphasis in original) are certainly on point when they stress that the creation of liquidity by central banks, as an ostensible solution to the problem of illiquidity in money and capital markets, was the creation of '*unredeemable debt*'. However, the monetary sovereigns are also endowed with a kind of agentic capacity by Amato and Fantacci, a capacity that they are held to have chosen to exercise in the crisis (2012: 45–6). Post-2007 crisis management is thus reducible to 'the paying of old debts with new debts, private debts with public debts' (2012: 236). Political economist Geoff Mann (2010a: 605) offers a similar view of contemporary crisis governance, meanwhile, when he traces the 'unlimited supply of highly liquid reserves' to the sovereign agency of the central banks. Conceiving of the sovereign power of central banks in the distinctly 'transcendent' terms of Hobbes' *Leviathan* (see Hardt and Negri 2000: 325), Mann (2010a: 602) holds that the autonomous, absolutist, and authoritarian exercise of that power is what provides 'contemporary capital's invisible infrastructure, the skeleton that keeps it upright when its muscles have failed'.

Post-Keynesian and political economy perspectives thus leave little scope for recognizing how contingent and dynamic last resort lending was made possible by multiple modalities of power, and was enacted as a distributed, relational, and strategic form of agency. A strict sovereign rationality of *raison d'État* did produce mercantilist central banking at its outset, at the end of the seventeenth century. From the nineteenth century, however, the development of modern central banking was made possible by modalities of power that gradually brought to the fore questions of national economic management and the stability of the monetary and financial conditions deemed necessary to securing life itself. Indeed, as Krippner (2007: 482) observes in relation to the US, 'monetary policy over the past quarter century' has been 'the site par excellence of neo-liberal policymaking'. Increasingly, modern central banking techniques and practices have not been prescribed in line with what might be best for the sovereign as such, but to incite or dampen market circulations such that they might not slow or accelerate too violently. There is thus no 'prescriptive norm' of what the interest rate should be in contemporary monetary policy, for instance, but the 'empirical norm' or 'mobile norm' of the market (Lemke 2011: 47; Amoore 2013). The market is to be both constantly modelled and measured on the one hand, and performed and 'modulated' on the other (Deleuze 1992; Holmes 2013). The minting of base money reserves by the Fed and the Bank in order to keep finance turning was thus an extension of modern central banking which, in Foucault's (2003c: 241) terms, 'does not erase the old right' of the sovereign, but 'does penetrate it, permeate it'. Furthermore, emerging in the processual composition of the discrete liquidity apparatus, revised sovereign techniques of emergency lending were mobilized as part of a distributed and relational *agencement.*

To illustrate this point further, consider an additional element, a market device of economics at large, which was also crucial to the exceptional operations of the liquidity apparatus: the balance sheet. Much like a commercial bank, the asset side of a central bank balance sheet typically includes sovereign bonds and bills, private debts (i.e. outright and collateralized loans and securities of all kinds), and official forex reserves. It is the liabilities side of a central bank balance sheet, however, that is quite different from that of a commercial bank. A central bank's liabilities include its debts in their various forms, but also the base money that it mints—i.e. the sum of the national currency in circulation, plus bank reserves held in deposit (Buiter 2008: 1–2). Unlike the deposits of a commercial bank, base money liabilities do not represent a claim on anything other than themselves. In the era of fiat money, base money is entirely self-referential and irredeemable.

In official reports (e.g. Cross et al. 2010; BIS 2008, 2009; FRB Markets Group 2008, 2009), as in critical academic accounts (e.g. Mann 2010a; Mehrling 2011; Thompson 2013), the balance sheets of the Bank of England and Federal Reserve feature strongly in the analysis of the liquidity injections which were undertaken by way of crisis governance. It is apparently on the balance sheets of the central banks that the staggering quantities and shifting qualities of the liquidity injections are to be found. What this obscures, however, is that the balance sheet actually contributes to making the actions of injecting liquidity possible. As a long-established body of scholarship on the corporation and capitalist enterprise attests (e.g. Schumpeter 1950; Sombart 1967; Weber 1978), balance sheets and double-entry bookkeeping do not merely measure and record the activities of an economic organization, but actually contribute to constituting that activity and its organization. While we will explore this scholarship in more detail in Chapter 5, what is of particular interest here is how the legacy of the initial legal formation of the first central banks as joint-stock companies manifests itself in modern central banks which continue to organize their operations through the device of the balance sheet. The balance sheet was not a passive descriptor of the liquidity injections, such that changes in the size and composition of central bank balance sheets were 'a by-product' of crisis governance actions (BIS 2009: 101). Rather, the balance sheets of the central banks were actually an active element in the apparatus that sought to render the crisis governable as a liquidity problem. It is the positioning of base money on the liabilities side of the balance sheet which ensured that, as they pumped liquidity on a monumental scale in the contemporary crisis, the Fed and the Bank themselves remained 'inherently liquid' and perpetually solvent (Buiter 2008: 2). As the central banks minted base money reserves, it was only through the metrics of the balance sheet that those reserves could fund the revisions to last resort lending techniques.

Conclusion

Beginning the book's concrete analysis of the governance of the global financial crisis, this chapter has addressed how the crisis was initially made up and managed as a problem of liquidity. The truly vast and wide-ranging liquidity injections of the Federal Reserve and Bank of England were shown to have been rooted in the OMOs and discount window techniques that are routine in central banking, and to have rested upon the well-established place of those techniques in last resort lending. The ways in which liquidity injections went significantly beyond the previously accepted parameters of last resort lending were also outlined and brought to the fore. The provision of liquidity embraced the money market operations of non-depository institutions and foreign banks in hitherto unseen ways, for instance. It also extended to directly funding and literally making capital markets; that is, the markets for securitized assets and corporate and government debt.

When set against the consensus on the ends and means of the governance of the global financial crisis, moreover, the chapter has begun to develop two of the main arguments advanced in this book. First, it has shown how the crisis was not initially governed as a general issue of the circulation of markets, banking, or capital, but as a specific and urgent need for 'liquidity'. At the outset, the crisis was rendered as a technical problem-object of liquidity in order that it could be acted upon. This abstraction was achieved through the relational mobilization of specific orthodox and heterodox economic discourses on liquidity, market devices of economics that measured and materialized liquidity, and the affective confidences of liquidity. Second, the chapter has shown that the rationality of monetary sovereignty institutionalized in the Fed and the Bank was indeed crucial to the provision of liquidity: without the minting of fiat, base money in the form of bank reserves, the circulation of transferable debt claims in the markets would have remained slow and unsteady at best. Yet, as has also been detailed, such strategic actions are not reducible to the ostensible agency of the central banks, but involved the distributed and relational agency of a discrete security apparatus in which sovereign last resort lending techniques were restyled and put to work in historically unprecedented ways. Even these exceptional liquidity injections were insufficient, however, and the crisis proved to be far more pervasive and persistent than it had first appeared. It could not be contained as merely a moment when liquidity had been lost.

Notes

1. Chuck Prince's remarks were made during an interview he gave in Japan to the *Financial Times* (Nakamoto and Wighton 2007).
2. Former Vice Chairman of the Federal Reserve Board of Governors, Alan Blinder (2013: 250, original emphasis), provides the following summary of 'quantitative easing':

   The name derives from the idea that a standard easing of monetary policy works on price—on the cost of borrowing money. When that price falls, related quantities— such as the quantities of bank reserves, money supply, and bank loans—are supposed to increase.... Once the *price* (that is, the interest rate) avenue is exhausted, the central bank can still boost the quantities of bank reserves, money, and credit directly—normally by buying assets.... The idea is to push more and more reserves into banks, at essentially a zero price, in the hope that the surfeit of reserves will induce banks to make use of them (e.g., to finance new lending).

3. Federal Reserve Board Press Release, 10 August 2007. Available at: <http://www.federalreserve.gov/newsevents/press/monetary/20070810a.htm> (accessed June 2014).
4. 'Repos' (repurchase agreements) are short-term loans (e.g. overnight) that are issued to finance the holding of a financial asset, where the asset itself provides the underlying collateral. The legal form taken by a repo combines the sale of an asset with an agreement to repurchase the asset at the original sale price plus some rate of interest. Moreover, the sale price is less than the prevailing market price for the asset, a difference (or 'haircut') that is smallest when the asset/collateral is perceived to be low risk (e.g. a US Treasury bill) (Mehrling 2011: 23–4).
5. Discount window liquidity techniques, also sometimes referred to as 'standing loan facilities' and 'liquidity backstops' (BIS 2008: 69), relate to the central bank's position within the clearing and payments system. Net payments between the reserve accounts of banks, held at a central bank, must be settled on a daily basis. If a bank is unable to settle payments by accessing money market debt, and does not have sufficient reserves at the central bank, it must take out a collateralized loan at the central bank's discount window to, in effect, access the central bank's own reserves. The rate of interest ('discount rate' or 'overnight rate') payable at the discount window is typically higher than that which prevails in the money markets and, thus, encourages settlement to take place through the money market in the first instance.
6. The precise nature of OMOs depends upon the specific legal arrangements and institutional norms that are at work in each central bank. The Bank of England, for instance, routinely engages in OMOs with a wide range of institutions, and this was reflected in the mechanisms through which it undertook to inject liquidity in the contemporary crisis. The Bank did not introduce a new Discount Window Facility into its operations until October 2008, a move that permitted lower-quality collateral to be swapped for government securities in a way that was not permitted in its OMOs (Fisher 2012). The Federal Reserve, in contrast, ordinarily conducts OMOs with a limited group of primary dealers, while depository institutions have to access its discount window.

7. Issued by the US Treasury, and sold at auction by the Federal Reserve to primary dealers who act as market-makers, 'Treasuries' are dollar-denominated debt instruments that come in three forms: 'T-bills', which have a maturity of one year or less; 'T-notes', which have a maturity of between two and 10 years; and 'T-bonds', with a maturity of between ten and thirty years.

8. Federal Reserve Board Press Release, 11 March 2008. Available at: <http://federalreserve.gov/newsevents/press/monetary/20080311a.htm> (accessed June 2014).

9. Mervyn King, quoted in Bank of England News Release, 21 April 2008. Available at: <http://www.bankofengland.co.uk/archive/Pages/digitalcontent/historicpubs/news/2008/029.aspx> (accessed June 2014).

10. See, for example, Federal Reserve Board Press Release, 17 August 2007. Available at: <http://www.federalreserve.gov/newsevents/press/monetary/20070817a.htm> (accessed June 2014). Federal Reserve Board Press Release, 16 March 2008. Available at: <http://www.federalreserve.gov/newsevents/press/monetary/20080316a.htm> (accessed June 2014).

11. Federal Reserve Board Press Release, 12 December 2007. Available at: <http://www.federalreserve.gov/newsevents/press/monetary/20071212a.htm> (accessed June 2014).

12. Federal Reserve Board Press Release, 16 March 2008. Available at: <http://www.federalreserve.gov/newsevents/press/monetary/20080316a.htm> (accessed June 2014). Federal Reserve Board Press Release, 14 September 2008. Available at: <http://www.federalreserve.gov/newsevents/press/monetary/20080914a.htm> (accessed June 2014).

13. Respectively, see Federal Reserve Board Press Release, 19 September 2008. Available at: <http://www.federalreserve.gov/newsevents/press/monetary/20080919a.htm> (accessed June 2014); and Federal Reserve Board Press Release, 21 October 2008. Available at: <http://www.federalreserve.gov/newsevents/press/monetary/20081021a.htm> (accessed June 2014). Typically providing a home for deposits by institutional investors such pension funds and insurance companies, the $3 trillion dollar money market funds industry in the US holds portfolios invested in short-term money market assets, especially commercial paper and including that issued by banks. The price of a share in each fund is historically just above one dollar, essentially a promise of return of capital invested plus a relatively small amount of interest. That one large money market mutual, Reserve Primary Fund, could not meet that guarantee and 'broke the buck' during the crisis produced a relatively brief but very intense rupture in money market circulations that the Federal Reserve acted upon (Madigan 2009).

14. Federal Reserve Board Press Release, 14 October 2008. Available at: <http://www.federalreserve.gov/newsevents/press/monetary/20081014b.htm> (accessed June 2014).

15. Federal Reserve Board Press Release, 12 December 2007. Available at: <http://www.federalreserve.gov/newsevents/press/monetary/20071212a.htm> (accessed June 2014). 'Swap lines' between central banks are a practice of crisis management that, according to Kindleberger (1996: 181–2), emerged from negotiations at the BIS and in response to problems in the Eurodollar markets during the early 1960s.

More recently, they were also utilized in response to the market volatilities pro-voked by the 9/11 attacks of 2001.

16. Federal Reserve Board Press Release, 25 November 2008. Available at: <http://www.federalreserve.gov/newsevents/press/monetary/20081125a.htm> (accessed June 2014).

17. Bank of England News Release, 5 March 2009. Available at: <http://www.bankofengland.co.uk/archive/Documents/historicpubs/news/2009/019.pdf> (accessed June 2014).

    Issued by HM Treasury and sold at auction by the Debt Management Office (DMO) since 1998 to so-called 'Gilt-edged market makers'. UK 'gilts' are sterling denominated debt instruments that come in two main forms, both with a wide range of maturities: conventional gilts and index-linked gilts. Gilts are denoted by the coupon rate and date of maturity (e.g. four per cent Treasury Gilt 2016), and circulate widely in secondary markets.

18. Federal Reserve Board Press Release, 3 November 2010. Available at: <http://www.federalreserve.gov/newsevents/press/monetary/20101103a.htm> (accessed June 2014).

19. The power of such metaphors in economic thinking and organization has been widely acknowledged (McCloskey 1998; Mirowski 2002), and, for Amin and Thrift (2004), is an important concern in cultural economy analysis. On watery meta-phors as 'instruments of communication' and 'instruments of inspiration' in global finance, see Clark (2005).

20. By establishing a fluctuating minimum level of the 'high-quality liquid assets' that a bank should hold—according to scenarios of future money market stress, and monitored by national regulators—the LCR is designed to ensure that the banking system is much less susceptible to a rupture in the circulations of short-term debt. See BIS Press Release, 6 January 2013. Available at: <http://www.bis.org/press/p130106.htm> (accessed June 2014). On the implementation of the LCR in the US, see Federal Reserve Board Press Release, 24 October 2013. Available at: <http://www.federalreserve.gov/newsevents/press/bcreg/20131024a.htm> (accessed June 2014).

21. Before coming to the Fed, Bernanke (2000) built his academic reputation on the contribution he made to debates over Federal Reserve policy decisions during the crisis of the 1930s. As he later put it, 'the Fed did not do enough to stabilize the banking system in the 1930s, and so the lesson there is that in a financial panic, the central bank has to lend freely, according to Bagehot's principle, to halt runs and to try to stabilize the financial system' (Bernanke 2012: 74).

4

Toxicity

Introduction: 'toxic Kool-Aid'

> It's sort of a little poetic justice, in that the people that brewed this toxic
> Kool-Aid found themselves drinking a lot of it in the end.
>
> Warren Buffett, Chairman, Berkshire Hathaway, 6 February 2008.

While the will to govern the global financial crisis concentrated initially on the problem of liquidity in money markets, a related but relatively discrete set of interventions forged and sought to act upon the problem of 'toxicity' in capital markets. Memorably referred to by Warren Buffet in early 2008 as the 'poetic justice' of 'toxic Kool-Aid' (Dabrowski 2008), the specific issue addressed by these initiatives was the value, valuation, and circulation of assets related to and derived from US sub-prime mortgages. Sub-prime MBS and CDOs had apparently become illiquid and untradeable, and were variously referred to in common currency as 'toxic assets', 'toxic refuse', and 'toxic waste'. Such assets, which had proffered massive returns during the preceding bubble, were now threatening huge losses for investors. What was particularly significant, however, was that the struggle to price toxic assets in capital markets also ensured that they were the source of 'incalculable costs' which extended indefinitely into the future, as there was 'no knowledge [of] how long they will have to be kept or how much they can be resold for' (Amato and Fantacci 2012: 74). Thus, and as the closure of the hedge funds operated by Bear Stearns and BNP Paribas at the very outset of the crisis appeared to demonstrate, toxic assets poisoned the credibility of the securitization and structured finance techniques, investment strategies, and webs of revolving short-term debt relations that had 'brewed' up their circulations over the preceding period. It was the toxicity of this particular class of assets, then, that supposedly gave rise to the liquidity problem in money markets, and this was crucial to marking them out for dedicated attention by way of crisis management.

The focus for the chapter is upon how the crisis was made legible as a dilemma of toxicity, and upon the attempts to create 'bad banks' designed to take toxic assets temporarily out of circulation. As detailed in the opening section, two sets of toxic asset interventions were enacted in the US during 2008, prior to the broader targeting of capital market liquidity and the unfurling of QE programmes by the Federal Reserve. The first set of interventions concentrated on the toxic assets of particular institutions: namely, the Wall Street investment bank, Bear Stearns; and the giant insurance company, American International Group (AIG). The second was the most high-profile and politically contentious governance action that was undertaken in the US during the crisis: the TARP which, in its planning phase, was known as the 'Toxic Assets Relief Program'.[1] Funded and organized under the auspices of the US Treasury, and announced on 19 September 2008, the $700 billion TARP was a comprehensive commitment to spend the equivalent of $2,300 for every man, woman, and child in America on the temporary purchase of toxic assets from the capital markets (Herszenhorn 2008). Covering the toxic asset problem with the TARP proved unfeasible, however, and the first $350 billion tranche of TARP funds were primarily spent to recapitalize US banking from mid-October 2008 (see Chapter 5).

The second and third sections of the chapter develop an understanding of the strategic and distributed agency of the security apparatus that—produced through a relational arrangement of heterogeneous elements, and transcending the seemingly separate domains of state/market and public/private—rendered the crisis governable as a discrete problem of toxicity. The second section concentrates on the specific economic discourses and market devices that figured the crisis in these terms. Unlike the resonance of orthodox and heterodox economics that contributed to the abstraction of the crisis as a liquidity issue, an orthodox economic discourse was to the fore as the apparatus figured the crisis in metaphorical terms as a contagious infection of the cardiovascular system of the economic body. The crisis appeared to be less an acute instance of the recurring illiquidity problem endogenous to financial markets and capitalist banking, and more an aberrant result of the creation and circulation of a particular and idiosyncratic class of assets. As such, financial market models and regulatory strategies that reified liquid capital markets were held in place rather than questioned. Market calculations of the premiums payable on CDS contracts provided the key device for measuring the nature and extent of the toxic asset problem to be addressed.

As the final section of the chapter will show, acting on the toxic asset problem entailed the gathering together of a number of further elements in the apparatus of governance. The apparatus featured the theory and practice of 'bad banks', the sovereign state institutions of the Federal Reserve and the US Treasury, dedicated legal provisions and statutes, and a discourse that portrayed the temporary purchase of toxic assets as critical to preventing the infection of the financial system from spreading to the rest economic body. The TARP also required the enrolment of a reverse auction process in order to purchase toxic assets, but this quickly proved to be impracticable and unusable. Thus, when attempting the 'sifting' of 'the good [assets] from the bad [assets], ensuring that things are always in movement, constantly moving around, continually going from one point to another' (Foucault 2007: 65), this discrete apparatus reconfigured sovereign monetary and fiscal techniques in an explicit attempt restore uncertain capital market circulations and the opportunities that they ostensibly afford for the financialized security of the population.

Bear Stearns, AIG, and the TARP

The last resort support that the New York Federal Reserve provided to Bear Stearns in March 2008 was of a qualitatively different order to the money market liquidity injections which had preceded it. It was the crisis governance action that, set in the context of the theory and practice of last resort lending, 'constituted crossing the Rubicon' (Blinder 2013: 105). First, and most obviously, this 'extraordinary intervention' was not a matter of lending to the markets in general via the routine mechanisms of OMOs and the discount window, but was focused upon an individual institution (BIS 2008: 112). Strict adherence to Bagehot's principle of last resort lending would have ruled out support for any single institution, not least because an institution that cannot post the collateral to cover emergency central bank loans is typically held to be insolvent rather than illiquid (Goodhart and Illing 2002: 2–3; see Chapter 5). However, in the case of Bear, the Fed judged that support for an individual institution was warranted to try to halt a self-fulfilling loss of confidence in markets. For example, in his 3 April 2008 Testimony to the Senate Banking, Housing, and Urban Affairs Committee, Timothy Geithner (2008), then President of the New York Fed, justified the action in the following terms:

> In our financial system, the market sorts out which companies survive and which fail. However, under the circumstances prevailing in the markets, the issues raised in this specific instance extended well beyond the fate of one company. It became clear that Bear's involvement in the complex and intricate web of relationships that characterize our financial system, at a point in time when markets were especially vulnerable, was such that a sudden failure would likely lead to a chaotic unwinding of positions in already damaged markets.

Testifying before the same Committee, Ben Bernanke (2008c) similarly stressed that the action to 'prevent a disorderly failure of Bear Stearns' should be seen as inseparable from 'the unpredictable but likely severe consequences for market functioning and the broader economy' that would have followed from such a failure. In this respect, it was not the sheer size of Bear Stearns that was said to justify a significant departure from the established practices of last resort lending, but the extensity of its market relations. In the parlance of the period, it was not simply that Bear was 'too big to fail', but that it was 'too interconnected to fail'.

Second, what was also unprecedented about the Fed's support for Bear Stearns was that the institution in question was one of Wall Street's investment banks, albeit the smallest of the big five, and not one of the commercial banks that the Fed was permitted to assist when acting as the bankers' bank. Thus, and as 'the fork in the river' that set the Fed's course for crisis management (Reinhart 2011: 72), the bailout of Bear required the Fed to invoke the special provisions of Section 13(3) of the Federal Reserve Act.[2] Support for Bear was accompanied by other precedent-setting liquidity measures: the PCDF, which opened the Fed's discount window to all investment banks and other primary dealers; and the TSLF, which permitted primary dealers to swap collateral in order to support their money market borrowing.[3] Explaining the exceptional nature of these actions to Congress, Geithner (2008) offered a reading of financial market innovation feeding into structural change that left the Fed with little choice but to intervene. As he put it:

> Over the past 30 years, we have moved from a bank-dominated financial system to a system in which credit is increasingly extended, securitized and actively traded in a combination of centralized and decentralized markets. In many ways, the business models of banks and non-bank financial institutions—especially large securities firms—have converged, with banks playing a greater agency role in the credit process, and securities firms doing more of the financing ... these changes in the relative roles of traditional commercial banks and investment banks have changed the nature of financial stability.

For Geithner, the Fed's 'tools' were outdated, and saving Bear demonstrated the Fed's willingness to 'adapt' in order to 'deal with current market realities'.

Third, what was particularly distinctive about the rescue of Bear Stearns by the Fed was the unique and idiosyncratic form taken by the action, announced on 16 March 2008 and finalized eight days later. The immediate source of Bear's problems were that it was unable to roll over the $100 billion or so of short-term repos through which it financed its routine operations (Blinder 2013: 102). However, the Fed did not support Bear with a liquidity loan of the kind that, within the parameters of the PCDF, would have required that assets were posted as collateral. Instead, the Fed provided a non-standard discount loan to acquire a portion of Bears' assets. What was more, the Fed's extraordinary $29 billion discount loan was not extended directly to Bear, or even to JP Morgan Chase, the clearing bank that regularly arranged the financing of Bear's business. Rather, to circumvent its own regulations and to grease the wheels of the deal that saw JP Morgan acquire Bear at a knock-down price, the Fed lent to a so-called 'bad bank'. This newly created limited liability company—named Maiden Lane LLC—was incorporated solely to buy £30 billion worth of Bear's toxic assets.

Prior to the crisis, mortgage securitization had been the largest component of Bear's fixed-investment activities which, in turn, generated more than half of the firm's profits. In addition, 'a series of acquisitions and expansions had turned Bear Stearns into a full-service, vertically integrated mortgage machine' (Blinder 2013: 101–2). Maiden Lane LLC—named after the street from which it is possible to gain backdoor access to the New York Fed—largely mirrored the legal arrangement of the SIVs that were a feature of the shadow banking sector in the run up to the crisis. Accordingly, it was an asset management firm, BlackRock, who were employed by the Fed to gradually liquidate the Maiden Lane LLC portfolio of toxic assets. Over a maximum ten-year period, the principal and interest on the Fed's loan, followed by the same for JP Morgan's $1 billion stake in Maiden Lane LLC, were to be paid down on a monthly basis via the divestment of the assets.[4] By June 2012, however, the Fed had been repaid, and Maiden Lane LLC was wound up.

Further bad banks were created in November 2008, this time for the toxic assets of the giant insurance company AIG. Called Maiden Lane LLC II and Maiden Lane LLC III, the AIG bad banks took on a similar legal form to their namesake which had been incorporated nine months earlier. The Federal Reserve Bank of New York announced that it would extend loans for up to six years of $22.5 billion and $30 billion to Maiden Lane LLC II and III, respectively, although the exact amounts loaned were slightly lower in each case. Amid the market chaos of mid-September that was prompted by the bankruptcy of Lehman Brothers and the fire-sale acquisition of Merrill Lynch by Bank of America, the Fed had already stepped in to save AIG from collapse. Then the Fed granted a two-year, $85 billion loan to AIG, in return for an eighty per cent equity stake (Andrews et al. 2008; Felsted and Burgess 2008).[5] The November loans to Maiden Lane LLC II and III by the New York Fed were thus in addition to the 'liquidity facility' of September that had been designed 'to assist AIG in meeting its obligations as they come due'.[6] The creation of the AIG bad banks was also accompanied by the purchase of a further $40 billion worth of new equity in AIG, under the rapidly evolving auspices of the US Treasury's TARP programme.[7]

The wide-ranging interventions in support for AIG were justified on grounds that were much the same as the 'too interconnected to fail' explanation which was given for the bailout of Bear. For instance, at a hearing of the Senate Banking, Housing, and Urban Affairs Committee in March 2009—itself provoked by a yet further extension of equity investment in AIG, which took the US Treasury's total stake in the company to $70 billion—the Federal Reserve Board Vice Chairman, Donald L. Kohn (2009), reported that:

> Our judgment has been and continues to be that, in this time of severe market and economic stress, the failure of AIG would impose unnecessary and burdensome losses on many individuals, households and businesses, disrupt financial markets, and greatly increase fear and uncertainty about the viability of our financial institutions.

Accordingly, and with specific reference to the AIG bad banks, the loan to Maiden Lane LLC II was for the purchase of the toxic, non-agency MBS that AIG had previously used as collateral in its repo market borrowings. This ensured that Fed funds flowed to the banks that were the counterparties to AIG's outstanding short-term debt relations. In lending to Maiden Lane LLC III, meanwhile, the Fed targeted the CDS operations of AIG that were head-quartered in London and worth in the region of $450 billion. Toxic CDOs were purchased from investors for whom AIG had written over-the-counter CDS contracts, such that these investors were able to unwind their positions via the receipt of Fed funds.[8] BlackRock was again employed by the Fed as the asset manager of AIG bad banks, and the divestment of the assets of Maiden Lane LLC II and III was such that the New York Fed was repaid within four years.

Established in the intervening period between Maiden Lane LLC I and Maiden Lane II and III, however, was a toxic asset bad bank that was designed to be much more extensive in scope and 'to fundamentally and comprehensively address the root cause of our financial system's stresses by removing distressed assets from the financial system' (US Treasury Department 2008a). First announced on 19 September 2008 by the then US Treasury Secretary, Henry ('Hank') Paulson, the initial three-page TARP proposal requested authority from Congress 'to issue up to $700 billion of Treasury securities to finance the purchase of troubled assets' (US Treasury Department 2008a). Under the terms of what was also known as 'the Paulson plan', such assets were to be purchased from investors by the US Treasury's newly created Office of Financial Stability through a reverse auction process, and at prices higher than those presently prevailing in markets. This was expected to indirectly boost banks' capital, as it would reduce the capital which they had to set aside against these assets on the liabilities side of their balance sheets.

Before the TARP was eventually passed by Congress on 3 October as the Emergency Economic Stabilization Act of 2008, it was initially rejected by the House of Representatives and considerable political horse-trading over add-itions to the legislation was necessary.[9] Within two weeks of coming into effect, however, the TARP had mutated from its initial design as a temporary bad bank for toxic assets, and became the principal funding mechanism that supported the direct recapitalization of US banking (see Chapter 5). The US Treasury did not ultimately feature significantly, then, in the action taken on the problem of toxicity. As already detailed in Chapter 3, it was the Federal Reserve that took the lead in addressing capital markets problems, most notably through the TALF and QE1 programmes, and under the rubric of liquidity and not toxicity. That said, November 2008 saw TARP monies set aside to contribute to public guarantees on the value of toxic assets purchased by so-called 'vulture investors' from the books of Citigroup. This insurance-style approach to the ongoing problem of toxic assets was repeated for Bank of America in January 2009 (Andrews 2009). The Obama administration's Public-Private Investment Program (P-PIP) of March 2009 announced a similar intention (Geithner 2009; US Treasury Department 2009a), creating a so-called 'aggregator bank' (rather than a bad bank) by providing public support for private investment in what were renamed as 'legacy assets'.

The Toxicity Problem

In order that the Maiden Lane LLCs and the TARP bad bank could be held out as solutions, the crisis was rendered as a problem of 'toxicity'. As Philip Mirowski (2013: 169) notes, the various metaphors of toxicity that were applied to sub-prime assets 'had no basis whatsoever' in the efficient markets theory of finance that prevailed in the run up to the crisis: from this perspective, 'the system as a whole simply cannot fail to price and allocate risks; hence there is no such thing as virulently "toxic" assets'. Nonetheless, the tendency to label unrealizable debts and, especially, untradeable secondary claims upon debts, as 'toxic' appears to have already begun on Wall Street a few years before the outbreak of the crisis.[10] It was the apparently anomalous quality of toxicity that was crucial to the traction that the metaphor gained in economic discourse during the first 12 months or so of the crisis. US Treasury Secretary Paulson had, for example, initially attempted to cajole the major banks to contribute to a 'superfund' for 'illiquid', 'distressed', and 'toxic assets' in October and November 2007 (Andrews 2007). Talk of toxicity served to reduce all that had gone wrong with global finance, and the more immediate complexities of MBS, CDOs, and CDS, in particular, to an apparently simple, singular, and historically unique object to be acted upon: sub-prime, toxic assets. Thus diagnosed, the crisis, like these assets, appeared as the exception that proved the rules of efficient and liquid capital markets.

The mobilization of the toxicity discourse played on the broader economic narrative that abstracted the crisis as a liquidity problem. It did this in four main ways. First, it was the loss of certain, supposedly normal qualities of liquidity that the designation 'toxic assets' typically invoked: there was temporarily no capital market within which sub-prime assets could be easily priced, traded, and liquefied. For Geithner (2008), for example, and with reference to the creation of Maiden Lane LLC I, JP Morgan Chase could not be expected to 'absorb some of Bear's trading portfolio' at the present time because of 'the uncertainty ahead about the ultimate scale of losses facing the financial system'. As such, it was the definition of liquid assets and markets provided by orthodox economic textbooks—and certainly not those of Bagehot, Keynes, and their heterodox successors—that was primarily emphasized by the toxicity discourse. The crisis appeared, in the first instance, to be a problem of capital market liquidity that had subsequently become manifest in a problem of money market or 'funding liquidity' (Borio 2010; Brunnermeier 2008, 2009). As Carruthers and Stinchcombe (1999: 353) remind us:

> By liquidity of a market, economists mean that standardized products can be bought and sold continuously at a price that everyone in the market can know, and that products are not normally sold at a price that diverges substantially from the market price. The idea is that everyone can know at all times what the price is, and only one price obtains in the market.

Illiquid sub-prime assets were said to be toxic, in short, because they could not be valued and priced as normal by the capital markets. In Geoff Mann's (2010b: 174) terms, there was certainly 'a quantitative decline in the magnitude of value' of sub-prime assets, but this did not fundamentally question 'the category of value or the value-form' that was encapsulated by the circulation of transferable claims on sub-prime debt. For many practitioners and commentators, such abnormal market outcomes were inseparable from the breakdown in the risk calculations of the bond rating agencies that, having provided the 'standardized' information on sub-prime assets, were now found to have been highly optimistic at best (Langley 2008a; 2010).

Second, the toxicity discourse reinforced the naturalized and circulatory envisioning of monetary and financial economies that is carried forward by notions of liquidity. For instance, when Hank Paulson (2008a) appeared before Congress to seek approval for his TARP, he positioned toxic assets as 'choking off the flow of credit which is so vitally important to our economy'. In figuring such circulatory representations of finance, however, talk of toxicity replaced the hydraulic and mechanical imaginary of liquid financial markets with a more embodied imaginary. Rather than a problem with the irrigation of the economic land, it appeared that the cardiovascular financial system of the economic body had been momentarily poisoned and needed to be flushed out. As it provided a diagnosis of the crisis, the toxicity discourse was thus part of the broader tendency to represent the crisis through an array of analogies with contagious diseases—as a virulent infection and pandemic, not unlike the global swine-origin influenza with which it coincided (Haldane and May 2011; Peckham 2013). In the terms of Timothy Geithner (2008), for example, 'Contagion spreads, transmitting waves of distress to other markets, from subprime to prime mortgages and even to agency mortgage-backed securities, to commercial mortgage-backed securities and to corporate bonds and loans'. Yet, the specific description of assets as 'toxic' also called up a much longer-standing imaginary, such that the crisis was explained as that which was infecting the monetary and financial lifeblood of the economic body.

Writing on the role of money in the modern metropolitan and liberal form of life that he saw to be emerging at the turn of the twentieth century, Georg Simmel (2004: 474) states that:

> money can be compared to the bloodstream whose continuous circulation per-
> meates all the intricacies of the body's organs and unifies their functions by
> feeding them all to an equal extent.

As Johnson (1966) details, however, what he calls the 'money = blood meta-phor' can actually be traced to Aristotle, and was commonplace during the medieval period. It gained particular force in mercantilist thought, moreover, and in the wake of William Harvey's early seventeenth-century analysis of the body's circulatory system. Despite the vital associations that this created between money and the various organs of the state—as articulated, for instance, in Thomas Hobbes' *Leviathan* (de Goede 2005: 22–3)—the blood metaphor was largely held in place as the physiocrats and classical political economists invented and separated out of the object of 'the economy' as a productive and circulatory system in the late eighteenth century (Buck-Morss 1995). The analogous representation of money as the blood of the economic body has also tended to continue, in part because it is able to occupy the conceptual space of 'the macro-economy' that is vacated as neoclassical and neo-liberal approaches largely reduce economic life to micro-economics (1995: 463). The toxicity metaphor, in short, invoked a deeply embedded and embodied diagram of monetary and financial circulations. It followed that what was needed were 'cleansing' actions (Madigan 2009), akin to a kind of purification or dialysis of the financial bloodstream.

Third, the toxicity discourse also served to hold in place the wide array of business models, techniques, and organizational strategies that, gaining sway from the mid-1990s, reified liquid markets. Markets during the boom appeared as a known thing or object regarded by practitioners as independent and external to them, as having an agency and 'life of their own' when setting and moving prices, facilitating exchange, managing risk, and so on. Take, for example, International Accounting Standard 39, authored by the Inter-national Accounting Standards Board (IASB) and introduced in 2005. In a move away from traditional practices of valuing an asset on the basis of an estimate of its underlying worth, assets included in financial statements were 'marked-to-market' at 'fair value' (i.e. at the price they could expect to fetch in present liquid markets, rather than their historical cost) (Nolke and Perry 2006; *Economist* 2008b). Similarly, and as was noted in the previous chapter, the reification of liquid markets was present in international risk management standards which made no provision for 'liquidity risk'. The assumption of liquid markets also underpinned the edifice of the 'originate-and-distribute' model of commercial banking (see Chapter 5). Moreover, it was also at the heart of the global expansion and reach of Wall Street's investment banks. Earning very healthy fees and commissions from the issue, structuring, and sale of sub-prime assets, the investment banks' highly leveraged, proprietary trading strategies ensured that they were also crucial to the circulation of those assets.

Fourth, as it held in place the liquid market models and practices of the pre-crisis period, the toxicity discourse also reproduced the envisioning of global financial circulations as serving to reduce so-called 'systemic risk'. Prevailing in regulatory and central banking practices prior to the crisis (e.g. Bernanke 2007), and often referred to as 'the completion' or 'the perfection of the markets' (Chinloy and MacDonald 2005; Engelen et al. 2011), this imaginary of self-stabilizing market circulations included the movements of 'over-the-counter' CDS markets.[11] While enabling trading in volatility and variance that is actually marked by an indifference to the performance of underlying assets (Martin 2007; Wigan 2009), CDS nonetheless held out the pre-emptive promise that the default risks of specific assets (e.g. a corporate bond) could be hedged through bespoke contracts. The aggregate effect of the valuation, pricing, trading, and hedging of transferable claims on underlying debts that were carried by liquid market circulations was therefore commonly held to be the 'decomposition' and 'distribution' of default risks among investors (see also Chapter 6). As the authors of an IMF working paper optimistically put it, for instance, when reflecting in July 2007 upon the impact of the already rising tide of defaults in the US sub-prime mortgage market:

> The dispersion of credit risk to a broader and more diverse group of investors has nevertheless helped to make the U.S. financial system more resilient. The magnitude and scale of losses being currently experienced in subprime mortgage markets would have materially impacted some systemically-important U.S. financial institutions in the traditional originate-and-retain business model. But, thus far, most subprime losses have been borne by, and contained in, the origination network's periphery of thinly-capitalized specialty finance companies, lower-rated ABS and CDO tranches, and some hedge funds.   (Kiff and Mills 2007: 12)

As the crisis developed, it appeared to be the case that, by cleaning the system of aberrant toxic assets, the 'dispersion' of default risks and attendant pre-emption of systemic risk could continue.

Crucial in this regard was ensuring that markets for CDS contracts held up. The scale of investor losses on toxic assets was partly dependent upon whether they were covered by CDS contracts on those assets (*Economist* 2008c), and Bear Stearns and especially AIG were hugely significant to the CDS market (Felsted and Burgess 2008). When establishing bad banks for their toxic assets, the Fed had, in effect, recognized that these institutions were 'too interconnected to fail' precisely because, if the CDS contracts that it had written became worthless, this would have forced a complete collapse in CDS markets and further investor losses on the assets that were underlying them. Although credit derivative contracts actually enabled the debt markets to be levered and speculated upon, the toxicity discourse perpetuated the representation of CDS markets as serving to hedge the debt markets.

In sum, a key element in the apparatus that abstracted the crisis as a toxicity problem was the discourse that made a series of largely metaphorical plays on the orthodox economics of liquid market circulations. Mobilized in relation with this discourse were several market devices that were also crucial to determining the known extent of the ostensibly toxic objects to be acted upon. By providing measures of the value of toxic assets, these devices necessarily contributed to the terms through which the crisis itself came to be understood. Banks' balance sheets, for instance, provided one set of calculations of the material givens of the toxicity problem. It was here that the presently declining values of sub-prime assets were literally 'booked' or 'written-down', an accounting move whereby these assets were revalued to a certain amount in the dollar. At the point at which the TARP proposals came before Congress, for instance, investors were widely known to have made a cumulative total of $500 billion worth of write-downs on sub-prime assets since September 2007 (Tett 2008). Doubts remained, however, as to whether balance sheets provided an accurate picture of the scale of the toxic asset problem, not least because the falling values of sub-prime assets had been consistently under-calculated throughout the crisis and banks had made successive revisions to write-downs when seeking to 'clean their books' (Brunnermeier 2008). With the balance sheets of commercial banks featuring the 'safety valve' of accrual accounting, whereby 'souring assets can escape the rigors of mark-to-market accounting', misgivings also persisted about the valuations that individual institutions were placing on their assets (*Economist* 2008b). For example, a *New York Times* article from the period during which the TARP proposals were being considered by Congress reported that Merrill Lynch had sold $31 billion worth of CDOs at 22 cents in the dollar in July, but that the balance sheet of Citigroup valued a similar set of assets at

61 cents in the dollar (Bajaj 2008). Mistrust in the capacity of balance sheets to accurately calculate the scale of present losses was compounded, moreover, by fears over what was yet to come.

The material givens of the toxicity apparatus were therefore typically established with reference to another set of calculations that, by definition, sought to price the future value of assets. CDS are specific to the assets that act as their underlying referent. As such, CDS contract prices provide a *de facto* market valuation of the assets in question. In the midst of the crisis, a spike in the price for CDS contracts written against bonds issued by a particular financial institution were commonly taken as an indication, usually alongside a sharp fall in that institution's share price, that it had not yet fully declared the extent of its losses on toxic assets (Larsen and Scholtes 2008). More directly, and in terms of contracts written on sub-prime MBS and CDOs themselves, rising CDS premiums were taken as an indication of the likely future value of the underlying instruments. Indeed, prior to the turmoil, the cost of purchasing a CDS contract was widely accepted as a key measure of value for CDOs derived from sub-prime mortgages and, as such, contributed to producing an apparently liquid CDO market (Tett 2009: 171). Moreover, ABX Home Equity indexes—which reference baskets of CDS written on tranches of CDOs backed by sub-prime bonds—provided not only charts that tracked the price of purchasing CDS contracts on the CDOs concerned, but also graphical images of the apparent value of the CDOs. The indexes record prices as a percentage of par value for a CDS contract on the underlying CDOs, hence they are calculated in terms of cents in the dollar. As images of theses indexes often featured in official and news media reports in September and October 2008, what was notable was that the precipitous falls that were typically recorded on their graphs in order to show sudden rises in CDS premiums were taken as proxy quantitative measures of the sharp decline in the value of the underlying CDOs.

Building the Bad Banks

In order that the discrete security apparatus could act upon the toxic asset problem, several further elements were mobilized. This included the theory and practice of 'bad banks', legally defined entities to which 'non-performing assets' are transferred for the purpose of divestment over time. The distinction between a 'good bank' and a 'bad bank' developed in the US during the mid-to-late 1980s (Faucette et al. 2009). For example, the 1984 bailout of Continental Illinois had, in effect, created a bad bank, as the Federal Deposit Insurance Corporation (FDIC) purchased $3.5 billion worth of the institution's bad assets and sought to manage them through either resale or debt collection. The good bank/bad bank distinction was used widely for the first time in popular parlance, however, with reference to a strategy employed by Mellon Bank in the US in 1988. In response to problems with the mortgage assets and other real estate loans on its books, Mellon created a bad bank called Grant Street. Grant Street was financed by a dedicated issue of junk bonds by Mellon, and was operated under the supervision of the Office of the Comptroller of the Currency.

Prior to the contemporary crisis, the two most prominent examples of bad banks that had been created with explicit public financial support were the 1989 Resolution Trust Corporation (RTC), formed in response to the US Savings and Loans debacle (Curry and Shibut 2000), and the aptly named Retriva and Securum bad banks that were established in 1992, in response to the Swedish banking collapse. It was the RTC that was influential in shaping thinking on the TARP bad bank, described by Gillian Tett (2008) of the *Financial Times* as an 'RTC repeat'. Indeed, just two days before the TARP was unveiled, Nicholas F. Brady (US Treasury Secretary, 1988–1993), Eugene A. Ludwig (Comptroller of the Currency, 1993–1998), and Paul A. Volcker (Chairman of the Federal Reserve, 1979–1987) contributed a co-authored piece to the *Wall Street Journal* entitled 'Resurrect the Resolution Trust Corp'. As they put their case:

> right now the system is clogged with enormous amounts of toxic real-estate paper that will not repay according to its terms. . . . Until there is a new mechanism in place to remove this decaying tissue from the system, the infection will spread, confidence will deteriorate further, and we will have to live through the mother of all credit contractions. . . . There is something we can do to resolve the problem. We should move decisively to create a new, temporary resolution mechanism.
>
> (Brady et al. 2009)

The RTC also seems to have been the main model advanced by the 'Break-the-Glass Memo'—the contingency planning document that was drawn up in the wake of the Bear Stearns fiasco, and submitted to the office of President George W. Bush by the US Treasury in mid-April 2008—which provided the basis for the TARP (Thomas 2013: 187). Moreover, once debate over the TARP took hold, key figures in the operation of the RTC, such as former director of the Office of Thrift and Supervision, Tim Ryan (2008), continued to give public voice to the case for a bad bank solution.

Also crucial to the composition of the governance apparatus which sought to act upon the toxic asset problem were the sovereign institutional elements of the Federal Reserve and the US Treasury. Not unlike the liquidity injections of last resort lending, the Maiden Lane LLC bad banks mobilized the monetary sovereignty institutionalized in the Fed. This was especially the case as the Fed drew on its own balance sheet when providing the discount loans that funded the purchase of the toxic assets of Bear and AIG. In this respect, what was notable about the TARP was, of course, that this seemingly more comprehensive bad bank mustered the fiscal rights of the sovereign that were institutionalized in the US Treasury. As it produces and centralizes the fiscal monopoly of the sovereign, the reason of state makes possible the issue of sovereign debts which are to be repaid at a later date by the receipts of taxation. So, and to meet the costs of funding the TARP by adding to the national debt, the US Treasury was thus able to pledge to its creditors the full faith and credit of the sovereign. This included the future capacity to tax populations as necessary, and, in effect, commitments to balance Federal budgets and control inflation.

Funding the TARP by issuing new sovereign debt into capital markets that had otherwise ground to a halt was not a difficult prospect for the US Treasury. Relative to the pressures for fiscal rectitude that are confronted by other states, US sovereign institutions enjoy the fiscal flexibility that follows from what Barry Eichengreen (2011) terms 'exorbitant privilege'. Given the status of the US dollar as global money, the Treasuries of different maturities issued by the US state continue to be the 'benchmark' which other debt instruments are priced-off in global wholesale financial markets. Treasuries, moreover, are widely known and understood as the ultimate, liquid 'safe haven' or 'safe harbour' for investors. So, rather than triggering investors to sell all their holdings of US financial instruments—and leading to the collapse of the dollar on foreign exchange markets that some expected (Calleo 2009)—the global financial crisis which was 'made in America' somewhat perversely opened the flood gates for a massive inflow of foreign capital into America (Helleiner 2014; Stokes 2014). There was, then, ample investor appetite for the new sovereign debt that was necessary in order that the TARP bad bank could be funded.

In order that the sovereign institutions could organize and fund each of the bad banks, specific statutes and legal-cum-economic provisions also had to be mustered, in relation, as elements of the governance assemblage. As illustrated by the legislative additions that were made to the US Treasury's initial plan of 19 September 2008, and especially by the initial refusal by the House of Representatives to permit the US Treasury to roll out the TARP on 29 September, this particular bad bank was dependent upon the legal authorization of Congress. Meanwhile the Fed was required to invoke the 'unusual and exigent circumstances' of Section 13(3) of the Federal Reserve Act in order that it could lend to Bear and AIG. At the same time the creation of the Maiden Lane LLCs enabled the Fed to circumvent the regulations that restricted its last resort lending to the making of liquidity loans. These bad banks were incorporated in Delaware, and utilized the registered agent services provided by CT Corporation, a subsidiary of the Dutch multinational Wolters Kluwer.[12] By taking advantage of the tax-fee and limited information reporting requirements of the shell-company incorporation provisions that are routinely offered in the US by the state of Delaware (*Economist* 2013), the Maiden Lane bad banks were thus effectively offshore, and had foreign LLC status in New York.

The comprehensive bad bank solution of the TARP also sought to enrol into the governance apparatus a mechanism through which toxic assets could be valued and priced. To borrow terms from Foucault (2007: 65), what the Paulson Plan envisaged was that 'the inherent dangers of this circulation' of toxic assets were to be 'cancelled out' by a reverse auction process. To make toxic assets knowable and actionable, the TARP had to achieve 'what financial experts have been unable to do for the last year—put a dollar value on mortgage-related assets that no one wants' (Landler and Andrews 2008). It was envisaged that the Treasury would offer to purchase certain classes of toxic assets at a particular price, and investors would decide whether to sell at that price. Following the passing of the TARP legislation, the Treasury was given a six-week period to work out the details of the reverse auction process and the subsequent arrangements for asset management, as it was at the end of this period that the first round of toxic asset purchases was due to take place.

The most immediate issue that the valuation of toxic sub-prime assets seemed to create was that the prices to be paid by the Treasury had to be higher than those currently prevailing in markets. Without higher prices, banks would have no incentive to sell in the reverse auction process, and this would have also prompted further write-downs under the terms of accrual accounting (*Economist* 2008d: 94). With this in mind, and in response to questions posed to him during his appearance before Congress while the TARP legislation was being considered, Ben Bernanke suggested that the Treasury would pay what he termed a 'hold-to-maturity price' for toxic assets; that is, a price that an investor would be willing to pay if they envisaged holding the instrument until its maturity (in Bajaj 2008). But, the prospect that the TARP auctions would pay over and above market prices for toxic assets served to undermine its already weak political legitimacy, as it bailed out Wall Street investors at taxpayers' expense.

For the small coterie of micro-economists that supplied the US Treasury with multiple designs for the reverse auction process, the most pressing issue posed by the Paulson Plan to value toxic assets was how to best aggregate dispersed market information and assign prices with a 'helping visible hand' (Mirowski 2013: 305). Yet, as George Soros (2008) warned in an article published in the *Financial Times*, for instance, not only were these opaque and complex assets 'hard to value', 'but the sellers know more about them than the buyer: in any auction process the Treasury would end up with the dregs'. So, while the passing of the Emergency Economic Stabilization Act led to an initial surge in stock market prices, continued public debates about whether the TARP could provide a workable response to the toxicity problem contributed to ongoing market turbulence. For example, the Chicago Board Options Exchange Volatility Index (VIX), also known as the 'Fear Index', came to the fore in the popular imagination as it spiked sharply in early-to-mid-October (Grynbaum 2008; Weitzman 2008). In our terms, the struggle to mobilize a mechanism through which toxic assets could be valued under the auspices of the TARP was animated by an affective atmosphere of doubt and scepticism. When attempting to provide a comprehensive solution, the distributed and relational agency of the crisis governance apparatus failed to come together and to act upon the toxic asset problem.

Of particular analytical importance, however, is not the failure of the TARP to produce its intended solution to the crisis, or the relative success of the Maiden Lane LLCs, but what the toxicity apparatus reveals more broadly about the will to govern the crisis. The rationale of the apparatus was to restore the uncertain circulations of the capital markets which appear to be vital to securing life itself. This apparent crisis management solution did not seek to 'help troubled families to pay back their mortgages', but instead aimed 'to help troubled securities to regain their liquidity' (Amato and Fantacci 2012: 85). To that end, the toxicity problem that had infected the cardiovascular circulations of the economic body was not to be nullified and governed by a 'form of prohibition', as would be have been characteristic of the sovereign rationality of power (Foucault 2007: 66). Toxic assets were not to be siphoned off into bad banks in order that they might be written off once and for all, and such that the techniques and practices which had produced the virulent infection could be outlawed or even standardized through a disciplinary mode of restrictive regulation. Instead, sovereign monetary and fiscal techniques were to be transformed and mobilized in a relational arrangement with the other elements of the apparatus, such that toxic assets were temporarily filtered out and the uncertain circulation of transferable debt claims could restart. In the terms of Ben Bernanke (2008a), the purchase of toxic assets would enable the aggregation of information and 'price discovery', encouraging investors to once again embrace the opportunities ostensibly afforded by the capital markets.

What was also notable, moreover, were the various ways in which acting on the toxic asset problem to revive financial market circulations was explicitly represented as securing the life of the population. Emphasizing, in effect, that cardiovascular toxicity poses a threat to the health of the economic body, inaction was portrayed as allowing the infection to spread beyond the immediate domain of financial circulation. As Geithner (2008) put it, for example, when explaining the Bear Stearns' bad bank to a Senate committee:

> if this dynamic continues unabated, the result would be a greater probability of widespread insolvencies, severe and protracted damage to the financial system

and, ultimately, to the economy as a whole.... Absent a forceful policy response, the consequences would be lower incomes for working families, higher borrowing costs for housing, education, and the expenses of everyday life, lower value of retirement savings and rising unemployment.

Not dissimilarly, in the televised address to the nation that he delivered during the period in which the TARP proposals were before Congress, President George W. Bush (2008) stressed that 'This rescue effort is not aimed at preserving any individual company or industry. It is aimed at preserving America's overall economy'. For Bush, it was clear that 'our entire economy is in danger', and that the costs of inaction would be high:

> without immediate action by Congress, America could slip into a financial panic and a distressing scenario would unfold. More banks could fail ... The stock market would drop even more, which would reduce the value of your retirement account. The value of your home could plummet ... Even if you have good credit history, it would be more difficult for you to get the loans you need to buy a car or send your children to college.

Bush's televised address thus left viewers in little doubt that toxic assets were a problem for the American way of life, and that the TARP provided the solution that would successfully act on that problem. As he later put it (in Politi 2008), the TARP was required 'for the financial security of every American'.

That the complex financial market interconnections of certain institutions had to be maintained for the good of the population was also made plain, and with reference to AIG in particular, by the continual assertion of the company's contribution to 'everyday life'. Readers of the popular media in the US were constantly reminded that AIG's toxic asset problem arose from the misguided activities of its London office, and not from its core insurance business. Similarly, and as described by Donald L. Kohn (2009) of the Federal Reserve, AIG had '30 million customers' and was the 'largest life and health insurer in the United States', 'the second largest property and casualty insurer in the United States', 'and the leading commercial insurer in the United States, providing insurance to approximately 180,000 small businesses and other corporate entities, which employ approximately 106 million people in the United States'. If that wasn't enough, Kohn also informed the Senate committee before which he was appearing that AIG 'is also a major provider of protection to municipalities, pension funds, and other public and private entities through guaranteed investment contracts and products that protect participants in 401(k) retirement plans'.

Conclusion

Talk of toxic assets, toxic waste, and toxic refuse was rife during the first twelve months or so of the contemporary crisis of global finance, and a number of crisis management interventions explicitly targeted the technical problem of capital market toxicity. However, this feature of the governance of the crisis is typically conflated by economists with the broader drive to address the problem of liquidity, which is said to have extended to both the 'funding liquidity' of money markets and the 'market liquidity' of capital markets (Borio 2010; Brunnermeier 2008, 2009). On the rare occasions when the will to govern the crisis as a toxicity problem is addressed by political economists, it tends to be ridiculed as a distraction from the social forces and processes which are said to have really been at work (e.g. Mirowski 2013). Yet it remains the case that, as the tumult intensified during the spring, late summer, and early autumn of 2008, the managerial interventions that were made in the US in particular sought to address the crisis as a matter of toxicity. Indeed, there was a moment when the fate of global finance appeared to turn on whether Congress would pass the Emergency Economic Stabilization Act of 2008. Without the requisite bad bank to temporarily purchase toxic assets that could not be valued and were poisoning circulations of the capital markets, it genuinely seemed as though the edifice of global finance would collapse.

Giving the governance of the crisis as a problem of toxicity the specific and critical attention that it deserves, this chapter has further developed the book's account of the multiple and discrete apparatuses that sought to make up and manage the crisis. Contributing to the book's challenge to the consensus view on the governance of the crisis, the chapter's analysis is especially notable in three respects. First, it has underscored that the 'option of circulation' (Foucault 2007: 49) was one of the key tendencies that were present across the crisis governance apparatuses to a greater or lesser degree. As with the extensive array of liquidity injections and liquidity facilities that were addressed in the previous chapter, it was significant that a distinct apparatus sought to strategically place toxic assets in bad banks such that the uncertain circulations of the capital markets could be restored. Toxic assets were not to be written off and taken out of circulation once and for all, and the various techniques (e.g. securitization) that had created those assets and sent them into circulation were not to be ruled out in the future. Second, and related, the chapter has begun to draw out how the crisis was explicitly governed, at its height in particular, as a biopolitical security dilemma. It has shown how acting on the toxic asset problem was not solely regarded as a question of restoring capital market circulations, but of securing the wealth and well-being of the population in which those circulations were positioned as being of essential importance. Removing toxic assets from markets for fungible and transferable claims on debt relations thus appeared as essential to the continuation of the credit and investment relations of housing, retirement planning, and so forth. Third, the chapter has underlined the contingency and fragility that was present as the will to govern the crisis was operationalized through discrete security apparatuses. It has shown how, through the TARP in particular, it was not possible to manage the crisis as a toxic asset problem. As Rabinow and Rose (2003: xvii) suggest, 'despite the initial intention that an apparatus will respond in a targeted way to a particular problem to achieve a specific strategic objective, diverse and unplanned effects can and do result'. The crisis, then, escaped the ordering interventions of the apparatus that sought to act upon it as a problem of toxicity. The TARP was folded into a quite different shape, as it was incorporated into an apparatus that rendered and governed the crisis as a predicament of the solvency of banking.

Notes

1. Confidential interview, representative of the FDIC, Washington, DC, March 2012.
2. Strictly speaking, it was the initial liquidity loan of $13 billion that the Fed made to Bear on the evening of Thursday 13 March—via JP Morgan Chase, the clearing bank that routinely arranged the financing of Bear's business—which was the first time in the course of crisis governance that the Fed was required to invoke Section 13(3) of the Federal Reserve Act. The loan was repaid, with interest, on the Friday evening, before the creation of the bad bank for Bear's toxic assets.
3. Federal Reserve Board Press Release, 16 March 2008. Available at: <http://www.federalreserve.gov/newsevents/press/monetary/20080316a.htm> (accessed June 2014).
4. New York Federal Reserve Press Release, 24 March 2008. Available at: <http://www.newyorkfed.org/newsevents/news/markets/2008/rp080324b.html> (accessed June 2014).
5. New York Federal Reserve Press Release, 29 September 2008. Available at: <http://www.newyorkfed.org/newsevents/news/markets/2008/an080929.html> (accessed June 2014).
6. Federal Reserve Board Press Release, 16 September 2008. Available at: <http://www.federalreserve.gov/newsevents/press/other/20080916a.htm> (accessed June 2014).
7. Federal Reserve Board Press Release, 10 November 2008. Available at: <http://www.federalreserve.gov/newsevents/press/other/20081110a.htm> (accessed June 2014).
8. Federal Reserve Board Press Release, 10 November 2008. Available at: <http://www.federalreserve.gov/newsevents/press/other/20081110a.htm> (accessed June 2014).
9. In the meantime, America's largest thrift institution, Washington Mutual, and Wachovia bank both collapsed, and were taken over with assistance from the Fed by JP Morgan Chase and Wells Fargo.

10. Confidential interviews, representatives of the FDIC and SEC, Washington, DC, March 2012.

11. CDS are derivative contracts written and sold by institutions that seek a stake in the risk/return characteristics of specific underlying debt instruments without investing in the instruments themselves. In return for premiums that are based on calculations about the likelihood of default on the underlying instruments, buyers in the 'covered' CDS market can thus hedge against the default risk of the underlying instruments that they hold in their portfolio. Buyers in the 'uncovered' CDS market, meanwhile, speculate and 'short' the underlying instruments (Lewis 2008). Should the 'credit event' of default occur, the buyer of a CDS receives the contracted pay-out from sellers and, in return, gives the seller the debt instruments underlying the contract or an equivalent based on the instruments' value.

12. Under US law, a registered agent provides a legal address (not a Post Office Box) within a state jurisdiction—in this instance, in Delaware—and is required to ensure that persons are available during normal business hours to facilitate legal processes in the event of any action being served upon the incorporated entity concerned. Typically, a registered agent also receives all official documentation pertaining to that entity from the state government, including that issued for tax purposes, and is required to forward such documentation accordingly.

5

Solvency

Introduction: 'underlying problems'

> Confidence in global financial institutions and markets has been badly
> shaken. Threats to systemic stability became manifest in September with
> the collapse or near-collapse of several key institutions.... The combin-
> ation of mounting losses, falling asset prices, and a deepening economic
> downturn, has caused serious doubts about the viability of a widening
> swath of the financial system.... One result has been sudden failures of
> institutions as markets have become unwilling (or unable) to provide
> capital and funding or absorb assets. Piecemeal interventions to address
> the attendant liquidity strains and resolve the troubled institutions did not
> succeed in restoring market confidence, as they have not addressed the
> widespread nature of the underlying problems.
>
> International Monetary Fund, *Global Financial Stability
> Report*, October 2008: xi

Surveying the wreckage as the global financial crisis reached its peak, the
opening paragraph of the Executive Summary of the IMF's (2008) *Global
Financial Stability Report* of October 2008 asserted that there were now 'threats
to systemic stability' and 'serious doubts about the viability of a widening
swath of the financial system'. The collapse of Lehman Brothers on
15 September—ten days prior to the completion of the *Report*'s research—
produced a standstill in money and capital market circulations, flows which
had already experienced acute 'liquidity strains' over the preceding fourteen
months. What the Lehman bankruptcy also provoked, however, was a precipitous collapse in banks' equity prices. It was these prices that provided a
particularly stark indicator of the 'doubts' about 'viability' to which the IMF
referred. Banks' equity prices had been falling throughout the crisis, as their
liquidity problems were taken to demonstrate that they were indeed over-
valued due to their holdings of toxic assets. A total of $8 trillion dollars had
been wiped off the value of US stocks since the onset of the crisis, and it was

the banks that were the hardest hit (Brunnermeier 2009: 90). Yet, the rout of the autumn 2008 seriously weakened banks' capital positions still further, and thus their capacities to 'absorb losses'. 'Sudden failures of institutions' were now said to be a manifestation of more 'widespread' and 'underlying problems': many banks were technically insolvent. As Ben Bernanke (2010a) was to later admit to the Financial Crisis Inquiry Commission (FCIC), of the thirteen institutions that he counted as the 'most important' in the US, twelve were 'at risk of failure within a period of a week or two'.

As the full violence of the crisis was being wrought, an array of further 'piecemeal interventions' were enacted to address the liquidity problem, as was detailed in Chapter 3. It was during this period that, as analysed in the previous chapter, the US Treasury unfurled its TARP in an attempt to cover the problem of toxic assets. Seeking to alleviate the pressures on banks' capital positions, the Financial Services Authority (FSA) and Securities Exchange Commission (SEC) (2008) also introduced a joint, four-month moratorium on the short-selling of thirty four financial stocks in the UK, and 799 stocks in the US. Moreover, while insolvent institutions that were deemed to be systemically significant were also saved from bankruptcy on an incremental and ad hoc basis, the introduction of the Bank Recapitalization Fund (BRF) by HM Treasury on 8 October heralded a decisive shift in the prevailing abstraction of the crisis (Darling 2008a). For the first time since its onset, the crisis was to be governed as a problem of the solvency of banking. Only programmatic interventions which committed the fiscal machinery of the state to purchasing equity stakes and funding the recapitalization of banking seemed capable of preventing widespread insolvency. In the terms of the Bank of England (2008: 30), for instance, the BRF and accompanying measures were 'a system-wide response' to 'system-wide volatilities'. In popular parlance, banking was 'under water' and in need of a very public 'bailout'.

This chapter focuses upon the governance apparatus that rendered the crisis as a problem of banking solvency, and which attempted to enact the programmatic solution of recapitalization. It opens with an overview of the main recapitalization interventions that were made on either side of the Atlantic, including, most notably, the BRF in the UK, and the reallocation of the TARP funds to cover the bailout of US banking. The second, third, and fourth sections of the chapter analyse the main elements that were strategically gathered together in the distributed and relational agency of the bailout apparatus. The second section will stress the performative power within the apparatus of the balance sheet, understood as a market device of economics at large. The metrics, measures, and materialities of the balance sheet were crucial to the way in which the apparatus figured the solvency problem. Furthermore, as the third section will highlight, it was through the relational arrangement of bank balance sheets and treasury institutions that sovereign fiscal techniques were reconfigured, and were put to work to enact the urgent solution of the 'recapitalization' of banking and not 'nationalization'. The fourth section of the chapter will analyse the ways in which the apparatus strategically sought to elicit an affective, atmospheric element; that is, the 'market confidence' which, for the IMF, had 'been badly shaken' and which previous 'piecemeal interventions . . . did not succeed in restoring'. The provision of the ostensible material resource of capital as a 'reserve', 'buffer', and 'cushion' for absorbing future bank losses will be shown to have been inextricably related with the restoration of confidence in banking and financial circulations. Moreover, the constant reiteration of the strategic importance of the bank bailouts to the security of the population will be held to have broadened this relation further, figuring an ostensibly vital relation of capital–confidence–life.

The Bank Recapitalization Fund and Capital Purchase Program

Meeting in Washington, DC, two days after the announcement of HM Treasury's BRF, the Group of 7 (G-7) Finance Ministers and Central Bankers (2008) stated that they would 'use all available tools to support systemically important financial institutions and prevent their failure'. This unequivocal affirmation of a will to govern the crisis now featured the commitment to:

> Ensure that our banks and other major financial intermediaries, as needed, can raise capital from public as well as private sources, in sufficient amounts to re-establish confidence and permit them to continue lending to households and businesses.

Returning from Washington to Parliament in order to detail the implementation of the BRF, for the then Chancellor of the Exchequer, Alistair Darling (2008b), it was 'increasingly clear that the measures I am announcing today form the basis of an international consensus on the right response to these events'. Indeed, by 'adopting new ideas and letting go of the old ones', he claimed later that month that the UK had 'led the way on global recapitalisation' (Darling 2008c; see Quaglia 2009). The bailout plan was, according to Bernanke (2012: 76), 'a great example of international cooperation'. Across the 11 major economies included in a study for the BIS, Panetta et al. (2009) calculate that, by June 2009, the amount of fiscal resources committed to recapitalization packages totalled around €5 trillion, with immediate outlays of €2 trillion (equivalent to nearly eight per cent of combined GDP).

Under the terms of the BRF, UK banks and building societies (and subsidiaries of global banks with significant UK business) committed to increase their Tier 1 capital by an amount agreed with the government (Bank of

England 2008: 31).[1] The scale of these commitments was calculated according to a methodology that combined the present market value of each bank's assets on the one hand, and a 'stress testing' element, which projected write-downs on those assets according to an adverse macroeconomic scenario, on the other (2008: 28–9; see Chapter 6). HM Treasury purchased equity in the institutions that were unable to raise high-quality capital in the markets; namely, Royal Bank of Scotland (RBS) and Lloyds Banking Group (which had come to include a near-collapse of Halifax Bank of Scotland (HBOS) in the previous month). The result was initial equity stakes of £20 billion in RBS and £17 billion in Lloyds, with a further £39 billion of public money invested in these institutions in November 2009 (NAO 2009b). Share coupons were set at a punitive rate, and conditions on dividend payments and executive pay were also attached. Ultimately, the government came to own eighty four per cent of RBS and forty one per cent of Lloyds, investments which it began, in June 2013, to attempt to sell off to the private sector (Osborne 2013).

The BRF was one component in a three-pronged intervention that sought to take 'decisive and extraordinary action to support the banking system during this period of exceptional financial turbulence' (Darling 2008b). The securities lending of the Bank of England's Special Liquidity Scheme (SLS) was also extended (see Chapter 3), in an effort 'to address weaknesses in some UK banks' funding structures' by supporting their capacities to raise short-term liquidity through repo markets (Bank of England 2008: 29). Significantly, provision was made for government guarantees against default on the unsecured debt instruments issued by institutions participating in the recap-italization programme. In return for an underwriting charge, the government stood behind the bonds, commercial paper, and certificates of deposit issued by the banks within an initial six-month window (Bank of England 2008: 31). A £250 billion ceiling was set on the cumulative value of these guarantees. In the course of the global recapitalization effort, the issuance of bonds covered by government guarantees tended to assist banks in rolling over and refinan-cing existing short-term debts which reached maturity in the period through to mid-2009 (Panetta et al. 2009: 3, 16). However, in the UK the government guaranteed bonds issued by banks facilitated a considerable expansion of bank capital, much of which funded the write-down of assets that had gone bad. Indeed, of the total volume of capital raised by UK banks during late 2008 and the first half of 2009, issues of guaranteed debt instruments accounted for a much greater proportion overall than direct government equity stakes.

The BRF was not, of course, the first time in the course of contemporary crisis governance that institutions on the verge of collapse had been bailed out by the sovereign treasuries on either side of the Atlantic. Neither did it prove to be the last. In February 2008, for example, and after six months of unsuc-cessfully searching for a private buyer, HM Treasury took Northern Rock into public ownership. It also facilitated the fire sale of Bradford & Bingley to Banco Santander in September 2008 (Darling 2009: 132–5). Planning for the BRF was informed by HM Treasury's experience of dealing with the Rock (NAO 2009b: 5), and also by the management of banking crises in Finland, Norway, and Sweden in the late 1980s and early 1990s which, according the BIS (2009: 104), was 'widely regarded as "best practice"'. HM Treasury was also fully prepared to bail out HBOS in mid-September 2008, had a hasty takeover by Lloyds TSB not been successfully engineered.[2]

In the US, meanwhile, and after months of speculation over their 'thin and poorly defined' capitalization, the US Treasury and Federal Housing Finance Agency concluded in early September 2008 that it was in 'the best interest of the taxpayers for Treasury to simply make an equity investment' in the government-sponsored mortgage market giants Fannie Mae and Freddie Mac (US Treasury Department 2008b). The aim here was to keep US mortgage markets open for business.[3] Moreover, as already discussed in the previous chapter, the US Treasury took an eighty per cent equity stake in the insurance giant AIG on 16 September, in return for a massive, two year, $85 billion emergency line of credit made available by the Federal Reserve. In late September, Washington Mutual was placed in receivership by the FDIC, and was quickly sold to JP Morgan Chase. In a move also facilitated by the FDIC, Wachovia announced on 29 September that it was selling its banking operation to Citibank, sparking a bidding war that ultimately saw a takeover by Wells Fargo.[4]

There were those on either side of the Atlantic, such as *Wall Street Journal* reporter Roger Lowenstein, who looked through the problems of liquidity and toxicity during the early months of the crisis, and instead questioned the solvency and capitalization of banking. As he later put it, by the autumn of 2008 'Banks had suffered horrendous losses that drained them of their capital', and 'capitalism without capital is like a furnace without fuel' (Lowenstein 2010: xxv). However, it was the unveiling of the Paulson Plan to temporarily purchase toxic assets that brought a vigorous debate among academics, politicians, and bureaucrats to a head. What, precisely, was the problem-object of the crisis, and how it could be best addressed? An array of economic luminaries gave public voice to the view that the issue was one of banking solvency which was best addressed by direct recapitalization (e.g. Krugman 2008; Soros 2008; Stiglitz 2008b). By way of illustration, for Martin Wolf (2008b), writing in the *Financial Times*, the Paulson Plan did not sufficiently recognize the ways in which the collapse in prices for toxic assets fed the unwinding of previously highly leveraged positions. As such, and 'above all, a scheme for dealing with the crisis must be able to remedy the looming decapitalisation of the financial system in as targeted manner as possible'. Critics such as Lowenstein and Wolf did not have to wait long for a *volte-face* in the US Treasury's approach to crisis management, however.

Less than two weeks after it had finally passed through Congress on 3 October as the Emergency Economic Stabilization Act, the first $250 billion of TARP monies were utilized to recapitalize US banks through the purchase of preference shares. Secretary Paulson had indicated this likely change of direction at the Washington meeting of the G-7 Finance Ministers and Central Bank Governors on 10 October. In a statement released following the meeting, Paulson (2008b) did not rule out 'the approach we are taking to broad mortgage asset purchases', but also set out the bare bones of 'plans to purchase equity'. Such intervention 'would be designed to encourage the raising of new private capital to complement public capital', and public purchases through 'a broadly available equity program would be on a non-voting basis'. The change of direction for the TARP was facilitated by provisions in the Act which gave the Treasury Secretary 'discretion . . . to purchase other assets, as deemed necessary to effectively stabilize financial markets' (US Treasury Department 2008a). The toxic asset problem was now to be addressed through the balance sheet of the Federal Reserve.

Through what was named the Capital Purchase Program (CPP), half of the $250 billion of TARP funds initially spent on bank recapitalization were invested in the nine largest US banks. These now included the main remaining investment banks—Goldman Sachs and Morgan Stanley—that changed their legal status to bank holding companies in late September.[5] Under the terms of the CPP, which came to cover over 200 institutions in total, banks which were deemed by regulators to require recapitalization could not turn it down. Special dividends and warrants ensured that taxpayers would benefit from any subsequent rise in a bank's share price, and some restrictions were placed on the levels of executive compensation (Landler 2008; Lohr 2008). The disassembly of the toxic asset apparatus continued as Congress granted the release of the second half of the TARP monies for the purposes of recapitalization in January 2009. This funded the Capital Assistance Program (CAP) of the newly elected Obama administration, a revamp of the CPP that was actually of greatest significance to proffering an apparent solution to the problem of 'risk' in the governance of the crisis (see Chapter 6). In between the CPP and the CAP, and seeking to address the apparent insolvency of individual institutions that were deemed systemically important, the US Treasury Department's (2008c) growing portfolio of bank equity came to include $20 billion of preferred stock in Citigroup in November 2008. In addition, $20 billion was invested in the preference shares of another banking giant, Bank of America, in mid-January 2009 (US Treasury Department 2009b). Prior to these standalone interventions, Citigroup and Bank of

America had already each received a direct $25 billion boost to their capitalization through the CPP.

Unveiled in conjunction with the CPP on 14 October 2008, and broadly mirroring the measures that accompanied the BRF in the UK, the US Treasury authorized the FDIC to put in place the Temporary Lending Guarantee Program which covered unsecured senior debt instruments issued by banks. While this entailed a staggering maximum commitment of $2.25 trillion (Panetta et al. 2009: 8), the total cost of payouts to investors by the time the Program closed at the end of 2012 amounted to just $113 million.[6] A distinctive feature of the US debt guarantees was that banks had to 'opt out' rather than 'opt in': in other words, new senior bank debt was automatically guaranteed by government, for a fee, unless the issuing institution specified otherwise. Nonetheless, the relatively large-scale equity stakes which were taken up through the CPP in the US meant that, in contrast with the UK in particular, issues of guaranteed debt did not feature so strongly in the overall recapitalization process. That said, the sums involved in the uptake of FDIC debt guarantees were still very considerable, and were the highest of all similar schemes globally (Panetta et al. 2009: 16–17, 49). By way of direct comparison, between October 2008 and May 2009 ten UK banks issued government guaranteed debt with an aggregate value of €113 billion, while 40 US banks did the same but to the tune of €192.5 billion.

Balance Sheets and Banking

Although the strategic and distributed agency of the bailout apparatus entailed the mustering and relational arrangement of a number of specific elements, there was a material-calculative element that was particularly crucial to the enactment of the apparatus: the balance sheet. The balance sheet is a market device of accounting and of economics at large. In a similar manner to the way in which the materialities of the balance sheet literally figured central bank's liquidity injections (Chapter 3), the balance sheet did not merely provide a mechanism for recording the perilous state of the banks as the crisis deepened. Rather, as the balance sheet named and gave an account of the problem with banks in terms of its categories (assets, liabilities, and so on) and quantitative, monetary measures, it held a significant and performative form of power within the apparatus. This power extended not only to bringing into being the technical problem of bank solvency that was to be acted on, but also to envisaging the apparent solution of recapitalization. To take a term from Deleuze and Guattari (1987: 325), the balance sheet was the 'operator', the material 'component of passage' between extant banking assemblages and the security apparatus that enacted the bailout of banking.

The performative power of the balance sheet in the bailout apparatus was a particular manifestation of the broad importance that its classifications and calculations hold for producing and reproducing capitalist enterprise. The significance of accountancy, and especially double-entry bookkeeping, has been attended to by social theorists such as Max Weber (1978), Joseph Schumpeter (1950), and Werner Sombart (1967). For Schumpeter (1950) and, especially, Weber (1978), the development of double-entry bookkeeping is a crucial component in the development of modern capitalist rationality, most notably because it is technically superior to other means of record keeping and makes possible calculations of the costs, valuations, profits, and so on of enterprise in terms of monetary units. Sombart (1967) goes further still, such that double-entry accounts are, in his analysis, the essential causal innovation of capitalism.

Such grand claims have sparked historical controversies over whether the emergence and uptake of these market devices, from the fifteenth century onwards, actually produced rational and calculative practices (e.g. Carruthers and Espeland 1991; Chiapello 2007; Funnell 2001). As Carruthers and Espeland (1991) argue, however, a narrow focus on the accuracy of double-entry bookkeeping practice obscures not only the technical achievements that it had slowly and fitfully secured by the nineteenth century, but especially the ways in which it operates rhetorically, symbolically, and cognitively to engender and legitimate enterprise. Miller and Napier (1993) make a similar point when they interrogate double-entry bookkeeping as an ensemble of both technique and rationale. Writing before the recent interest of cultural economy in the performativity of economics (Callon 1998; de Goede 2005; MacKenzie 2006; MacKenzie et al. 2007), what Carruthers and Espeland (1991) and Miller and Napier (1993) nonetheless reach out for is the kind of analysis that is prompted by the category of performativity. Indeed, in Miller and Napier's (1993: 633) terms, the 'grammars' of accounting are 'not merely contemplative or justificatory', but are 'performative'. There are strong parallels, then, between a concern with the technical and rhetorical significance of double-entry bookkeeping, and the distinction drawn by Chris Clarke (2012) between performativity and performance: a specific economic theory or market device may be performative and make itself true in financial practice, and economic discourses may also act as continuous performatives that constitute the generic categories of finance.

As the bailout apparatus rendered and acted on the crisis as a problem of solvency, the performative power of the balance sheet was at work in three main ways. First, the balance sheet was the key generic, calculative device in the envisioning of what was wrong with banking and the financial economy more broadly. For the Bank of England for example, the problem-object of the crisis was expressed as one of 'the overextension in banks' balance sheets'

(2008: 26), 'balance sheet fragilities' (2008: 29), and 'balance sheet weaknesses' (2008: 29). What was notable about the generic performativity of the balance sheet in this respect was how the spatial materiality of the device—which 'balances' assets against liabilities—served to symbolically represent orthodox conceptions of economy as a natural domain which tends to equilibrium. The financial economy, diagrammed through banks' balance sheets, appeared as momentarily out of kilter and in danger of collapse. It was through the generic performativity of the balance sheet device that the bank bailouts thus displayed the tendency of security apparatuses to seek 'a sort of homeostasis' and 'to compensate for variations' in apparently vital processes (Foucault 2003c: 246). Stabilizing the temporarily unbalanced books of the banks seemed likely to have the cumulative effect of restoring systemic financial stability.

Second, it was through the practical performativity of the metrics of the balance sheet that the crisis was rendered as a problem of bank solvency. 'Solvency' and 'insolvency' are financial standings that can only be named and known in terms of the balance sheet. In this respect, the classifications and calculations of the balance sheet produced the material givens of the urgent need upon which the bailout apparatus was to act. In banking, and to put this in necessarily schematic terms, the balance sheet places loans and the other income generating instruments on the asset side, while deposits and mandatory debts of all kinds (with varying but finite maturities) occupy the liabilities side. Although international and US accounting standards use a vertical as opposed to horizontal format, the assets and liabilities positioned on each 'side' must balance with the other. Regular, daily imbalances are funded via short-term money market debt, reserves, and, if necessary, by borrowing from the bankers' bank. However, an insolvent bank that is likely to default on its obligations to depositors and creditors is one where, in the basic equation of the balance sheet, the value of total assets is less than total liabilities plus equity capital (i.e. shareholder investments where claims are discretionary). So, to return to the Bank of England (2008: 26–9) report of October 2008, the problem of 'the overextension in banks' balance sheets' was 'exposed by rising uncertainty about banks' asset portfolios' and 'compounded for many banks by concerns about their dependence on wholesale market funding'. The result was that 'Financial markets began to perceive that banks globally, including in the UK, had potentially inadequate capital and assured sources of finance to insure against these balance sheet risks'. There was the prospect, in short, of 'default risk . . . at a system-wide level'.

Third, that the solvency problem could be acted on through the proposed solution of recapitalization was also a consequence of the performative power of the balance sheet. An action called 'capitalization' only takes on meaning in the context of a balance sheet. The balance sheet, then, was critical to the appearance of 'recapitalization' as the practicable solution towards which the bailout apparatus had to work. For Sombart, 'The very concept of capital is derived from this way of looking at things; one can say that capital, as a category, did not exist before double-entry bookkeeping' (in Carruthers and Espeland 1991: 33). To be more specific, as Francesco Boldizzoni (2008) details, although the idea of capital has many meanings across history, it is through the balance sheet that 'capital'—in terms of its etymology from the Latin *caput*, meaning 'stock'—appears as a kind of material resource belonging to an economic entity. It was in these terms that the BRF came to be cast as having 'invested' or 'infused' otherwise insolvent banking via a 'capital-strengthening exercise' (Bank of England 2008: 31). Moreover, it is through the classifications of the balance sheet that equity capital is positioned, by definition, as both an ownership claim against total assets, and a liability that can act as a so-called 'reserve', 'buffer', or 'cushion' which is capable of absorbing future losses that cannot be subjected to a capital write-down.

As the bailout apparatus rendered the crisis as a problem of banking solvency and an urgent need for capital, the market device of the balance sheet was enrolled in a relational arrangement with an economic discourse that gave context and depth to this diagnosis. The onset of the crisis provoked something of a reassessment of the economics of banking during the boom years. Issues of bank balance sheets and capital reserves featured strongly, for instance, in the discourse on the 'originate-and-distribute model' of banking briefly discussed in Chapters 3 and 4. What became clear as the crisis unfolded was that the bulging portfolios of toxic assets which banks had built up during the boom years could not ultimately be held 'off-balance sheet'—in wholly or partly owned shadow banking subsidiaries and vehicles, such as hedge funds and SIVs—and without the coverage of capital (e.g. *Economist* 2008a). The liquidity problems of 'margin calls', as creditors refused to roll over the short-term debts that sustained these vehicles, turned out to be solvency problems for the banks that owned them. As Ben Bernanke (2010a) later put it, in his testimony to the FCIC, 'many small vehicles, and a few big ones, that were spread across a lot of banks added up to a systemic vulnerability'. By the autumn of 2008, and as techniques of securitization and structured finance unravelled and money and capital markets ground to a halt, the various and previously unquestioned dividing lines which separated on- from off-balance sheet businesses became regarded as untenable.

Banks were now also held to have taken on excessive 'leverage' prior to the crisis. Significant growth on the asset side of banks' balance sheets was funded by increases in debt on the liabilities side (typically, short-term, money market debt), and not by a rise in deposits or through the issue of new equity capital. Indeed, the leveraging of banking had served to enhance returns on equity, helping banks to deliver 'shareholder value' to investors and to their executives who held stock as a result of compensation packages (Admati and Hellwig 2013; Engelen et al. 2011). In the UK in 2007, for example, the leverage ratios (i.e. total assets divided by equity capital) of the major banks ranged from roughly 20:1 to a staggering 60:1, while the median ratio had climbed over the preceding decade from approximately 25:1 to 35:1 (Bank of England 2008: 9). Although excessive leverage had enabled the maximization of profits during the bubble, it also magnified losses and made the prospect of insolvency much more likely once the bubble burst. For some, such as the IMF (2008), for instance, the crisis could thus be understood as a necessary but painful process of the 'deleveraging' of banking that was manifest in the shrinking of banks' debt to equity ratios.

The crisis discourse on the economics of banking also highlighted that the models and practices which threatened widespread insolvency had not been prevented by the international standards that, translated into binding national and/or European Union regulations, were supposed to guarantee that banks held sufficient capital to absorb losses. Originally introduced in part as a response to the longer-term tendency for banking leverage to increase (MacKenzie 2013), the standards in question dated to the Basel Accord on Capital Adequacy that was negotiated through the BIS Basel Committee on Banking Supervision (BCBS) in 1988 (Kapstein 1994; Porter 1993). Under the terms of the 1988 Accord ('Basel I'), minimum capital requirements for banks were based on the combination of two ratios that set the numerator of capital against the denominator of risk-weighted assets; a two per cent ratio of Tier 1 equity capital to risk-weighted assets, and an eight per cent ratio of Tier 1 plus Tier 2 capital to risk-weighted assets. Probabilistic calculations of the default risks of different asset classes were placed within risk-weighting categories ('buckets') that were relatively simple and very limited in number. So, for instance, all government bonds held on the asset side of a bank's balance sheet were given a zero per cent risk-weighting, loans to major economy banks had a twenty per cent risk-weighting, and corporate loans came with a 100 per cent risk-weighting that required the full eight per cent of their value had to be held as so-called 'regulatory capital'.

What drew the fire of the crisis discourse on banking, however, was the process of revising the Basel I capital adequacy standards which had begun in 1999. Aggregate levels of global bank capitalization did initially rise as national and European Union regulators introduced the Basel I standards and made them binding upon the banks, but then declined relatively quickly in the decade that followed. The limited number of risk-weighting buckets specified under Basel I was subject to 'regulatory arbitrage', as the banks exploited rules that made it possible for them to take on more risky and potentially higher-yielding assets within each bucket and without setting aside additional capital. At the same time, the off-balance sheet techniques and securitization programmes of the originate-and-distribute model that were typically extolled as 'financial innovation' began to make it possible for banks to further minimize regulatory capital requirements. Unveiled in June 2004, what Basel II introduced was a three 'pillar' system that, while continuing to specify minimum capital requirements (Pillar 1), added guidelines on supervision for national regulators (Pillar 2) and new information disclosure standards for banks in order to enhance transparency for investors and creditors (Pillar 3). However, and leaving aside the somewhat slow progress made on implementation across national jurisdictions, including in the US, it was the changes that Basel II made to the Pillar 1 standards which was the specific focus for criticism in the context of the crisis.

As the crisis took hold, the so-termed 'advanced-internal ratings-based (A-IRB) approach' of Basel II became widely recognized to have, in effect, rubber-stamped banks' own 'value-at-risk' (VaR) models for the calculation of Pillar 1, regulatory capital requirements (see Chapter 6).[7] While supposedly more accurate and holding greater granularity when calibrating probabilistic default risks—at a representative bank, the number of buckets for risk-weighted assets increased, for example, from seven under Basel I to around 200,000 under the VaR models legitimated by Basel II (Haldane 2011)—the result was a further fall in the capitalization of banking and a significant increase in leverage, especially at the larger banks that were able to gain A-IRB status. In the parlance of the period, then, Basel II was complicit in the 'gaming' of regulatory capital requirements by the banks.[8]

As a relational element enrolled in the bailout apparatus, the criticism of Basel II thus contributed in the autumn of 2008 to the rendering of the crisis as a problem of bank solvency which demanded urgent recapitalization. This immediate crisis governance also set a trajectory for the ongoing recapitalization of banking, in which the most high-profile intervention to date has been the third iteration of the Basel Accord. Unveiled in December 2010, and complementing the introduction of standards for liquidity risk management that were noted in Chapter 3, the Basel III standards include a number of initiatives aimed at 'raising the resilience of the banking sector' (BCBS 2010: 2). As will be shown in the next chapter, the Basel III initiatives also emerged from the apparatus that governed the crisis as a problem of risk and which embraced the ideas of macro-prudentialism. In terms of the ongoing recapitalization of banking, however, what the national implementation of Basel III will require of banks is an increase in the quantity and quality of capital that they hold on their balance sheets. In short, all banks, and especially those deemed to be of 'global systemic importance' (BCBS 2011), are to be required to hold more regulatory capital, and a greater proportion of that capital is to take the form of common equity.

Recapitalization and Fiscal Sovereigns

In order that the problem of banking solvency could be strategically acted upon in the UK and US, the bailout apparatus mobilized the resources and techniques of the sovereign treasury institutions. The markets were apparently in no position at this time to provide banking with the new capital that it so desperately required in order to stay afloat. What was also apparent was that banks' existing creditors (i.e. those holding bonds, not equity) were protected under prevailing juridical provisions. Once banks' equity capital had been wiped out and losses were borne by shareholders, creditors could not be required to take losses on the capital that they had made available to banks, apart from in the legally defined event of insolvency. Indeed, in the wake of the bank bailouts, how to enable the so-called 'bail-in' of creditors became a focus for international and domestic attention (e.g. Financial Stability Board 2011; ICB 2011). While respecting the established hierarchy of claims in liquidation, this juridical reform agenda sought to create what is typically termed 'orderly resolution' that includes creditor write-downs or debt to equity conversions, and thereby improves the 'loss absorbency' of capital on banks' balance sheets.[9]

In the absence of a market supply of new capital and given the legally enshrined claims of the banks' creditors, it was thus the sovereign fiscal institutions that were primarily deployed in the banking recapitalization programmes which were cast in the media and popular political discourse as a 'taxpayer bailout'. The division of responsibilities between central banks and treasuries for financial stability was, as Federal Reserve officials recognized during the crisis (Madigan 2009), a long-standing but often complex separation. Bagehot's principles of last resort lending required central banks to make liquidity available, against good collateral, to solvent banks. As such, while the solvency or otherwise of an individual bank was likely to be impossible to determine in the context of a liquidity crisis (Goodhart 2002: 229–34), central banks were not typically viewed as the institutions charged with dealing with insolvency. For Mervyn King (2008), then, in a speech delivered in October 2008:

> Central bank liquidity is sticking plaster, useful and important, but not a substitute for proper treatment. . . . Recapitalisation requires a fiscal response, and that can be done only by governments.

In the bailout apparatus, these in-principle divisions of responsibility between central banks and treasuries nonetheless required specific legislative provisions. The collapse of Northern Rock had exposed omissions in the agreement which established the different competences of the UK Tripartite Authorities (Bank of England, HM Treasury, and FSA) (NAO 2009a). The Banking (Special

Provisions) Act of February 2008 followed, and it was this legislation which authorized HM Treasury to bail out British banking later in the same year (NAO 2009b). Not dissimilarly, and as discussed in Chapter 4, the TARP legislation, which eventually struggled its way through Congress as the Emergency Economic Stabilization Act, was necessary to the authorization of US Treasury actions.

Underpinning these particular legal provisions in the governance apparatus, and thus making the bailouts possible more broadly, was the sovereign rationality of power that institutionalized monopoly fiscal rights within the treasuries. Both treasuries were already running fiscal budget deficits as the crisis took hold, and their outstanding sovereign debts were the equivalent of sixty two per cent of GDP for the US, and forty three per cent for the UK (OECD calculations, in Cecchetti et al. 2010). However, as already noted in relation to the initial construction of the TARP bad bank, issuing new sovereign debt was certainly not a problem for the US Treasury. Funding the bank bailouts by issuing government gilts was a somewhat harder proposition for HM Treasury. Because of the role of the City of London as an *entrepôt* global financial centre, the UK banking sector was very large relative to the size of the national economy. Bailing out the banks would thus place a particular strain on the public finances that was not present in the US, even leaving aside the standing of the dollar as global money. The additional issue of gilts during the crisis therefore tended to manifest itself in considerable volatility in the value of sterling on foreign exchange markets, especially against the US dollar. That said, what the Debt Management Office (2009: 5) describe as the ' "flight-to-quality" ' that was provoked by the tumult of the last quarter of 2008 and early 2009 was found to create 'investor appetite' for new gilts, and this was also reflected in the lower yields on shorter-duration gilts on secondary markets.

One of the most notable dynamics of the distributed agency of the bailout apparatus, however, was how the relations between specific elements gave a particular form to the way in which sovereign fiscal techniques were deployed in crisis governance. For the bailout apparatus, programmatic actions and the taking of direct equity stakes in individual institutions were brought into being not as 'nationalization', but as acts of 'recapitalization'. The Treasury institutions did not become the 'owners' of banks on behalf of the sovereign and the population, but were 'investors'. Put another way, from the time when capital was first pooled in mercantile partnerships and joint ventures, and chiefly since the seventeenth-century emergence of joint-stock companies, lenders and investors been the key 'audience' for double-entry accounts (Carruthers and Espeland 1991: 44–7). Once the crisis was abstracted as a problem of solvency through the metrics, measures, and materialities of the balance sheet, the bank bailouts were enacted before an audience of investors and were 'set above the fray, apart from political interests and intrigue' (Miller

1994: 3). This was especially the case when, as under the CPP, investment was explicitly made in preferred stock because it comes without voting rights. Arguments for nationalized banks and the democratic, public utility of banking were sidelined and closed down. As a seemingly rational and technical decision, public investment in the banks could only be a temporary and stabilizing measure, and one that was only made on the expectation that it would yield returns in due course.

That the treasuries were 'not a permanent investor in the banks', as Alistair Darling (2008b) put it when outlining the BRF before Parliament, also highlights how the bailout apparatus was not simply made possible by the rationalities of the sovereign mode of power. Neither, for that matter, did the disciplinary mode of power provide the conditions of possibility for the bailout apparatus, rationalities which would have conceivably governed the solvency problem as a question of how best to manufacture national banks in order to strengthen the national economy. The biopolitical mode of power was present in producing the bailout apparatus as a governance assemblage that addressed an urgent need for bank recapitalization. Acting on bank balance sheets and supporting recapitalization through temporary public equity stakes and debt guarantees was held to be necessary to restore the ostensibly vital circulations of banking, and as holding the added potential of proving the opportunity for returns to a society in which citizens were summoned up not merely as taxpayers, but as taxpayer-investors.

Banking on Confidence, Banking for Life

For all of the technicalities of bank balance sheets, excessive leverage, calculations of regulatory capital, and so on, the bank bailouts were far from an exact science. The bailout apparatus also sought to elicit a seemingly less tangible but nonetheless highly significant element: an affective atmosphere of confidence. Provoking and restoring confidence in banks and banking was consistently reiterated on both sides of the Atlantic as an inherent goal of the bailout apparatus. In the Parliamentary statements of Alistair Darling (2008a, 2008d), for instance, the BRF and accompanying measures were 'designed to restore confidence in the banking system'; and 'The objective' was 'to ensure that each eligible institution has sufficient capital to sustain confidence in the institution'. Similarly, in Hank Paulson's (2008c) terms:

> there is a lack of confidence in our financial system—a lack of confidence that must be conquered because it poses an enormous threat to our economy. Investors are unwilling to lend to banks, and healthy banks are unwilling to lend to each other and to consumers and businesses....We must restore confidence in our

financial system. The first step in that effort is a plan to make capital available on attractive terms to a broad array of banks and thrifts, so they can provide credit to our economy.

As these statements also show, the bailouts were based on the assumption that, potentially at least, capitalization programmes could produce the affective conditions of confidence that they prioritized. Whether this would be the result, however, was not certain. On the evening before the announcement of the BRF (Darling 2009: 157–61), for instance, the leaders of the largest UK banks continued to give voice to the view that making the plan for bank capitalization public might have the opposite effect to that which was intended, and spook the markets still further.

As was the case when the provoking of an atmosphere of confidence featured in the governance of the liquidity problem, the bailout apparatus targeted a restoration of 'confidence' in banks and banking without clearly specifying what that precisely entailed. What an 14 October 2008 statement by the US Treasury Department (2008d) called 'public confidence in our system' was often hazily articulated through an analogy with the banking of textbook economics. Here confidence is often said to be critical to fractional reserve banking, and to preventing so-called 'liquidity' and 'maturity mismatches' from producing a 'run' on banks by depositors. It was this that motivated Adam Smith and Milton Friedman, for example, to write about the stability or otherwise of banking as they each encountered moments of financial crisis in their own lives (Rockoff 2011). Interestingly, both concluded that banks should be required to hold reserves at the central bank that were equivalent to 100 per cent of their assets in order to ward off bank runs. As the contemporary crisis set in, however, deposits contributed only a small slice of the liabilities on banks' balance sheets. Deposits had also been insured by the FDIC in the US since 1933, and were quickly covered in the UK in response to the run on the Northern Rock. It was thus the stalling of banks' securitization programmes, margin calls on shadow banking vehicles, and the 'freezing over' of money market lending that were explained, by analogy, as a loss of confidence in banking, and as a 'run' by banks' creditors, not their depositors (e.g. King 2008; NAO 2009b). In the first instance, the 'public confidence' referred to in the Joint Statement of the US Treasury, Federal Reserve, and FDIC (2008) was the confidence of a professional, financial market public. For banks to be known differently in the markets and to each other, it was financiers and bankers on Wall Street in and the City that apparently had to feel differently about them.

In order that the confidences of creditors and investors might return to stabilize and re-energize banking, the bailout apparatus drew a close and tight relation between the capitalization of banks on the one hand, and the affective atmosphere of the financial markets on the other. Material and affective registers were combined. The calculated materialities of capital deemed necessary to cushion banks from their losses were to be supplied or guaranteed by sovereigns, such that creditors and investors could be reasonably confident about the future of banking. Put differently, with the iteration and reiteration of the material-affective relation of capital–confidence, the ostensible rationalities of capital and the desires and passions of markets were invoked as mutually sustaining.

Significantly, however, the attempt to cajole confidence and stabilize banking was not a matter of establishing the kind of certainty created by deposit insurance, for example, or by a 100 per cent reserve requirement. The bailouts were not a disciplinary move to standardize and guarantee the safety of each and every bank. Rather, as the NAO (2009b: 7) noted in the UK for instance, the 'Success of the support will be linked closely with sentiments and events in world markets'. The 'center of gravity' for the bailout apparatus was thus a 'present-future axis wobbling with uncertainty' (Massumi 2005: 4), and provoking confidence in the present about the future of banking depended upon whether the financial market public could be lured and attached to the recapitalization programmes themselves. If recapitalization was to amount to what, following Massumi (2005: 5), we might think of as a kind of governance 'lightning strike' that was capable of turning the tide of events and countering the threat of banking insolvency, then it was necessary that the bailout actions themselves became regarded with confidence.

Two sets of numbers are particularly revealing as to the ways in which the bailout apparatus sought attach Wall Street and the City to measures and programmes that recapitalized banking. First, consider the sums that the bailouts provided and earmarked in support of bank recapitalization. Backed by the sovereign fiscal and monetary pledges discussed above, these sums were truly vast, and typically took the form of noticeably round numbers. In the terms of the Bank of England (2008: 29, original emphasis), the BRF package *'was scaled to remove solvency fears'*. It represented 'the largest UK government intervention in financial markets since the outbreak of the First World War' (2008: 32). Hank Paulson, meanwhile, provided an insight into the presumed significance of the size of bailout packages for eliciting market confidence when he appeared before the Senate Banking Committee on 14 July 2008. Fearful that Freddie Mac and Fannie Mae would shortly collapse, but unsure precisely as to the volume of their losses, Paulson was attempting to secure Congressional approval for an unspecified amount of capital to be used at the Treasury's discretion should the need arise. He famously put his argument in the following terms:

> If you've got a squirt gun in your pocket, you may have to take it out. If you've got
> a bazooka, and people know you've got it, you may not have to take it out. By

having something that is unspecified, it will increase confidence, and by increasing confidence it will greatly reduce the likelihood it will ever be used.

(Quoted in Paulson 2010: 151)

Similarly, as part of the planning for the intervention that became the TARP, the Break-the-Glass Memo seemingly 'guesstimated that a government fund of $500 billion would do the trick' (Blinder 2013: 179). When putting the finishing touches to the TARP proposal for Congress in September, however, $500 billion didn't seem to be enough. As Paulson (2010: 265) put it when later recounting the decision to request $700 billion from Congress: 'I did want a bigger number, and I knew the market would too'. Moreover, when it came to distributing the TARP monies, the nine largest banks were required to take $125 billion worth of investments by the US Treasury, regardless of whether the banks themselves deemed them necessary. The figure $125 billion was exactly half of the first tranche of TARP monies, and it was only a general rule of thumb that framed the scale of specific capital injections into individual institutions. As Paulson (2010: 367–9) later described it, the banks were 'forced to take the money' and, by the following day, 'World markets had responded enthusiastically'.

Second, the numbers for banks' share prices and, especially, premiums for CDS on bank bonds, became akin to barometers that made visible the affective atmosphere of market confidence in banking. Sharp increases in the cost of a CDS contract on an individual bank's debt was taken to indicate a loss of confidence in that bank, while substantial increases across the board were felt to signal a negative turn in the affective givens upon which the bailout apparatus sought to act. CDS premiums were thus the pragmatic point of reference through which the success or otherwise of recapitalization interventions were assessed, both in real time and retrospectively (e.g. Panetta et al. 2009). For instance, in a speech he delivered only two weeks after the introduction of the BRF package, Mervyn King (2008) felt able to assert that 'The recapitalisation plan is having a major impact on the restoration of market confidence in banks'. The basis for his assertion was a significant fall in the 'CDS premia' payable by the UK's five largest banks that had taken hold since the announcement of the BRF. For King, as 'an indicator of market concerns about solvency of banks', CDS premia were 'the single most important diagnostic statistic'. Indeed, these price changes were such that he felt able to claim that 'the plan to recapitalize our banking system' will 'come to be seen as the moment in the banking crisis of the past year when we turned the corner'.

As the bailout apparatus sought to elicit an affective atmosphere of confidence by figuring and acting on the capital–confidence relation, the strategic and essential importance of bank recapitalization to the life of the population was also constantly reiterated. Speaking on 14 October 2008, for instance, Hank Paulson (2008c) put it thus:

> In recent weeks, the American people have felt the effects of a frozen financial system. They have seen reduced values in their retirement and investment accounts. They have worried about meeting payrolls and they have worried about losing their jobs. Families all across our Nation have gone through long days and long nights of concern about their financial situations today, and their financial situations tomorrow. Without confidence that their most basic financial needs will be met, Americans lose confidence in our economy, and this is unacceptable.

A day earlier, the other side of the Atlantic, the then Prime Minister Gordon Brown (2008) was no less dramatic:

> banks aren't just economic entities, they are woven into the fabric of all our lives, vital to savers, to mortgage holders, to businesses and to ordinary families everywhere. And this isn't abstract, this is about the conversations mothers and fathers will be having on their sofas tonight once they have put their children to bed. For when problems in America can lead to people in Britain wondering if they can get a mortgage—then we know that we are in extraordinary times. And when in these times normal markets have ceased to work, we cannot just leave people defenseless and on their own.

The problem-object of impending bank insolvency and a loss of confidence in banking was consistently positioned, then, as having security implications which extended well beyond the immediate financial market domain, and to 'the American people' and 'ordinary families everywhere'.

It is perhaps tempting to view these representations as the window dressing that, obscuring the 'class and institutional power' of 'finance capital', was necessary to make the taxpayer bailouts more palatable to 'the masses' who 'have an interest, however contradictory, in the daily functioning and repro-duction of financial capitalism because of their dependence on it' (Albo et al. 2010: 61). However, what this representational element of the apparatus achieved was, in effect, to draw a particular, neo-liberal ontology of 'the good life' into relation with the recapitalization and restoration of confidence in banking. What might be called a capital–confidence–life relation was forged, such that the capital and confidences of solvent banking became a security problem for 'ordinary families everywhere'. As such, the bailout apparatus was not just a matter of saving banks or finance capital, but of explicitly preserving a form of valued and financialized life. The discourse of capital–confidence–life travelled through the existing and extensive mediated spaces of the 'finance-entertainment complex' (Taylor 2004: 191), as it was blasted out at the height of the crisis in mainstream press, radio, and television news, and was churned over on dedicated satellite stations and on Internet blogs and advice forums. The result, to paraphrase from Marieke de Goede

(2012: 5), was the 'fostering' of a 'broad cultural space' in which bank solvency 'became perceived as an urgent security problem' for all.

That the bailout apparatus featured a representational and extensively mediated element that played up the fundamental security threat posed by the immanent banking collapse did give rise, however, to a further and related issue: how to get the circulations of bank lending moving again. If the financialized security of the population was what was at stake as the banks were recapitalized and confidence in banking was restored, then what were the indicators that mortgage markets were picking up, consumer credit was available at reasonable rates of interest, and that small businesses could access overdraft facilities as necessary to pay salaries and wages? As Congress considered whether to release the second $350 billion of TARP monies in January 2009, for example, the Congressional Oversight Panel (2009) was highly critical of the way in which the previous purchase of preference shares by the US Treasury had not been combined with accountability mechanisms that would have required lending to consumers and businesses. Further, as will be noted in Chapter 6, those banks that were permitted during the latter half of 2009 to repay the TARP monies which they had received by way of recapitalization were only permitted to do so once they were found to be materially capable of producing sufficient flows of credit.

Similar issues beset HM Treasury and the Bank of England in the UK, leading to a number of initiatives designed to translate the bailout actions into increased flows of bank lending to households and the productive economy. This culminated in the Funding for Lending scheme that, launched in July 2012 (Bank of England 2012b), remains in place at the time of writing in early 2014. Under the scheme, banks are permitted to borrow government gilts from the Bank in exchange for eligible collateral, with the fees charged and the amount banks are able to borrow dependent upon their lending growth. The strange irony here, however, is that as interventions such as Funding for Lending seek to influence and shape bank lending, they reach out for precisely the kind of control over credit creation that would be 'the normal expectation of nationalisation' (Watson 2009: 189). While the bailout apparatus has been hailed for warding off the immediate threat of banking insolvency in the UK in particular (e.g. NAO 2009b), it certainly did not lead to the restoration of the uncertain financial circulations upon which the security of the population ostensibly depends.

Conclusion

As the tumult of the global financial crisis reached a crescendo in the autumn of 2008, there was a significant sea change in the governance of the crisis.

With the unveiling of the BRF, a more-or-less discrete security apparatus quickly began to consolidate, an apparatus that rendered the crisis governable as a problem of banking solvency that required systemic recapitalization. It was significant, therefore, that the locus for crisis management partially shifted away from money and capital markets to banks and banking, and that the bailouts were funded by fiscal borrowing rather than by the minting of base money reserves at the central banks. What this chapter has also shown, however, is that the means and ends of the bank bailouts cannot be comprehended effectively when they are framed by the consensus view on the governance of the global financial crisis. The bailouts were not simply a matter of sovereign states and taxpayers propping up the ailing banks, and of the public socialization of private banking losses.

As it has further developed the book's critical encounter with the consensus view on how the crisis was governed, the chapter's analysis of the bank bailout apparatus is of particular import in three main ways. First, when highlighting and exploring the performative power of the balance sheet in the bailout apparatus, the chapter has called specific attention to the immanence of market devices in the management of the crisis. If contingent and multiple attempts to control the crisis were a matter of governing by rather than over economy as this book contends, it was not merely the theories and concepts of economics that mattered. Relations between the balance sheet and the crisis discourse on banking were critical to the rendering of the problem-object of banking solvency, and relations between the balance sheet and treasury institutions were essential to the technical, depoliticized solution of recapitalization by temporary equity investment. Second, by stressing how the bailout apparatus sought to draw and work on a material-affective relationship between capital and confidence in banking, the chapter has underscored how cajoling an atmosphere of confidence was a key characteristic of crisis governance. Whether or not creditors and investors regarded recapitalization interventions with confidence appeared to be crucial to determining a return of confidence and solvency in banking. As with the actions proposed at the height of the crisis to address the toxic asset problem, the recapitalization and restoration of confidence in banking was explicitly portrayed as the preservation of the circulations of a valued form of life. Third, when noting how longer-term agendas for the recapitalization and resolution of banking followed from the bailout apparatus, the chapter has begun to reveal how new, post-crisis technical fixes for finance emerged from the experiments of contingent crisis governance.

Notes

1. Tier 1 capital is that which is regarded as the highest quality capital. Under the Basel III capital adequacy standards, for example, Tier 1 capital includes the common equity capital issued to establish joint-stock corporation status, retained earnings, and other perpetual share capital that has no maturity date and which can be drawn upon for the purposes of asset write-downs (BCBS 2010: 12–17).
2. Confidential interview, representative of HM Treasury, London, September 2011.
3. Subsequently, these bailed-out institutions did indeed purchase the vast majority of new mortgages issued in the US from autumn 2008 (Moseley 2013), supported by the Federal Reserve which has made massive purchases of their debt and, especially, the MBS that they have issued against their bloated mortgage books.
4. The final days of September also witnessed the Dutch and French states taking part in the recapitalization of Fortis and Dexia, in concerted actions with the governments of Belgium and Luxembourg.
5. Federal Reserve Board Press Release, 22 September 2008. Available at: <http://www.federalreserve.gov/newsevents/press/orders/20080922a.htm> (accessed June 2014).
6. The figure for the final cost of the Temporary Liquidity Guarantee Program is taken from the pages of the FDIC website. See: <http://www.fdic.gov/regulations/resources/TLGP/> (accessed June 2014).
7. The 1996 Market Risk Amendment to the Basel I Accord had already permitted banks 'considerable freedom to use their own analyses of risk in calculating their capital requirements . . . caused by fluctuations in interest rates and market prices, and Basel II allowed them to do it for credit risk: the risk of borrowers defaulting' (MacKenzie 2013: 17).
8. Confidential interview, former representative of the FSA, London, September 2011.
9. Confidential interview, representative of HM Treasury, London, September 2011.

6

Risk

Introduction: 'modern risk management'

> a vast risk management and pricing system has evolved, combining the
> best insights of mathematicians and finance experts supported by major
> advances in computer and communications technology.... This modern
> risk management paradigm held sway for decades. The whole intellectual
> edifice, however, collapsed in the summer of last year because the data
> inputted into the risk management models generally covered the last two
> decades, a period of euphoria. Had instead the models been fitted more
> appropriately to historic periods of stress, capital requirements would have
> been much higher and the financial world would be in far better shape
> today.
>
> Testimony of Alan Greenspan, US House of Representatives'
Committee of Government Oversight and Reform, 23 October 2008

As illustrated by the October 2008 Testimony of former Federal Reserve Chairman Alan Greenspan, 'risk' and 'risk management' were a significant concern
in the governance of the global financial crisis. The crisis was oft diagnosed, at
the outset at least, as a 'mispricing' or 'under-pricing of risk'. With their prices
in free fall and bond ratings in serious doubt, it seemed that previous valuations and assessments of 'risky assets'—especially those related to and derived
from sub-prime mortgages—had been optimistic at best. In August 2007, for
example, ECB President Jean-Claude Trichet appraised the situation thus: 'we
see increased volatility in many markets and a significant re-appreciation of
risks. In some respects, what has been observed can be interpreted as a nor-
malisation of the pricing of risk'.[1] That the crisis could be rendered in such
terms was, moreover, a consequence of 'the vast risk management and pricing
system' that Alan Greenspan (2008) described to the US House of Representatives' Committee of Government Oversight and Reform. At the heart of this
system was the faith that 'mathematicians and finance experts supported
by major advances in computer and communications technology' could

correctly calculate the uncertainties of credit-debt as probabilistic risks—risks which could be valued, managed, priced, and traded accordingly.

After the first few months of the crisis, however, risk came into common currency in the figuring of the tumult in a different and more pervasive way. The problem of risk was now framed less as one of miscalculation and mispricing, and more as surfeit and excess. When combined with the massive salaries and bonuses earned by those packaging and trading in risks, it seemed that the 'intellectual edifice' had fed a dangerous and highly leveraged 'euphoria'. As with previous financial crises that have been similarly represented in terms of sinful excess and abandon, it again appeared to be the case that markets had recklessly and immorally gone beyond what was rational and reasonable (Cameron et al. 2011; de Goede 2009; Mirowski 2013: 207). However, in the contemporary crisis it was the 'excessive risk taking' of the purported 'search for yield' that was said to have destabilized market circulations and threatened the disintegration of global finance (Ashton 2009). In the parlance of the period, markets which were supposed to efficiently price and 'distribute risk' between investors, and thereby minimize so-called 'systemic risk', had produced dangerous 'concentrations of risk' in institutions that were 'too big to fail'.

For Greenspan, the collapse of risk management amid the crisis could be easily explained, and how best to respond was also a relatively straightforward matter. Given that it was 'the data inputted into the risk management models' which had been defective, all that was needed was for the 'models' to be 'fitted more appropriately to historic periods of stress'. In short, the crisis did not pose a fundamental challenge to the 'paradigm', and to the presumption that the uncertainties of credit-debt could be calculated and managed as risks. What concerns this chapter, however, is how the crisis was rendered and acted on as a problem of risk in ways that did indeed question the probabilistic paradigm. Within four months of Greenspan's testimony, it was announced that the second round of the recapitalization of US banks—which rebranded the US Treasury's CPP of October 2008 as the CAP—would not turn on the use of historical data, probabilistic calculations, and the bell-shaped curve of normal distribution which had 'held sway for decades'. Instead, as part of the opening intervention in the crisis by the new administration of President Barack Obama, major US banks would be subjected to a stress test that featured a pair of quantitatively imagined scenarios of US macroeconomic performance, 'as if' fictional futures which had not taken place, and were not necessarily expected to do so.

The first section begins, then, with a brief summary of the Supervisory Capital Assessment Program (SCAP) of the CAP. Commonly known as 'the bank stress test', the SCAP projected whether the nineteen largest American bank holding companies had adequate capital on their balance sheets going forward, and if they required further recapitalization. Between October 2008 and February 2009, these banks had already received over $200 billion between them in previous rounds of recapitalization and one-off bailouts, but this was widely held to have failed to restore market confidence in US banking. The second section of the chapter will turn to consider how the crisis was made up as a problem of risk calculation and management. The apparatus that governed the crisis as one of risk will be shown, in this respect, to have assembled a number of specific economic discourses and devices. Critiques of probabilistic risk management reached out to an understanding of financial markets as complex adaptive systems in need of macro-prudential regulation, and resonated with longer-standing theoretical lineages in liberal and hetero-dox economics that underline the fundamental uncertainty of the economic future. Also enrolled were scenario stress testing techniques that, previously underdeveloped in finance relative to their growing presence in security practices and risk management across other domains, produced the imagined 'low probability, high impact' futures upon which the crisis governance apparatus was to act.

The third section of the chapter asks what additional elements were assem-bled such that the apparatus could enact the SCAP stress tests as an apparent solution to the problem of risk. With the benefit of hindsight, official and media accounts often view the SCAP as the turning point in the governance of the crisis in the US, 'the decisive step in bringing the acute phase of the financial crisis to an end', in Alan Blinder's (2013: 257) terms. And, in doing so, they tend to pinpoint the significance of the concerted and cooperative action taken by the Federal Reserve and US regulatory agencies in conducting the stress test exercise, and the transparency of the SCAP process. Here, however, the apparatus will also be shown to have elicited an atmosphere of confidence, as market publics became attached to stress testing techniques and the apparent methodological precision with which they were applied by the SCAP. The recapitalization of the major US banks was thus achieved without further recourse to the public purse. Emerging from the apparatus that governed the crisis as a problem of risk, stress testing was rapidly incorp-orated into a range of macro-prudential regulatory initiatives that sought to improve the so-called 'resilience' of banks and banking systems by preparing them for the destructive eventualities of financial uncertainties, including the possibility of future financial crises.

The Supervisory Capital Assessment Program

The SCAP formed part of the much-anticipated Financial Stability Plan of 10 February 2009, the Obama administration's first major governmental intervention in the crisis. While new Treasury Secretary Timothy Geithner was widely seen as the architect of the Plan, the SCAP was announced as a joint statement of the leaders of the main government and regulatory agencies (US Treasury Department 2009c). The stress tests were a contributory mechanism in the CAP, itself an update on the CPP of the US Treasury's TARP. As was detailed in Chapter 5, the CPP had emerged when, only two weeks after the introduction of the TARP, the focus for crisis management shifted to the purchase of equity stakes in order to directly recapitalize the major banks. The remit of the CAP and its SCAP was the capital adequacy of the nineteen largest bank holding companies in the US, especially the degree to which the Tier 1 common equity capital that appeared on the liabilities side of their balance sheets was sufficient to cover growing volumes of defaults and trading losses on the asset side.

The broad parameters of the SCAP stress test exercise were announced in late February, and details about its methodology were made public in the last week of April (Board of Governors 2009a). The results of the tests for individual institutions appeared two weeks later, on 7 May (Board of Governors 2009b). Under the methodology, banks were required by supervisors to undertake tests on the adequacy of the capital that they currently held against two different macroeconomic stress scenarios. These 'plausible "what if" scenarios' featured quantified assumptions about real GDP growth, unemployment rates, and house prices for 2009 and 2010 (Board of Governors 2009a: 10). The 'baseline' or 'consensus scenario...reflected expectation among professional forecasters on the depth and duration of the recession', while the 'more adverse scenario was designed to be severe but plausible' (Tarullo 2010). While the baseline scenario posited falls in house prices of minus fourteen per cent and minus four per cent in 2009 and 2010, for example, for the more adverse scenario these projections were minus twenty two per cent and minus seven per cent. As with the other projections within the baseline scenario, the figures for decreases in house prices were arrived at by averaging the projections found in three respected and regular private economic forecasts in the US—the Blue Chip Economic Indicators and Financial Forecasts surveys, Consensus Forecasts, and the Survey of Professional Forecasters.[2] Meanwhile, projected figures in the more adverse scenario were established by supervisors through an analysis of 'the historical track record of private forecasters as well as their current assessments of uncertainty', the latter including 'subjective probability assessments' present in private forecasts from early 2009 (Board of Governors 2009a: 5). For the main variables in the adverse scenario—real GDP growth, unemployment, and house prices—there was a probability of roughly ten–fifteen per cent that each could be worse than projected.

Under each scenario, and using their year-end 2008 financial statement as a starting point, banks first produced projections of losses and shrinking revenues, where losses for 2009 and 2010 covered at least twelve separate categories of loans and other asset classes. Supervisors assisted in a process that was 'interactive and iterative' (Tarullo 2010), providing indicative loss-rate ranges for asset markets as a whole which were based on historical experiences and quantitative modelling of relations between loan perform-ance and macroeconomic variables. Next, supervisors evaluated banks' own projections in order to identify any methodological weaknesses, missing information, and overly optimistic assumptions. This appears to have led to 'numerous modifications of the banks' submissions', often arising from a combination of 'comparative analysis across the firms' and 'supervisors' own judgements' (Tarullo 2010). As a third step in the process, supervisors ran standardized information from banks, on such matters as detailed loan and portfolio characteristics, through their own probabilistic model. Finally, and based on these three steps, supervisors produced loss, revenue, and reserve estimates for each institution that, combined with information on existing reserves and capital, were used to project the capital that banks would need to remain solvent under each of the scenarios.

The nineteen banks included in the SCAP were estimated to have collect-ively incurred losses of $400 billion across the six economic quarters through to the end of 2008, including charge-offs, write-downs on securities in invest-ment and trading portfolios, and discounts on assets acquired when taking over failing or failed institutions (Board of Governors 2009a: 3). The more adverse scenario of the SCAP projected that further losses at the nineteen firms would amount to $600 billion across 2009 and 2010, with more than two-thirds of these losses arising from residential mortgages and other consumer-related loans (Board of Governors 2009a: 3). Moreover, under the adverse scenario, ten of the nineteen bank holding companies included in the Pro-gram were projected to need to raise a cumulative total of $75 billion in equity capital in order to meet the required adequacy thresholds at the end of its two-year horizon. The ten were given thirty days to produce plans that, over the next six months, would raise this capital from the markets and/or via the CAP as necessary.

It proved unnecessary, nonetheless, for any of the ten bank holding com-panies to directly receive CAP funds in order to meet their projected shortfalls of capital. Of the ten, only car finance company and fourth-largest mortgage lender in the US, General Motors Acceptance Corporation (GMAC), received a capital injection from the Treasury after May 2009, but this was through the TARP's Automotive Industry Financing Program. The CAP was closed on 11 September 2009, and by November the ten banks which were required to raise additional capital had done so to the tune of $77 billion. This was achieved by issuing new equity, converting existing preferred equity to common equity, and selling business arms and portfolios of assets. The ratio of Tier 1 common equity capital to risk-weighted assets across the nineteen institutions included in the SCAP increased from 6.7 per cent to 8.5 per cent by the end of 2009 (Bernanke 2010b). It was the banks themselves, and the markets of which they were part, that acted on the scenarios of the SCAP. The markets had shown themselves to be capable of advancing the preparedness of recapitalization, in conjunction with the regulators, supervisors, and the Treasury. Indeed, almost a month to the day after the results of the SCAP were announced (Dash 2009; *Economist* 2009c), a number of the nineteen firms included in the Program began to pay back the TARP monies that, from the previous autumn, funded their public recapitalization. By the end of the financial year 2010–2011, the TARP held only $30 billion worth of bank preference shares on which the Congressional Oversight Panel (2011: 177) expected eventual losses to tax-payer-investors be 'relatively small'.

The Riddles of Risk Management

The stress testing techniques deployed by the SCAP were one of the relational elements within a security apparatus that rendered the crisis as a problem of risk management. What this crisis governance assemblage produced, in short, was a 're-problematization' of how the financial future should be best managed in the present (Collier 2008: 238). The single summary box that features in the SCAP methodology paper is especially revealing in this respect (Board of Governors 2009a: 10). Entitled 'Assessing Capital Needs in an Uncertain World', it begins by stating that 'Projecting estimated losses and revenues for BHCs [bank holding companies] is an inherently uncertain exercise, and this difficultly has been amplified in the current period of increased macro-economic uncertainty'. The SCAP thus worked with, rather than against, the idea that the future is 'unknown, with a wide range of plausible outcomes'. In doing so, it cut sharply against the grain of the pre-crisis economy of global finance, wherein multiple and increasingly complex calculations of probabilistic risk were pivotal to the ways in which the uncertainties of both credit-debt relations and their related transferable claims were embraced and managed.

Probabilistic risk enabled and legitimated a vast array of opportunities for risk taking and speculative profit making before the crisis (Blackburn 2006; Partnoy 2004). While diverse organizational cultures did sometimes produce a healthy scepticism of the powers of quantification (Mikes 2011), highly mathematized risk management was nonetheless crucial to how the dangers of financial expansion were apparently diminished by banks and their burgeoning staff of 'wild-eyed quants' (*Economist* 2010a: 2). Especially when combined with the off-balance sheet accounting and securitization techniques of the originate-and-distribute model of banking, pre-crisis risk management apparently assured the decomposition and distribution of default risk among investors to the extent that, in aggregate, systemic risk was contained. Moreover, while enabling trading in volatility and variance which was actually marked by indifference to the performance of underlying assets (Martin 2007; Wigan 2009), rapidly growing 'over-the-counter' markets for credit derivatives held out the 'pre-emptive promise' that the default risks of specific assets (e.g. a corporate bond) could be insured through bespoke contracts (Amoore 2011).

Despite the pre-eminence of probabilistic risk management, stress testing techniques were certainly not new to finance at the point at which the contemporary crisis took hold. Rather, until the SCAP, stress testing remained 'the poor relation in the family of analytical techniques to control risk', 'a second-class citizen' (Rebonato 2010: 1). Stress testing was present in the early-to-mid-1990s, as risk management models and devices became fully integrated into banks' organizational procedures. It also became more prevalent in banks' risk management models after the collapse of Long-Term Capital Management in 1998 (Aragones et al. 2001), a debacle in which the pitfalls of probabilistic risk management loomed large (de Goede 2001).

In-house stress testing methods took various forms. They typically focused on 'individual business lines' rather than the totality of a bank holding company, for instance (Board of Governors 2009a: 2). Scenarios could be 'drawn from historical events' (i.e. past crises), or 'from plausible economic and political developments' (Jorion 2007: 357–8). Nonetheless, stress tests were positioned as a supplementary to VaR, the prevailing probabilistic risk management technique. Emerging at JP Morgan in the wake of the 1987 stock market crash, VaR puts a probabilistic number on the amount a bank can expect to lose on its portfolio of assets on the day in question (Partnoy 2004; Power 2005; Triana 2012). So, for example, VaR models in mid-2007 typically calculated that, with a ninety five per cent degree of statistical confidence, a large Wall Street firm would stand to lose no more than $50 million on a trading book worth several hundred billion (Triana 2012: xi–xii). It was VaR that the Basel II revision of the international standards on the capital adequacy of banks had adopted, in effect, when it moved towards an A-IRB approach to the risk-weighting of assets (Chapter 5). And, although stress testing was also one of the seven protocols which had to be met under Basel II if an organization was to be permitted to substitute external regulatory oversight for an A-IRB approach (Jorion 2007), the result was that 'stress-testing was not being meaningfully used to manage risk', but 'to manage regulation' (Haldane 2009a: 13).

In the apparatus that rendered the crisis as a problem of risk management, two economic discourses were arranged such that stress testing could be 'meaningfully used'. The first was the trenchant critique of the probabilistic risk calculations of VaR, a discourse that was given loud and highly visible expression in popular debate by Nassim Nicholas Taleb's (2007) metaphor of 'the black swan'. Some high-profile figures did continue to defend the old paradigm and suggest that, in the terms of Nobel prize winning economist Myron Scholes, 'a lot of models...were pretty good, but the inputs were awful' (in *Economist* 2009d). However, for Taleb probability calculations based on historical statistics are a poor guide to the frequency of the random and unexpected events which appear as the 'tails' of the normal, bell-shaped distribution curve. Black swans are rare relative to white swans, then, but there is no way of knowing when a black swan will show up. This was especially the case with VaR which, only ever promising statistical confidence of either ninety five per cent or ninety nine per cent, effectively ruled out the possibility of extreme 'tail risks' and large-scale losses.

The basic neglect of 'low-frequency, high-impact events' by VaR was further compounded by the assumption that future event correlation (e.g. defaults on debt obligations, simultaneous falls in prices for different asset classes) could be predicted on the basis of the historical statistical relationships between those events. Indeed, under VaR, a 'negative correlation' between several classes of assets in the past served to cancel out future exposures between them, 'yielding lower overall portfolio risk estimates' (Triana 2012: xii). This had a significant effect on portfolio management, as it led investors to chase so-called 'non-correlating' asset classes in ways that, for example, contributed to rising commodity market prices prior to the outbreak of the contemporary crisis.[3] For Taleb, in contrast, there was no way of knowing whether black swans might swim together. The widespread adoption of VaR as the market standard also created a further weakness, something that became plain as the crisis took hold. As one of Taleb's collaborators, Pablo Triana (2012: 100), subsequently summarized the issue: 'VaR encouraged the group thinking that led to the accumulation of similar portfolios across the industry', and it 'ordered the massive en masse liquidation of positions, leading to snowballing losses'. The result, as we saw in Chapter 4, was the burgeoning of 'toxic assets' that could not be priced and valued.

The critical observations on probabilistic risk management and VaR that were advanced with great effect by Taleb's black swan metaphor gained particular traction, moreover, when accompanied by widespread suspicions that VaR had also been 'gamed' by the banks and their employees. As noted in Chapter 5, the adoption and manipulation of risk management systems by banks assisted the minimization of regulatory capital provisions, as written in the Basel Committee codes and required by national supervisory rules. In addition, the gaming of VaR was directly implicated in the excesses of risk taking that provoked the crisis. This was because there was nothing to stop

VaR being engineered within banks' trading operations. As Triana (2012: xv) explains:

> Trading decisions and traders' compensation began to depend on what VaR said; if the number churned up by the model was deemed unacceptably large, a trader would be asked to cut down their positions, if the number was deemed comfortably tame the trader would be assigned more capital. If you made good money while enjoying a lowish VaR, you would be considered a hero by your bosses, someone capable of bringing in big bucks with seemingly minimal risk.

There were thus significant incentives to lower a portfolio's VaR number, and to 'subdue mathematical risk estimates' (2012: xv). Tactics employed included, for example, arbitrarily changing the historical timeframe of the data about assets which was included in the model's probabilistic calculations, and tweaking volatility and correlation calculations.[4]

Macro-prudentialism was the second economic discourse that contributed to the diagnosis of the crisis as a problem of probabilistic risk management. In the wake of the governance of the crisis as a dilemma of banking solvency, macro-prudentialism has been written into the revised Basel III standards on capital adequacy in banking (BCBS 2010). Key in this regard is the authorization of national supervisors to add 'counter-cyclical' capital buffers during financial upswings, thereby rendering minimum regulatory capital requirements as variable, and as an important focus in efforts to modulate financial circulations in the terms of Deleuze (1992). As the President's Working Group on Financial Markets (2008) had recommended in March 2008, for example:

> Regulators should adopt policies that provide incentives for financial institutions to hold capital and liquidity cushions commensurate with firm-wide exposure (both on- and off-balance sheet) to severe adverse market events. These cushions should be forward looking and adjust appropriately through peaks and valleys of the credit cycle.

Macro-prudentialism has also closely informed post-crisis institutional change in the UK regulatory regime, most notably in the creation of the system-wide, financial stability remit of the FPC (see Chapter 7). However, as a sprawling economic discourse and regulatory agenda that initially developed over a decade or so prior to the crisis, macro-prudentialism also advanced a strong suspicion of the effectiveness of 'micro-prudential' probabilistic risk management techniques, most notably VaR.

The distinction between micro- and macro-prudential approaches to risk appears to have emerged around the turn of the millennium, gaining currency at international organizations such as the Financial Stability Board (FSB) and BIS.[5] Advocates included Hans Tietmeyer of the Bundesbank and Andrew Crockett, then General Manager of the BIS. As Baker (2013: 115) summarizes,

Crockett's key insight was that 'aggregate risk was endogenous, or dependent on the collective rather than the individual behaviour of financial institutions'. It followed that 'while an institution's actions could appear individually rational, in the aggregate that behaviour could generate undesirable outcomes for the system as a whole'. The differentiation between micro- and macro-prudential approaches to risk was manifest, furthermore, in the development of the techniques of so-called 'macro stress testing'. As defined in a BIS working paper published five years before the SCAP, 'Macro stress-testing refers to a range of techniques used to assess the vulnerability of a financial system to "exceptional but plausible" macroeconomic shocks' (Sorge 2004: 1). These techniques featured globally after 2001 in the guise of the IMF's *Financial Sector Assessment Program*, for instance. Of most immediate relevance to the CAP and its SCAP, however, was that the BRF had employed a macro stress testing element in the calculations it made about the solvency and recapitalization of UK banking in October 2008 (Bank of England 2008: 28–9). So, when the Federal Reserve and US regulatory authorities prescribed and supervised the 'common forward-looking conceptual framework' of the SCAP (Board of Governors 2009a: 2), this contrasted not only with the probabilistic paradigm that was entrenched in financial risk management prior to the crisis, but was also a significant and highly visible departure from micro-prudentialism.

In the apparatus which rendered the crisis as a problem of probabilistic, micro-prudential risk management, the relational enrolment of the specific economic discourses and devices described above was a resonance that folded and blended various heterodox, liberal, and neo-liberal theoretical positions. What the resonance of these otherwise competing conceptions of financial markets centred upon was the conviction that, by their very nature, credit-debt relations and the circulations of transferable debt claims are fundamentally uncertain. As Andrew Baker (2013: 115–17) suggests, the macro-prudential economic discourse has a 'diverse and eclectic intellectual genealogy' that draws on Keynes and Minsky, among others. Informing macro-prudential stress testing techniques, for instance, is the Keynesian concept of 'fallacy of composition', and the idea that systemic developments are not simply the aggregate of individual actions. Minsky's financial instability hypothesis also undergirds the emphasis that macro-prudentialism places upon the pro-cyclical character of the short-term, probabilistic calculations of risk made by VaR. The tendency for VaR to produce uniformity across banks' asset portfolios is explained, meanwhile, in terms of the 'herding' effect that follows from the intersubjective and psychological qualities of markets, as identified by Keynes and behavioural economics.

Yet, macro-prudentialism also recovers from liberal economics the fundamental distinction between calculable risk and incalculable uncertainty made by Frank Knight (1921; e.g. Haldane 2009a; Turner 2009a: 45). It also draws from complex adaptive systems theory (Baker 2013: 116), an ontological and epistemological move in the economics of financial markets that was trumpeted during the crisis by staff from the Bank of England in particular (Haldane 2009b; Haldane and May 2011).[6] When viewed from a complex adaptive systems perspective, financial market outcomes do not result from the isolated and successive actions of market agents, but from interactions and interrelations in a dynamic and non-linear network that is replete with feedback loops and prone to tipping points. As Taleb (2009) put it, for example, when delivering his testimony to a Congressional hearing on VaR that was held during the crisis, 'We are in the worst type of complex system characterized by high interdependence, low predictability, and vulnerability to extreme events'. In the aggregate, then, markets are not envisaged as efficient and equilibrating machines by complex adaptive systems theory, but as essentially uncertain ecosystems that may achieve an extemporary order that is far from equilibrium.

For Giselle Datz (2013: 464), the mobilization of the metaphor of 'complexity' in diagnoses of the financial crisis fuelled 'a materialisation of doubt, an acceptance of extant limits to knowledge'. The attendant flowering of macro-prudentialism encouraged regulatory approaches that work with, rather than against, complexity and uncertainty. Similarly, as Jeremy Walker and Melinda Cooper (2011: 144, 150–1) detail, one manifestation of the complex adaptive systems reading of financial markets and its questioning of the 'epistemic limits to prediction' is 'a repertoire of practical methodologies' that, critiquing micro-prudential risk management, insist on 'the systematic introduction of non-predictive, futurological methods of vulnerability analysis such as scenario planning'. What Walker and Cooper also highlight is that the turn to these 'practical methodologies' at the Fed and especially the Bank in the years immediately preceding the crisis arose, in part at least, from their capacities to travel across and between domains which are also figured in the terms of complex systems. For Walker and Cooper, there are thus strong parallels between the step-wise growth in the application of macro-prudential stress testing in financial crisis governance, and the anticipatory techniques recently deployed more widely to advance 'resilience', whether in critical infrastructures of US national security policy, for instance, or in the sustainable urbanization of global development agendas. Such parallels would not seem to stop there, however. Macro-prudential stress testing scenarios also share much with a broader anticipatory turn in the techniques which, as a growing body of scholarship attests (see Anderson 2010; Amoore 2013), are at work in the securing of the uncertain future of terrorism, pandemics, and ecological disaster.

In the apparatus that rendered the crisis as a problem of probabilistic risk management, then, it was the macroeconomic stress scenarios of the SCAP that created the material givens upon which the CAP was to act. That which was to be acted upon, at a system level, were the low-probability, high-impact tail risks that were necessarily left to one side by the major US banks' own micro-prudential VaR calculations of risk-weighted capitalization. In the process, the SCAP produced the kind of 'enactment-based knowledge' about the state of US banking which, as a reading of Stephen Collier's (2008: 225) research would suggest, had clear parallels with the estimates and likelihoods which figure in the anticipatory techniques of catastrophe planning.[7] The SCAP had a particular 'inventory', 'event model', and assessment of 'vulnerability' that is typical of enactment-based knowledge. Given the unravelling of probabilistic risk management in the crisis, and the continuing sense in early 2009 that these were still uncharted financial waters, the starting point for the SCAP tests was that there was 'no archive of past events whose analysis might provide a guide to future events' (Collier 2008: 228). As Rebonato (2010: 1) puts it, during the tumult of autumn 2008 in particular, 'events of one-in-many-thousand-years rarity kept on occurring with disconcerting regularity'. Thus, instead of an archive, the SCAP included a dozen or so categories of loans and asset classes held by the banks, and their revenue in its various forms, as the 'inventory of elements' which were deemed most relevant to the impact of future quantified 'events' (e.g. house price falls) included within the macroeconomic scenarios (Collier 2008: 227). It was the 'vulnerability data' about these assets to future events which fed into loss and revenue estimates on bank's balance sheets, and to projections of capital adequacy (2008: 235).

Although the apparatus that rendered the crisis as a risk management problem served to reproblematize how the financial future should be best managed in the present, what the anticipatory techniques of macro-prudential stress testing deployed by the SCAP also featured was the 'recombination' and 'redeployment' of existing risk management techniques (Collier 2008: 238). Indeed, there is clearly a sense in which the tendency to regard stress testing as something of a remedy for the pitfalls of VaR served, in effect, to buttress existing 'archival-statistical knowledge' and the probabilistic risk techniques it enables (2008: 225). By way of illustration, consider the calculations of the thresholds on the levels and composition of capital that banks were required to hold on the liabilities side of their balance sheets at the end of the two-year horizon of the SCAP stress test: Tier 1 capital had to be greater than six per cent of risk-weighted assets, not total assets, with Tier 1 common equity capital similarly required to be in excess of four per cent of risk-weighted assets (Board of Governors 2009a). Thus, through calculations of asset values that took probabilistic account of their risks, the SCAP held in place and did not sweep away one of the basic premises of VaR. Similarly, the assumptions that underpinned the modelling of the vulnerability of particular asset classes to the impact of future events were also largely probabilistic, based on the analysis of archives of historical data about each of those loans and instruments. In acting to anticipate uncertainties in order to mitigate future dangers, the macro-prudential stress tests of the SCAP remained a complex calculative interweaving of the imaginative and probabilistic, the novel and historical.

Testing Out Banking

The macro-prudential stress testing of the commanding heights of US banking are widely regarded, with hindsight, as the beginning of the end of the crisis in its heartland. In a speech he made one year to the day after the announcement of the results of the SCAP, Ben Bernanke (2010b), for instance, described the intervention in the following terms:

> Last year's stress assessment was a watershed event—unprecedented in scale and scope, as well as in the range of information we made public on the projected losses and capital resources of the tested firms. We are gratified that market participants and private analysts viewed the exercise as credible. It helped to restore confidence in the banking system and broader financial system, thereby contributing to the economic recovery.

It was certainly the case that, prior to the SCAP, governmental interventions in the crisis were largely unsuccessful at restoring market confidence in the solvency of US banking. There was also initially very little indication that the SCAP would later be regarded as such a success. The Obama administration's plans of early February were heavily criticised for their lack of detail by the financial press, and were greeted by sharp falls on global stock markets (*Economist* 2009e, 2009f; Luce and Guha 2009). As Alan Blinder (2013: 257, original emphasis) recounts, the US stock market fell by five per cent on the day the plans were announced by Timothy Geithner, the new US Treasury Secretary, 'not on any *bad* news, but on *not enough* news. Much worse, stock prices continued to drop for a month, falling a frightening twenty two percent before they finally stopped'. Recall, however, that the action on recapitalization which the SCAP called forth was to be undertaken, just two months or so later, by the markets themselves and without direct recourse to the CAP funds of the US Treasury. So, what additional elements were present, in relation, such that the apparatus could enact the SCAP stress tests as an apparent solution to the problem of risk, and thereby 'restore confidence in the banking system and broader financial system'?

For Bernanke (2010b), and, typically, for other Federal Reserve insiders (e.g. Tarullo 2010), practitioners, and financial media commentators (e.g. Blinder 2013), the success of the SCAP hinged on its 'unprecedented... scale and scope', and 'the range of information...made public on the projected losses and capital resources of the tested firms'. In the terms of the analysis offered here, the apparatus that acted on the problem of risk management featured an important institutional element, in relation with an open process that laid bare the state of the major US banks to an anxious market public. The SCAP involved the kind of direct cooperation between supervisory and regulatory institutions that is not a usual feature of US governmental arrangements, and included the Board of Governors of the Federal Reserve System, the Federal Reserve Banks, FDIC, and the Office of the Comptroller of the Currency (OCC). Meanwhile, what was known as 'stress test transparency'—a departure from standard supervisory practice that made available the stress test methodology and opened the books of the major banks, which together accounted for two-thirds of banking assets in the US at the end of 2008—'played an important role in stabilizing the financial system' (Tarullo 2010). That a newly confident market public became attached to the collaborative institutional enactment of the SCAP would appear, at first blush, to have turned on the more-or-less complete information about concentrations of risk in US banking that it ostensibly revealed.

The SCAP did not restore confidence in US banking because the stress test results cast the major banks' preparedness for future uncertainties in a positive light. Recall that, under the adverse scenario, ten of the nineteen BHCs included in the Program were projected to need to raise a cumulative total of $75 billion in equity capital in order to meet the required adequacy thresholds. Neither was it the case, by the very anticipatory nature of macro-prudential stress testing, that the apparent success of the SCAP apparatus could be a matter of the correctness, proof, or empirical validity of the results that were produced. Risk information about the solvency of US banks could not be found by markets and analysts to be 'right' in realist terms and at the time at which it was made available. Rather, what mattered about the information that the SCAP produced, in the first instance, was that it chimed with market expectations. The SCAP told market publics what they felt they already knew. As Alan Blinder (2013: 258–9, original emphasis) puts it, 'For the stress test to ease market anxieties, the numbers would have to be, as in the tale of Goldilocks and the three bears, *just right*'. However, what was also crucial to the luring and attachment of the market public to the SCAP process were the ways in which the anticipatory techniques of macro-prudential stress testing themselves became invested with confidence and animated by a positive affective charge. For 'the numbers' to be 'just right', the security apparatus also had to elicit confidence in the techniques and calculations that produced those numbers.

As Yuval Millo and Donald MacKenzie (2009) show, the historical emergence and consolidation of financial risk management over recent decades did not turn on the 'facticity' of techniques for dealing with the uncertain financial future in the present (Latour 1988), even when those techniques typically claimed to render the uncertain future knowable as probabilistic risks. Following Michael Power (2007), and combining institutional economic sociology with the actor-network theory of Bruno Latour, what Millo and MacKenzie (2009: 639–41) highlight is that the rise of risk management in financial organizational life is a story of 'hybrid human-machine networks', and the 'integration' and 'fusion of knowledge' of risk calculations into managerial and regulatory practice. So, to borrow terms from Millo and MacKenzie, the suggestion is that the 'remarkable success' of the SCAP did not hinge on the 'accuracy' of its results (2009: 638). Rather, what mattered was the 'practical usefulness' of the macro stress testing technique, the growing 'reputation among the different organizational market participants' of stress testing, and its 'constitutive (or performative)' power (2009: 638–9), that is, its capacity to socially and materially bring into being and produce action on that which it names.

In her account of the historical continuities of scientific techniques of quantification, Lorraine Daston (1995) makes a similar distinction to that which Millo and MacKenzie (2009) draw when analysing financial risk management. For Millo and MacKenzie (2009: 641, original emphasis), what is of particular import to the practicality and performativity of financial risk management devices is that knowledge about the future appears as '*methodologically* valid' and 'not always realistically valid'. Meanwhile for Daston (1995: 8), quantification, as one of the main 'aspects of how scientists come to know', is not simply marked by a drive for 'accuracy' but also for 'precision'. While the former 'presupposes that a mathematical model can be anchored in measurement; precision concerns the clarity, distinctness, and intelligibility of concepts, and, by itself, stipulates nothing about whether and how those concepts match the world'. For Daston, moreover, the search for precision—and, thus, for concepts and methods of quantification that are held by a scientific community to be credible, valid, and useful—is necessarily and always shot through with affective energies. As she has it, there is a contingent 'web of affect-saturated values' that circulates within and through scientific communities and their ways of knowing (1995: 4). These are collective mental states that make the apparent rationality of scientific endeavours possible, such that affect and rationality are not opposites, but are two sides of the same coin. In relation to techniques of quantification specifically, collectively held desires within those communities for 'communicability', 'impersonality', and 'impartiality' inform and imbue the drive for precision and, ultimately, their power (1995: 8–10). Signalling and acting through a subtle but high-profile change in financial risk management, the SCAP stress tests were thus a practical and useful intervention in markets that had been rocked by the 'mispricing of risk' and 'excessive risk taking'. But, as Daston's insights also serve to highlight, for a market public to become attached to the SCAP it mattered that it was 'precise': it brought to the fore, conceptually stabilized, and carefully applied a somewhat latent anticipatory turn in financial risk management techniques that was filled with positivity by markets and analysts.

As the reckonings and imaginings of the SCAP exercise were present on Wall Street in the first half of 2009, the credibility and reputation of stress testing techniques were also rapidly gaining ground. As the *New York Times* reported on the eve of the results of the SCAP process, for instance, they were animated by 'hope more than fear' (Leonhardt 2009). More broadly, when the *Economist* (2008a: 11) magazine had published a special report on international banking in May 2008, financial risk managers were cast as 'professionally gloomy', and as taking 'a hard look at themselves'. However, in a similar report published exactly a year later, and in the same month as the results of the SCAP, there was said to be a 'revolution within' banks' in-house financial risk management practices (*Economist* 2009d: 14). Crucial to this 'revolution' were the techniques of stress testing, especially as they came to have greater clarity and intelligibility through ongoing innovation and development. Stress testing was apparently in the process of becoming of strategic significance to banks, 'more important to boards as they seek to define institutions' risk appetites' (2009d: 14). In short, at the point at which the SCAP was undertaken stress testing was very much in vogue. While the SCAP produced the imagined 'low-probability, high-impact' futures upon which the crisis governance apparatus was to act, stress testing was also held out as the significant addition to the repertoires of financial risk management.

Indeed, and in the wake of the perceived success of stress testing in the governance of the crisis in the US in particular, these techniques came to feature very strongly in the updated approaches to financial risk management that have been typically framed under the rubric of making banks and banking systems more 'resilient'. For example, the integration of stress testing into micro-prudential risk practices, reported by the *Economist* (2009d) to be rapidly developing in May 2009, has been subsequently reinforced in the revisions of the Basel III standard on the capital adequacy of banks (BCBS 2010: 46–7). Reflecting the resonance between competing economic theories, which centres on the fundamental uncertainty of the financial future, moreover, Basel III also introduced a leverage ratio that sets the numerator of equity capital against total assets as the denominator.[8] While clearly seeking to dampen the tendencies to excessive leverage that were held to have contributed to creating solvency problems during the crisis (Chapter 5), the leverage ratio was also envisaged to serve 'as a backstop to the risk-based capital measures' and to provide 'an extra layer of protection against model risk and measurement error' (BCBS 2010: 2). There was thus an explicit recognition of the limits of probabilistic risk management, even when plans for 'enhanced risk coverage' require 'a stressed value-at-risk (VaR) capital requirement based on a continuous twelve-month period of significant financial stress' (2010: 3). Furthermore, and staying with the same international standards, SCAP-like macro-prudential stress tests came to be regarded as a crucial tool to be employed by regulators as they seek to advance so-called 'capital conservation'; that is, 'the build-up of adequate buffers above the minimum that can be drawn down in periods of stress' (2010: 6). The pro-cyclical tendencies of VaR capital calculations are thus to be offset by counter-cyclical capital provisions which are anticipated to be sufficient for the uncertain future.

For regulators and supervisors in the US, meanwhile, the macro-prudential stress testing of the banking system proved to be a far from one-off exercise. The SCAP inaugurated the now annual macro stress testing exercise for the 30 largest BHCs, which takes place under the auspices of the Federal Reserve's Comprehensive Capital Analysis and Review (CCAR). It also produced much of the impetus behind the macro stress testing, introduced under the Dodd–Frank Reform Act of 2010, which applies to a wider array of financial market institutions, such as savings and loan institutions. CCAR 'builds on lessons learned during the financial crisis about the importance of taking a forward-looking and comprehensive approach to assessing capital adequacy' (Board of Governors 2011: 2). It requires that banks project their capital adequacy across three scenarios:

> a baseline scenario generated by the bank holding company and reflecting its expectations of the most likely path of the economy; a stress scenario generated by the bank holding company that is tailored to stress its key sources of revenue and most vulnerable sources of loss; and an adverse 'supervisory stress scenario' generated by the Federal Reserve.   (2011: 12)

The 'key innovation' of CCAR, however, was that Federal Reserve officials examine, and may object to, the annual capital plans submitted to them by the largest BHCs (2011: 3). These plans cover a two-year horizon, must have a view as to how the new Basel III international capital adequacy standards will be met before the implementation deadline of 2019, and include intended 'capital actions' such as the payment of dividends and share repurchases and issuance (2011: 5). As such, while making risk information about banking publicly available for market consumption was a primary objective of the SCAP—and, indeed, is a main driver in the regular and additional stress tests that the wide-ranging reforms now require of US banks—CCAR 'includes, but is much broader than, an assessment of stress scenario results and a firm's sensitivity to different assumptions about potential losses' (2011: 18). In the terms of this book's analysis of the legacies of crisis governance, CCAR firmly positions stress testing techniques in relation to the supervision of the preparedness of US banking for the necessarily uncertain financial future.

Across the Atlantic, stress testing has recently and similarly been positioned as part of the Bank of England's approach to implementing a rounded, macroprudential regulatory agenda for financial stability. One of the first recommendations of the FPC was to require the Prudential Regulatory Authority (PRA) to produce a framework for the stress testing of the UK banking system. As detailed in the resulting discussion paper, and building on principles articulated in the June 2013 *Financial Stability Review*, the Bank of England (2013: 7) now envisages that an annual, concurrent stress test exercise 'will deliver an integrated process for deliberations around bank capital adequacy, both at a system-wide and an individual-institution level'. Given the new institutional arrangements at the Bank, the stress tests are also viewed as providing 'a device through which the Bank can be held accountable to Parliament, and the wider public, on its financial stability objective, by allowing the FPC and the PRA Board to articulate the resilience standard against which they hold the banking system' (2013: 7). Broadly in line with CCAR, and with the Basel Committee's vision of the role of macro-prudential stress testing in counter-cyclical capital provisioning, the Bank thus set out not 'a simple "pass–fail" regime', but a process feeding into 'a more graduated policy framework, where the magnitude of remedial actions taken would be a function of policymakers' judgement around the adequacy of banks' capital plans' (2013: 8). This was also something of a continuation of the Bank's existing practice where, for instance, a 'capital shortfall exercise' involving the eight largest UK banks and building societies, conducted in June 2013 by the PRA, required that five of the eight produce plans to make provisions of capital worth a total of £13.7 billion.[9]

Adoption and experimentation with macro-prudential stress testing techniques also included the European Union (EU) exercises of 2010 and 2011, which largely failed to restore market confidence in the solvency and capitalization and of European banking. In terms of the analysis advanced here—and, especially, with regard to the ways in which the cajoling of market confidence was a necessary relational element in the apparatus that governed the crisis as a problem of risk management—it is notable that coverage of the EU tests in the specialist media, for example, tends to roundly praise macroprudential stress testing while commonly drawing comparisons between the SCAP and EU exercises. By way of a broadly typical illustration, consider an extended 'Analysis' piece in the *Financial Times* during the week in which the results of the 2011 EU stress tests were due to be released. Here Patrick Jenkins and Brooke Masters (2011) acknowledge that 'internal tests that model for isolated stresses' were reasonably well-established in banking organizations for the best part of a decade before the crisis, and that during this period 'regulators began to use their own scenarios to evaluate soundness'. But, as they continue, 'only since the financial crisis has stress-testing become a vital part of the regulatory arsenal'. This is said to be because 'Attempts by increasingly sophisticated tests to model the effects of simultaneous, interdependent changes reflect the big lesson of the financial crisis—that systemic risk resulting from the interconnectedness of an increasingly complex financial sector can be economically disastrous'. Macro-prudential stress testing is, then, widely regarded in positive terms as an anticipatory financial risk management technique which has considerable efficacy for advancing the resilience of the complex and adaptive financial system. It is, as another article from the *Financial Times* has it, 'all the rage in the post-financial crisis world' (FT Reporters 2010: 16). In our terms, stress testing has the organizational practicality, kudos, and scientific status to potentially inspire an atmosphere of confidence among the market public, engendering their action in the present and on the basis of its quantitatively imagined futures.

There is clearly a sense in which the European and national supervisory and regulatory agencies charged with undertaking the EU-wide tests of the summers of 2010 and 2011 lacked the collective authority that was a significant institutional element in the enactment of the SCAP. The relative opacity of the information made available for market consumption in the EU exercises also contributed to their failure to lure a confident market public to them. That said, what comes through most strongly from the specialist media reports that compare the SCAP and EU tests is the misgivings that the markets had about the latter on the grounds of their apparent methodological imprecision. Even before the 2010 EU test gave a clean bill of health to all but seven of the ninety one banks that it covered, for example, the *Economist* (2010b) magazine expressed fears that the exercise would be 'stress test lite'. This was said to be likely because, as the backwash from the global financial crisis had come to take the form of a fiscal crisis in certain European states (see Chapter 8), it was 'tricky politically' for the test 'to factor in Europe's sovereign debt jitters'. When the results of the 2010 test were made public (CEBS 2010), the adverse scenario's 23.1 per cent discount on Greek sovereign debt instruments was, in particular, greeted as 'too benign' such that 'the exercise was a largely wasted opportunity' (FT Reporters 2010: 16).[10] Responsibility for conducting the 2011 tests moved to the newly created European Banking Authority (EBA). Despite very public efforts to address the perceived methodological imprecision of the 2010 tests (EBA 2011a; Jenkins and Masters 2011), and when only nine out of ninety one banks failed the test a month later and to the tune of a meagre €2.5 billion in total (EBA 2011b), the exercise was again affectively charged with distrust, doubt, and a degree of frustration among markets and analysts (e.g. Lex Column 2011).

Much of the scientific validity of macro-prudential stress testing techniques turns on their capacity to address the problem of so-called 'disaster myopia' resulting from the neglect of 'tail risk' by VaR models. As such, the imprecision of EU tests—which failed to anticipate the potentially disastrous uncertainty of Greek sovereign default, even though this was largely taken for granted in the markets at the time—thus continued to forestall the revival of confidence in the solvency of European banking.

Conclusions

This chapter has continued to examine the multiple and contingent ways in which the global financial crisis was governed, analysing the relatively distinct apparatus that rendered the crisis manageable as a problem of risk. Although the crisis was variously articulated under the rubric of risk, it has been shown how the particular problem-object that was forged and acted upon was the probabilistic calculation and management of default risk. Just when one might have expected financial risk management to have reached the kind of limit point suggested by Beck's (1992) insurability thesis, the ostensible threshold was extended through the SCAP's very public turn to the anticipatory techniques of macro-prudential stress testing. As such, while the SCAP process was part of the second major systemic attempt to act upon the solvency of US banking through the recapitalization solution, it was arguably of greater significance to the apparent resolution of the crisis as a problem of risk. Rooted in the creativity, experimentation, and remarkable fungibility of calculations of risk (Ewald 1991; Lobo-Guerrero 2011), the low-probability, high-impact future events that were bracketed-out by the micro-prudential risk management of VaR were incorporated into a rejuvenated financial risk management that again appeared capable of establishing the capital that banking required in the present.

When furthering the challenge that the book poses to the consensus on the governance of the global financial crisis, the upshot of this chapter's analysis of the apparatus that made up and managed the crisis as a problem of risk is primarily three-fold. First, by teasing-out the economic discourses that were arranged to abstract the crisis as a problem of probabilistic risk management, this chapter has emphasized the multiplicity of the economic theories which were immanent to crisis governance. Tenets of Keynesian and post-Keynesian thought, lineages of liberalism and neo-liberalism, and precepts from complex adaptive systems theory were all present in a resonance that folded together their shared verdict on the fundamental uncertainty of credit-debt relations. Second, as this chapter has shown how the financial market public became attached to the SCAP stress tests, it has elaborated upon the ways in which crisis governance sought to elicit an affective atmosphere of confidence. Previous chapters have detailed how luring market publics to confidence-restoring interventions largely turned on the signalling of a willingness not to stop at any cost when injecting liquidity, for instance, or when constructing bad banks and bailing out banking. Here, however, the SCAP and the recapitalization of banking became invested with market confidence by virtue of the precision with which anticipatory, macro-prudential stress testing techniques were brought to the fore, worked-up, and applied. Third, by tracing the seemingly successful mobilization of stress testing from the SCAP through to subsequent national regulatory practices and international standards, this chapter has shown how certain crisis management solutions came to provide blueprints for post-crisis financial governance. Stress testing now occupies a prominent place in the revised risk management systems designed to ensure banks that are better prepared and more resilient—it is now front and centre in macro-prudential experiments with the modulation of financial circulations. In the wake of crisis management, stress testing emerged, in short, as a key technique for governing through, as opposed to against, the uncertainty of the financial future.

Notes

1. European Central Bank Press Release, 14 August 2007. Available at: <http://www.ecb.int/press/pr/date/2007/html/pr070814_1.en.html> (accessed June 2014).
2. Details on each of these forecasting agencies is available at: <http://www.aspenpublishers.com/blue-chip-publications.htm>; <http://www.consensuseconomics.com/>; and <http://www.philadelphiafed.org/research-and-data/real-time-center/survey-of-professional-forecasters/> (accessed June 2014).
3. Confidential interview, representative of the Investment Management Association, London, September 2011.
4. Confidential interview, former representative of the Financial Services Authority, London, September 2011.
5. Confidential interview, former representative of the Financial Services Authority, London, September 2011.
6. The complex adaptive systems theory of finance can be traced to the ecological science of Crawford S. Holling and the distinctive variant of neo-liberal economics offered by Friedrich Hayek, especially as the latter emphasizes the futility of rational economic planning and critiques classical liberal conceptions of market equilibrium in favour of the 'spontaneous order' that is said to be achieved through the decentralized information processing of the market. For an excellent and detailed overview, see Taylor (2004: 265–301).

7. By carefully tracing the genealogy of a new form of calculative knowledge of catastrophe that works through estimates and likelihoods—from US civil defence planning for possible nuclear attack during the late 1940s, to natural hazard modelling in the 1960s and 1970s, and, more recently, to terrorist risk assessments and their integration into federal budgetary rationalization—Stephen J. Collier (2008) makes a distinction between 'apparatuses of collective security' that are produced through 'archival-statistical knowledge' on the one hand, and those produced through 'enactment-based knowledge' on the other. There are important differences between catastrophe planning and macro-prudential stress testing, to be sure. As the SCAP methodology paper makes clear, for example, even the adverse macroeconomic scenario was not 'a "worst-case" scenario' (Board of Governors 2009a: 5). Notwithstanding such differences, drawing parallels between these techniques assists in identifying what was distinctive about the uncertainties which the SCAP figured as the material state of the US banking system.

8. On the issues surrounding the national implementation of leverage ratios, see Braithwaite and Jenkins (2013).

9. Bank of England News Release, 20 June 2013. Available at: <http://www.bankofengland.co.uk/publications/Pages/news/2013/081.aspx> (accessed June 2014).

10. Indeed, and as if to justify the negativity that animated the exercise in July 2010 Irish banks which had passed the test's adverse scenario were recapitalized as part of the joint EU and IMF bailout shortly thereafter.

7

Regulation

Introduction: 'socially useless'

> It is hard is to distinguish between valuable financial innovation and non-valuable. Clearly, not all innovation should be treated in the same category as the innovation of either a new pharmaceutical drug or a new retail format. I think that some of it is socially useless activity.
>
> Adair Turner, *Prospect Magazine*, 27 August 2009

When, in August 2009, the then head of the regulatory regime in the UK, Adair Turner (2009c), described certain aspects of apparently innovative pre-crisis banking and financial market practice as 'socially useless', it sparked a media storm.[1] Turner, who had taken over as the Chairman of the now defunct FSA at the height of the crisis in September 2008, was largely unrepentant, however. The *Turner Review*, which he had completed in the preceding March on the regulatory challenges posed by the crisis, held that 'financial innovations can sometimes achieve economic rent extraction, rather than delivering valuable customer and economic benefits' (Turner 2009a: 106). During September 2009, Turner (2009b) went on to reiterate his view on the social utility of banking in a speech he delivered to the City Banquet at Mansion House. An audience at the Cass Business School was party to a more developed, academic version of his views on social utility in March 2010 (Turner 2010). Those which concerned Turner were the regulatory failures that had permitted self-referential and self-serving financial innovations, innovations that had led, as his *Prospect Magazine* interview put it, to certain 'bits of the financial system' growing 'beyond a socially reasonable size'. The issue, as he summarized it, was that in the years preceding the crisis 'the "efficient market hypothesis"' had 'been in the DNA of the FSA and securities and banking regulators throughout the world'. This had prompted 'the idea that more complete markets and more liquid markets are definitionally good, and the more of them we have the more stable the system will be'. Put another way, regulation had filled financial innovations that liquefied credit-debt relations, and which ostensibly distributed and circulated their attendant risks, with a progressive social meaning. The crucial question for the future, as Turner posed it, was whether the crisis meant that 'regulators have to sometimes ban new products and say, "I'm going to ban that unless you can prove to me that it is socially useful"?' (Turner 2009c).

Adair Tuner's remarks are a high-profile example of one of the various ways in which, in the governance of the global financial crisis, 'regulation' was held out to be a problem to be addressed and a solution to be enacted. In schematic terms, the problem was typically said to be that a lack of regulation of one form or another had enabled an excessive boom that collapsed to produce the crisis. That the crisis was rooted in Anglo-American markets and centred upon Wall Street and the City of London was seemingly of little surprise, as it was in these spaces that the state had been particularly aloof and the regulation of retail and wholesale finance was known to be relatively permissive, lax, and 'light touch' (FSA 2011). For instance, US sub-prime mortgage products, providing the crucial underlying income streams for the toxic assets that were related to or derived from them, were themselves found to have been written and sold by predatory lenders and brokers who escaped the regulatory reach of Federal government agencies (e.g. Rushton 2007; Shiller 2008). At the other end of the mortgage securitization chain, as Chapter 6 detailed, the surfeit of risk taking by the major Wall Street and City banks was now said to have been made permissible by very limited and ineffective regulations. The role of Wall Street in the frenzied 'slicing and dicing' of risk, for example, was largely unhindered by regulation, as investment banking had been made exempt from the direct Federal oversight of the SEC by the Gramm–Leach–Bliley Act of 1999 (Cox 2008; US Senate Permanent Subcommittee on Investigations 2011).[2]

When proffered as a solution to the crisis, meanwhile, regulation typically appeared as that which would purge global finance of its pre-crisis excesses, and return it to a state that was more-or-less reasonable and stable. The crisis was thus acted on through an array of regulatory responses, both domestically and internationally, and a number of these responses have been touched upon across the previous chapters of this book. Take, for example, the development of the third iteration of the Basel Committee regulatory standards that provide an important basis for national banking rules and supervisory arrangements. In Chapter 3, attention was drawn to how the pre-crisis absence of regulations pertaining to 'liquidity risk' provoked the BCBS to introduce the liquidity coverage ratio. Moreover, the changes to capital adequacy requirements under Basel III, as the primary initiative designed to make banks more resilient, were discussed in Chapter 5. And, as was noted in Chapter 6, Basel III also encourages the counter-cyclical interventions of macro-prudential regulation, including the integration of anticipatory, stress testing techniques into national supervisory assessments of the capital adequacy of banking.

The particular focus for this chapter, however, is upon the headline governance interventions on either side of the Atlantic that, when managing the crisis as a regulatory dilemma, cast the problem largely in the terms expressed by Adair Turner. In the US, the intervention in question is the 'Volcker rule' that, announced in January 2010 and appearing as Section 619 of the Dodd–Frank Wall Street Reform and Consumer Protection Act of later the same year, was finally agreed upon by regulatory authorities in December 2013. Put baldly, the Volker rule prohibits deposit-taking institutions from undertaking proprietary trading and from investing in, or sponsoring, hedge funds and private equity funds. In the UK, meanwhile, the 'ring-fencing' of retail and investment banking operations within BHCs, as recommended by the Independent Commission on Banking (ICB 2011) in the Vickers' Report of September 2011, came into effect as part of HM Treasury's Banking Reform Law that passed through Parliament in late 2013. What characterized both the Volcker rule and the Vickers' ring-fence was the way in which, like Turner's incendiary remarks, they raised regulatory questions about the purpose of banking and finance. Rather than merely regulating processes of competitive market innovation, they attempted to reorder and shape the future structure of banking. The Volcker and Vickers regulations were also the most politically high-profile domestic responses to the regulatory deficits that had permitted pre-crisis excesses—excesses which had seemingly left governments with little choice but to bail out institutions which were 'too big to fail' in order that they could continue to perform their supposedly essential intermediary functions.

The chapter will analyse the structural regulation of the Volcker rule and Vickers' ring-fence, understood as the assembled actions of a strategic and distributed apparatus of security. It will proceed in three main sections, beginning with a summary of the content and passage of these particular regulatory interventions. The second section will ask how the apparatus that governed the crisis as one of regulation abstracted the problem to which it sort to respond. While mustering an array of economic discourses on the pre-crisis regulatory deficit, the apparatus will be shown to have enrolled specific discourses and devices concerned with the size and substance of banks and banking when framing the issue of structural regulation. Permissive and lax regulation thus appeared to have enabled commercial banks to become 'too big to fail' when the crisis came. This burgeoning of banking was held to have been rooted in the taking of excessive, speculative risks in the wholesale markets. The final section of the chapter concentrates upon the ways in which the governance apparatus mobilized and reworked sovereign regulatory techniques in order to address the perceived problem of structural regulation.

To take and extend terms from Foucault (2007: 6), it is shown that 'instead of a binary division between the permitted and prohibited', the Volcker and Vickers regulations established 'a bandwidth of the acceptable that must not be exceeded' for the deposit-taking, ring-fenced banks that they delineate. Once separated out, the practices and circulations of commercial and investment banking were each differently positioned in positive relation to the security of the population, and mechanisms designed to mitigate inherent dangers were applied to the specific contingencies of commercial banking.

The Structural Regulation of Anglo-American Banking

Reflecting on the wide range of regulatory interventions made in the face of the crisis, the most recent annual report of the BIS (2013: 57–8) draws attention to those actions which have furthered what it calls the 'structural regulation' of banking. The vast majority of regulatory interventions are said to have taken 'banks' business models and structure as given', and to have updated and extended 'capital and liquidity requirements' in the light of the experience of the crisis. The 'rationale' of structural regulation, in contrast, is 'to protect financial stability by shielding core functions of commercial banks from losses related to investment banking and securities markets activities'. The report identifies and briefly compares three prominent examples of structural regulation: the Volcker rule in the United States, the Vickers' ring-fence in the UK, and the recommendations for EU banking reform which were made by the Liikanen Report of October 2012.[3]

The Volcker rule was initially recommended by the President's Economic Recovery Advisory Board (PERAB). Created in February 2009 and running for two years, PERAB sought to provide Barack Obama with 'independent, non-partisan information, analysis, and advice as he formulates and implements his plans for economic recovery and enhancing the strength and competitiveness of the Nation's economy'.[4] It was PERAB's Chairman, Paul Volcker, head of the Board of Governors of the Federal Reserve System between 1979 and 1987, who was the driving force behind the regulation that bears his name. As the chair of a G-30 working group on financial stability that reported in January 2009, Volcker's recommendation was that:

> Large, systemically important banking institutions should be restricted in undertaking proprietary activities that present particularly high risks and serious conflicts of interest. Sponsorship and management of commingled private pools of capital (that is, hedge and private equity funds in which the banking institutions own capital is commingled with client funds) should ordinarily be prohibited.
>
> (G-30 2009: 28)

Subsequently, and while chairing PERAB, Volcker appeared before a Congressional committee hearing in September 2009 that was dedicated to the various regulatory reform proposals circulating in Washington. Here Volcker (2009) largely reiterated the position taken by the G-30 report of earlier in the year:

> I would exclude from commercial banking institutions, which are potential beneficiaries of official (i.e., taxpayer) financial support, certain risky activities entirely suitable for our capital markets. Ownership or sponsorship of hedge funds and private equity funds should be among those prohibited activities. So should in my view a heavy volume of proprietary trading with its inherent risks.

Given Volcker's previously expressed views on the need for structural regulation, it was perhaps of little surprise that what was to become known as the 'Volcker rule' emerged from PERAB in January 2010.

Announced with considerable fanfare by President Obama (2010), the Volcker rule was positioned in the context of an 'economic crisis that began as a financial crisis, when banks and financial institutions took huge, reckless risks in pursuit of quick profits and massive bonuses'. The rule was also represented as a follow-up to actions wherein 'the American people—who were already struggling in their own right—were forced to rescue financial firms facing crises largely of their own creation'. More specifically, the regulation was said to be a response to the pre-crisis situation in which 'rules' had permitted banks 'to benefit from taxpayer-insured deposits while making speculative investments; and to take on risks so vast that they posed threats to the entire system'. As summarized by President Obama (2010), and in strikingly similar terms to that of the aforementioned G-30 report, what the Volcker rule was designed to ensure was that 'Banks will no longer be allowed to own, invest, or sponsor hedge funds, private equity funds, or proprietary trading operations for their own profit, unrelated to serving their customers'.

In order that it could become law, the Volcker rule was incorporated into the process wherein Senate and House financial regulatory reform bills were reconciled by Congress. It emerged as Section 619 of the Dodd–Frank Wall Street Reform and Consumer Protection Act of July 2010, which added a new Section 13 to the Bank Holding Company Act of 1956 (Richardson et al. 2011: 198–206).[5] The Dodd–Frank Act charged the newly created Financial Stability Oversight Counsel (FSOC) with overseeing the implementation of the Volcker rule by July 2012, a process which required collaboration between the five Federal regulatory agencies that would put it into practice (OCC, FDIC, SEC, Commodity Futures Trading Commission (CFTC), and the Fed). To that end, the FSOC (2011) produced an initial study and set of recommendations on the implementation of the Volcker rule in January 2011. Further work by the five agencies led to a set of proposals and a public consultation process that, from October 2011, debated the now highly complex exceptions to the original prohibitions (Stewart 2011). While it seemed possible that the legislation would remain bogged down in these technical controversies, it gained fresh impetus after huge losses emerged in May 2012 from the so-called 'whale trades' made on derivatives markets by the London offices of JP Morgan Chase. The precise statutory details of the Volcker rule were finally agreed by the agencies in December 2013, and the rule will become effective from July 2014 with the expectation that banks will fully conform to its requirements by July 2015.[6]

Volcker's initial vision for the rule was that, when interpreting the differences between the prohibited and permitted practices of commercial banks and other depository institutions, regulators should have considerable discretion and flexibility. For instance, when contributing to a Senate Banking Committee hearing of February 2010, he argued that definitions of prohibited practices should be 'broad enough to encompass efforts sure to come to circumvent the intent of the law' (Volcker 2010). However, given the opposition that the proposed rule generated from the US banking industry which typically cited high compliance costs and damage to international competitiveness (Sorkin 2012), and also the need to write the supervisory competencies of the five regulatory agencies into the guidelines, what ultimately emerged in December 2013 was an 800-page document that fully delineated the permitted and prohibited practices of depository institutions. Take, for example, the ban on proprietary trading. As Daniel K. Tarullo (2012) of the Board of the Federal Reserve summarizes, what constituted 'proprietary trading' under the Volcker rule was gradually narrowed down to a concrete and specific definition: 'taking a position as principal in any security, derivative, option, or contract for sale of a commodity for future delivery' that is 'for the purpose of selling that position in the near term or otherwise with the intent to resell to profit from short-term price movements'. This followed from efforts to untangle proprietary trading from trading that, exempted from the rule's prohibitions, is undertaken by banks in conjunction with long-term investment, underwriting, risk management, and, especially, market-making operations. Similarly, in terms of the restrictions on owning or sponsoring 'covered funds', the specified prohibitions were gradually narrowed down in terms of both the fund entities to which they apply (primarily private equity and hedge funds), and the organizational and investment relationships with those entities which are not permissible. The final version of the rule also requires banking entities to establish a comprehensive program of data collection designed to ensure compliance with the requirements of the statute, and to demonstrate that compliance to the appropriate supervisory agencies on an ongoing basis.

Governing the global financial crisis by enacting the structural regulation of banking was a similarly slow, complex, and hotly debated process in the

UK. Under the leadership of Sir John Vickers—a retired Oxford University economist who formerly served as a Chief Economist at the Bank of England, a member of the Bank's Monetary Policy Committee, and Director General of the Office of Fair Trading—the ICB was given a reform brief by Chancellor George Osborne in June 2010 to address the 'heavily concentrated' UK banking sector.[7] The precise remit of the ICB was to consider 'structural measures to reform the banking system and promote stability and competition, including the complex issue of separating retail and investment banking functions'. It was thus created to develop one of the core elements of the 'systemic approach' to regulatory reform called for by *The Turner Review* (Turner 2009a; also Bank of England 2009a: 53). Rather than adopting the Volcker rule solution to structural regulation, the principal recommendation to emerge from the ICB (2011) report was the idea of 'ring-fencing'. What this required was that BHCs establish a separate legal entity, within their corporate group, to provide retail banking services in the UK. The purpose of the ring-fence was said to be, first, to insulate retail banking operations from riskier wholesale financial activities and, second, in the event of future crisis, to ensure the continuous provision of retail banking services without extensive and expensive taxpayer bailouts.

As with the Volker rule's restrictions on the activities of deposit-taking institutions, the archetypal ring-fenced, retail banking entity envisaged by Vickers was not to be permitted to engage in certain wholesale market practices. In this regard, a ring-fenced bank was to be only allowed to engage in transactions with other entities within a bank holding company on an 'arm's length' basis. For Vickers, however, the practices which a ring-fenced bank was not permitted to undertake were broader, explicitly extending beyond the proprietary trading and covered funds that were the focus of the Volcker rule to include the full range of investment banking activities (e.g. underwriting, market-making, securities trading, derivatives) (ICB 2011: 45–6). This reflected a subtle but significant difference between the Volcker rule and the Vickers' ring-fence: while Volcker sought to prohibit commercial banks from undertaking certain business activities perceived to be highly risky, Vickers primarily concentrated on insulating so-called 'core' and 'essential' banking services from potential losses caused by other, 'casino' activities within a banking group.

The recommendations of the ICB were broadly accepted by the UK government and, in mid-2012, HM Treasury and the Department for Business, Innovation and Skills (2012) published a white paper on implementation. Placing the Vickers' ring-fence in the context of a wide range of domestic and international interventions designed to provide a regulatory response to the crisis, the white paper somewhat blurred the diving lines of the original recommendations by arguing that permitted retail banking activities should include 'simple hedging products' within the 'essential banking services' provided to small- and medium-sized enterprises (2012: 4). The Vickers' ring-fence eventually passed through Parliament as the lead part of the Financial Services (Banking Reform) Act of 2013.[8] The legislative culmination of UK regulatory reform, the Act also responded to the findings of the Parliamentary Commission on Banking Standards (2013) which had reported on the organizational culture of UK banking in the wake of the scandal over the manipulation of LIBOR.

The Problem of Bank Regulation

Developing across a decade or so and holding sway in Anglo-America in particular, the prevailing view on the regulation of banking and finance prior to the crisis was that it had become, and indeed should be, 'market based' and 'light touch'. The roots of this view and its implications for the organization of finance and the macro-economy stretch back through the latter half of the twentieth century (Krippner 2011). During the 1980s and 1990s, however, financial regulation witnessed 'a project of social reconstruction in the image of a deregulated system of free market capitalism', such that by the 2000s there was a 'complacency' and 'overbearing self-confidence' in the financial market innovations that had followed from deregulation (Engelen et al. 2011: 9). Given the ostensible efficiency and supremacy of markets as aggregators of information, the primary purpose of regulation was thus envisaged as enabling the so-called 'market discipline' of banking that follows from the assessments of creditors and investors. Consider, for example, the elaboration of this view offered by Ben Bernanke (2007), in a speech delivered to New York University Law School in April 2007. For Bernanke, this was 'regulation by the invisible hand', 'as opposed to' by 'the very visible hand of direct government regulation and enforcement'. He continued:

> The invisible-hand approach to regulation aims to align the incentives of market participants with the objectives of the regulator, thereby harnessing the same powerful forces that allow markets to work so efficiently. In the financial arena... this approach often takes the form of creating incentives for market participants to monitor and control the risk-taking behavior of financial firms—that is, to exert market discipline—thereby reducing the need for direct oversight by the government.

Understood in this way, the remit of regulation was limited largely to ensuring information flows in transparent markets, providing protections against fraud, and specifying and supervising minimum, risk-based capital provisions that were calculated by banks' own in-house models. Even then, and as

Bernanke warned, 'the benefits of regulation' held 'direct and indirect costs'; that is, costs 'arising from compliance with a thicket of complicated rules', and 'reductions in innovation or competition that can result from overly restrictive regulations'.

Read in the round, official commentaries on either side of the Atlantic which rendered the crisis as a problem of regulation tended to only partially run against the grain of such pre-crisis presumptions and practices. The presence of a more 'visible hand' of regulation was certainly considered to be necessary (Griffith-Jones et al. 2010). After all, and in terms that circulated in the popular media and public debates, regulators had been, at best, 'asleep at the wheel' as the financial crash approached. At worst, they had been 'captured' by the idea of the efficient market and/or the interests of Wall Street and the City (e.g. House of Commons Treasury Select Committee 2009; Sorkin 2010). Yet, as subsequent academic commentaries suggest, the crisis was a wasted opportunity to enact substantive regulatory reform that would reconstitute the forms and functions of finance (e.g. French and Leyshon 2010; Froud et al. 2010; Rethel and Sinclair 2012). Diagnoses of the crisis that called for an expanded remit for regulation and a more intrusive reach for regulators tended not to fundamentally reject market-based regulation. While the apparatus that governed the crisis as a problem of regulation certainly questioned the effectiveness of limited, market-reinforcing regulation, in the main it also did not frame this problem in such a way as to produce interventions that transformed banking and repressed financial circulations by way of a solution.

Consider, by way of illustration, *The Turner Review* (Turner 2009a), described as the 'most serious official response' to the crisis by the foremost academic observers of the UK regulatory scene (Engelen et al. 2011: 15). Citing heterodox economic insights taken from Keynes, Minsky, and behavioural economists, the *Review* is clear that 'market discipline expressed via market prices cannot be expected to play a major role in constraining bank risk taking, and that the primary constraint needs to come from regulation and supervision' (Turner 2009a: 47). Rather than preventing excesses by carefully monitoring available market information, investors hungry for shareholder value actually reinforce pro-cyclical debt creation and leveraged speculation by banks. The *Review* thus recommends an extensive list of regulatory reforms that include: increases and extensions of existing regulations on capital requirements, liquidity, leverage, and orderly resolution; the movement of over-the-counter CDS markets on to centralized and standardized clearing and counterparty systems; and the development of macro-prudential policy tools, such that regulators can intervene in a counter-cyclical manner by varying capital and liquidity requirements. Yet, *The Turner Review* explicitly creates what it calls 'wider issues—open questions' when it considers whether 'the failure of market discipline' is such that it necessitates legal prohibitions on certain retail and wholesale products, and upon speculative, short-selling practices (Turner 2009a: 105–14).

By way of a further example regarding how the problem of regulation was typically framed, consider the discourse which was enrolled to identify disjointed institutional arrangements and license reform. If regulators were indeed asleep at the wheel, then this discourse suggested that effective regulation was undermined by pre-crisis institutional composition. In the UK, as the aforementioned *Turner Review* and a number of other official reports and subsequent legislative proposals highlighted (HM Treasury 2010a, 2012), the division of responsibilities between the Tripartite authorities created a significant regulatory deficit. The FSA's attention to micro-prudential regulation and risk management, alongside the Bank of England's principal focus on monetary policy, created a gaping hole in regulatory coverage: issues of aggregate, financial stability were largely ignored, and addressing this regulatory deficit was widely held to require that the Bank be given a broader remit. As George Osborne (2010) described the issue, for instance, shortly after becoming Chancellor of the Exchequer in the Conservative–Liberal Coalition Government:

> only independent central banks have the broad macroeconomic understanding, the authority and the knowledge required to make the kind of macro-prudential judgments that are required now and in the future. And, because central banks are the lenders of last resort, the experience of the crisis has also shown that they need to be familiar with every aspect of the institutions that they may have to support. So they must also be responsible for day-to-day micro-prudential regulation as well.

Thus, the Financial Services Act of 2012 created the FPC at the Bank of England. It also dissolved the FSA, giving responsibility for micro-prudential regulation to the newly formed PRA inside the Bank, and created a separate body (the Financial Conduct Authority) to deal with retail consumer issues.

Similarly, in the US, as Ben Bernanke (2012: 50–1) later summarized, the distribution of responsibilities between different US regulatory institutions meant that 'many important financial firms did not really have any serious, comprehensive supervision by a financial regulator'. However, the 'vulnerabilities' created by 'what was missing' from these institutional arrangements also resulted from the fact that 'Nobody was in charge of looking to see whether there were problems related to the overall financial system'. The Financial Crisis Inquiry Commission reached the same conclusions (FCIC 2011: 52–66). What resulted were the provisions of the Dodd–Frank Act that disbanded the Office of Thrift Supervision (OTS) (Donelson and Zaring 2011), created the FSOC and the Consumer Financial Protection Bureau, enhanced the 'systemic risk' responsibilities of each individual regulatory institution, and restructured the internal supervisory divisions of the Federal Reserve. So, on either side of the Atlantic, the abstraction of the crisis as a problem of regulatory architecture suggested that regulation had not been sufficiently broad or intrusive prior to the crisis. Yet, while prompting changes in the character of regulation—most notably by authorizing new, macro-prudential regulatory responsibilities at the central banks and calling for improved cross-institutional working—framing the problem in these terms did not license the imposition of new legal constrains or disciplinary specifications.

As the governance apparatus rendered the crisis as a particular problem of the structural regulation of banking, further and specific economic discourses were enrolled. The focus was upon the size and substance of banks and banking, and upon how juridical regulation could be employed to effect change. In terms of size, the crisis discourse on 'too big to fail' was brought to the fore in regulatory debates, often in conjunction with concerns over moral hazard (e.g. Tarullo 2009b). In the terms of President Obama (2010), for instance, what mattered was ensuring that 'the American taxpayer' should 'never again be held hostage by a bank that is "too big to fail"'. The notion of too big to fail dates to 1984, when it was used by Congressman Stewart B. McKinney during a Congressional hearing concerned with the FDIC's bailout of Continental Illinois, then the seventh largest bank in the US (Stern and Feldman 2004: 11–13). In the contemporary crisis, for the ICB (2011: 251), 'Financial institutions whose collapse would have such adverse impacts on the financial system and the wider economy that they will be bailed out by the government rather than be allowed to go insolvent are defined as those which are "too big to fail"'. And, for the ICB, its 'recommended reforms' could 'be explained in relation to the "too big to fail" problem'. This was said to be because the ring-fencing of retail banks 'gives them some protection from problems elsewhere in the international financial system', and also 'curtails risks to the public finances' (2011: 14) in the event of future crises by limiting potential bailouts to retail operations. Similarly, for Volcker (2010), while his rule was justifiable on the grounds that it would reduce excessive risk taking by depository institutions, it was also 'designed to help deal with the problem of "too big to fail" and the related moral hazard that looms so large as an aftermath of the emergency rescues of financial institutions'.

The too-big-to-fail metaphor provided a common touchstone for diverse economic accounts of the problem of structural regulation in banking, enabling a resonance between otherwise divergent views on what was at stake. It was revealing, for example, that the remit of the ICB (2011) in the UK included questions of concentration and competition in banking markets, as well as structural regulation. The recommendations of the Vickers' report thus sought to work towards an ideal-typical, orthodox economic understanding of the supposed benefits of competitive markets that naturally tend to equilibrium, where 'suppliers compete vigorously with each other, and with the real threat of entry by other firms, to provide a choice of products to well-informed customers' (2011: 153). At the same time, however, too big to fail was also identified as a significant regulatory problem by those taking insights from complex adaptive systems theory. Drawing an analogy between biological food systems and the 'financial ecosystem', for instance, Haldane and May's (2011: 351) essay in the magazine *Nature* very publicly suggested that too-big-to-fail banks were the outcome of 'evolutionary forces' that had encouraged the 'survival of the fattest rather than the fittest'. Significantly, for the governance of the crisis as a problem of structural regulation, Haldane and May identified too-big-to-fail banks as the 'super-spreaders' that serve to amplify relatively isolated shocks throughout the financial system. For them, it was thus possible to make a complex adaptive systems case for structural regulation. As they put it:

> The structure of many non-financial networks is explicitly and intentionally modular. This includes the design of personal computers and the world wide web and the management of forests and utility grids. Modular configurations prevent contagion infecting the whole network in the event of nodal failure. By limiting the potential for cascades, modularity protects the systemic resilience of both natural and constructed networks.   (2011: 354)

With explicit reference to the separations of the Volcker rule and the remit of the ICB, it followed for Haldane and May that 'encouraging modularity and diversity in banking ecosystems' provides 'a means of buttressing systemic resilience'.

The mobilization of the too-big-to-fail discourse was accompanied, in relation, by a number of calculations on the size of banks and the benefits they accrue by dint of their size. Relatively simple market devices of economics at large provided quantitative measures of the problem at hand in terms, for instance, of market concentration. As such, official discussion on either side of the Atlantic of the structural regulation of too-big-to-fail banks was usually accompanied by figures, graphs, and charts that showed the growing share of total national banking assets accounted for by the major banks in the run up to the crisis (e.g. Bank of England 2009a: 53; FCIC 2011: 52–3). More complex calculations were also attempted that put a number on the so-called 'implied subsidy' enjoyed by the too-big-to-fail banks; that is, how implicit government guarantees on the future of huge banks were effectively already priced in by investors in terms of the interest payable on debt issued by those banks (e.g. Haldane 2012). Big banks, in short, pay less interest on their debt. So, when HM Treasury and the Department of Business, Innovation and Skills (2012: 7–10) adopted the ring-fencing recommendation of the ICB, for instance, the 'wider context' was described largely with reference to a range of calculations of the implied subsidy enjoyed by too-big-to-fail banking conglomerates. The

Vickers' ring-fence was accordingly cast as not breaking up holding company arrangements and reducing the size of banks, but as ensuring that 'all banks should be subject to normal competitive market forces' in line with 'investors' true risk appetite'. In the pre-crisis terms of Ben Bernanke (2007) discussed above, the regulatory ring-fencing of banks sought to ensure that market discipline applied to all banks, regardless of their size.

The second specific economic discourse that made up the crisis as a particular problem of structural regulation focused, meanwhile, on the substance of the banking business. Pre-crisis regulation was said to have permitted a transformation of banking, as increasingly speculative banks moved too far away from their supposed intermediary functions in the 'real' economy. In the terms that became common to media and political debates in the UK, especially in the wake of the bailout of RBS, commercial banks appeared as having been allowed to succumb to the excesses of the 'casino' (e.g. *Guardian* 2010; Turner 2009a: 94). Critical academic analyses went further still, arguing that regulation which heralded market discipline and shareholder value actually prompted competitive imperatives for volume growth on fee-income and spread-based profits rather than margin improvement (Erturk and Solari 2007). Regulation was rounded on for making possible the originate-and-distribute banking model that criss-crossed the commercial, investment, and shadow banking sectors. In sum, as the financial system had become geared to creating 'the wrong kind of credit' that inflated asset price bubbles (Engelen et al. 2011: 202–11), regulation had failed to ensure that banks provided for more productive forms of investment.

In the US, this discourse on speculative banking was refracted through the longer-standing and deeply engrained suspicion of the universal banking model that flowered after the Wall Street Crash of 1929. While the rendering of the crisis as problems of liquidity and toxicity in the US often represented universal banking as the new reality that necessitated the update of crisis management measures, this was not the case in the framing of the problem of structural regulation. For example, when Volcker (2009) appeared before a Congressional committee hearing in September 2009, he was dismissive of the domestic and international agenda that singled out so-called 'systemically important institutions' for particular, prudential regulatory treatment (e.g. Financial Stability Board 2011). Instead, positioning himself as the contemporary Carter Glass, Volcker explicitly invoked the past success of the New Deal banking legislation—especially the Glass–Steagall Act of 1933, which separated investment banking from commercial banking—and described himself as taking 'a more traditional view'.[9] For Volcker (2009), and because of their role 'to provide vital basic services to customers', it is commercial banks that 'taken collectively', are 'systemically important'. What further provoked the ire of Volcker, and many others (e.g. Johnson 2010; Obama

2010), was that pre-crisis regulation had, in effect, permitted the system of FDIC guarantees on retail deposits to be leveraged in support of proprietary trading. That which had been originally introduced to protect vital banking functions in the wake of widespread failures during the early 1930s had been utilized for speculative purposes which undermined those functions once again when the contemporary crisis hit. First and foremost, then, the US version of structural regulation sought to limit excessive risk taking by Federally insured depository institutions.

In the UK, meanwhile, the discourse that critiqued pre-crisis regulation on the grounds that it had permitted a transformation of the form and function of banking was somewhat different. Here the originate-and-distribute variant of the universal banking model ran up against calls for so-called 'narrow' or 'utility banks' (e.g. Kay 2010). While present but less prominent in US debates over structural regulation, what these proposals typically called for was regulation that would create state-guaranteed banks for the sole purpose of providing critical, intermediary services to the economy. In line with *The Turner Review* (Turner 2009a: 93–6), however, the ICB rejected the idea of utility banking. For Turner (2009a), the supposed benefits for credit creation and default risk management that followed from the securitization techniques of the originate-and-distribute model continued to hold, but required regulation to prevent excessive risk taking. Much of the disintermediated business (e.g. bond issues) that was once the preserve of investment banks was also held to have become 'core elements within an integrated service to corporate customers' (2009a: 94).

The case for rejecting utility banking was also buttressed in the UK by wider considerations about the competitiveness of the City of London as a global financial centre. Amid the debates over how to govern the crisis as a problem of regulation, these considerations were given force by the report of Sir Winfried Bischoff (2009). Commissioned by HM Treasury in 2008, Bischoff (2009: 38) warned that:

> Policy-makers should continue to recognize the international context of the UK's financial sector when making rules and proposals specifically designed for the UK. The UK should not introduce regulations that are inconsistent with international practices unless there has been a consistent and long-term failure to act at the international or regional level.

When HM Treasury and the Department of Business, Innovation and Skills (2012: 8) adopted the Vickers' ring-fence, the purpose of structural regulation was thus said to be to 'strengthen the universal banking model' and ensure to that 'the UK's reputation as the world's leading financial centre will be further enhanced'.

As the governance apparatus rendered the crisis as a problem of structural regulation, the economic discourse on the substance of banking was often arranged in close proximity to certain calculations that provided indicators of the extent to which banking had become overblown and decoupled from its intermediary functions. That an excess of speculative, wholesale operations had been permitted to develop in banking was found to be evidenced, for instance, by the divergence between executive compensation levels in banking and non-financial corporations. The FCIC (2011: 61–4), for example, drew attention to the way in which this growing divergence began in the mid-1980s, at the moment when the separations of the Glass–Steagall Act began to gradually unravel. More broadly, the payment of staggering bonuses to traders became symbolic in the popular imagination of all that had gone wrong with banking. National accounting measures of the relative contribution of the finance sector to economic performance and profitability—significant to the pre-crisis manufacture and celebration of banking as a productive part of economic life (Christophers 2013)—were now invoked as indicators of banking gone bad. The discussion of 'regulation redux' by the aforementioned report of the FCIC (2011: 64–6), for instance, marshals a range of aggregate measures of US GDP, corporate profits, leverage, and debt when working towards the conclusion that the business of banking had been allowed to become divorced from the needs of the 'real' economy.

The Solutions of Volcker and Vickers

As the crisis was made governable as a regulatory problem and as an issue of structural regulation in particular, sovereign regulatory institutions were enrolled in order to enact the ostensible solutions of the Volcker rule and Vickers' ring-fence. Implementation and supervision of the Volcker rule required cooperation between the five Federal regulatory institutions involved, most notably the FDIC and the Fed. The Vickers' ring-fence, meanwhile, required the activation of the rehashed UK regulatory architecture that was firmly centred on the Bank of England. The newly diagrammed and more extensive regulatory remit of these institutions certainly went well beyond the minimal responsibilities that, prior to the crisis, were deemed necessary to enable the invisible hand of market discipline. As the question of regulation centred on 'governing at the border between too much and too little' (Foucault 2007: 19), apparent solutions to the crisis affirmed that more regulation was indeed required. This was especially the case for the structural regulation of Volcker and Vickers that was (and remains) politically contentious precisely because legal prohibitions were explicitly called upon to address the form and function of banking.

Yet, as with the contingent and relational deployment of sovereign institutions in the crisis governance apparatuses previously discussed in this book, the structural reform of regulation did not simply centralize authority in the sovereign regulatory agencies. Governing more by creating new regulations did not equate to an exercise of the sovereign mode of power. Rather, the Volcker rule and Vickers ring-fence rearticulated sovereign regulatory techniques, and marshalled them in new ways. The problem of regulation was not rationalized in such a way that 'the protection and codification of market practices' was 'conceived of as the exercise of sovereign rights' (Foucault 2008: 18). Even under the auspices of the apparently more radical structural regulation of the Volcker and Vickers interventions, juridical regulatory techniques were not deployed to rule out, close down, or prohibit that which, in the run up to the crisis, had transformed Anglo-American banking and threatened its complete collapse. Certain wholesale market circulations that were deemed speculative and high risk were not placed outside of the law by structural regulation, but were positioned at one remove from deposit-taking, ring-fenced banks.

When deploying sovereign regulatory techniques to separate out commercial banking and wholesale finance, moreover, the structural regulation of Volcker and Vickers positioned each domain of banking as playing different but nonetheless positive roles in securing the life of the population. Most obviously, the circulations of savings and credit that are intermediated by deposit-taking institutions and commercial banks were consistently reiterated as being 'vital', 'essential', and 'critical'. For the then Deputy US Treasury Secretary, Neal S. Wolin (2010), for instance, the Volcker rule boiled down to 'limitations' designed 'to prevent a banking firm from putting its clients, customers and the taxpayers at risk by conducting risky activities solely for its own enrichment'. At the same time, however, structural regulation largely affirmed the apparently constructive contribution to the security of the population made by wholesale banking circulations. Despite the consistent labelling of proprietary trading as 'speculative' and of investment banking as 'casino banking', such gambling and gaming in this instance did not appear to question the social and political legitimacy of wholesale markets. Put another way, while commercial banking appeared as a critical infrastructure that provides the financial essentials of life, it certainly did not seem to provide all that is necessary. So, for Volcker (2010) for instance:

> Recurrent pressures, volatility and uncertainties are inherent in our market-oriented, profit-seeking financial system. By appropriately defining the business of commercial banks . . . we can go a long way toward promoting the combination of competition, innovation, and underlying stability that we seek.

Not dissimilarly, in the terms of the Vickers report (ICB 2011: 9), 'A number of UK banks combine domestic retail services with global wholesale and investment banking operations. Both sets of activities are economically valuable'. Somewhat contrary to the ostensible rationality and science of risk taking that has tended to legitimate modern finance (de Goede 2005), structural regulatory solutions to the crisis accepted and worked with, rather than against, the fundamental uncertainties of wholesale financial circulations and the opportunities that they apparently afford for speculative and competitive entrepreneurialism.

Furthermore, once delineated through structural regulatory techniques, each domain of banking practice was made amenable to a distinctive logic of activist, market-based regulation. Instructive in this respect is the comparison that is typically drawn between the Volcker rule and the Glass–Steagall Act, with the former commonly described as 'Glass–Steagall lite'. What is significant about this description is not that contemporary structural regulation is different because the business of banking has fundamentally changed since the 1930s. Such a view holds that a firm regulatory separation between commercial and investment banking in the mould of Glass–Steagall has become impossible, and it is this that led the Volcker rule to put in place the more limited aim of singling out narrowly defined sets of transactions and business lines for regulatory attention (e.g. Acharya et al. 2011; Richardson et al. 2011; Turner 2009a). In our terms, however, what is notable is that the Glass–Steagall Act and contemporary structural regulation each deploy sovereign regulatory techniques to achieve quite different ends.

Glass–Steagall rationalized sovereign regulatory interventions in disciplinary terms, and erected regulatory walls that 'enclosed' and 'isolated' commercial and investment banking in what were, in effect, distinct cellular spaces (Foucault 2007: 45). Once separated out, both commercial and investment banking were 'entirely regulated' (2007: 46), and subjected to close supervisory surveillance. Both were tamed and made docile, as their 'obligatory' functions were 'prescribed' in support of the productive economy and national economic competiveness (2007: 46–7; Foucault 1977: 220). Consider, for instance, the section of the Banking Act of 1933, known as Regulation Q, that established the power of the Federal Reserve to set interest rate ceilings on deposit accounts, or the way that mass stock market investment products such as mutual funds were outlawed (Nocera 1994). In the wake of World War II, and via such regulations and capital controls, it was thus obligatory for US banks, pension funds, and other investors in long-term debt instruments to hold large amounts of government bonds that were issued to fund the war effort and subsequent Cold War and welfare expenditures (Blyth 2013: 241; Reinhart and Belen Sbrancia 2011). Accordingly, US investment banking and commercial banking each became cartelized and ossified in the post-1945 period.

In contrast with Glass–Steagall, the Volcker rule and Vickers' ring-fence make 'use of some instruments of prescription and prohibition' to delineate domains of banking and financial circulation which are modular spaces that 'function in relation to each other' (Foucault 2007: 47). Once differentiated and defined in relation to each other and to the security of the population, both commercial and investment banking are relatively free from the kind of regulation that would specify and standardize their business. Each is enabled in 'the development of ever-wider circuits' (2007: 45). In the terms of Paul Volcker (2010), the 'literally thousands of hedge funds, private equity funds, and other private financial institutions' that are 'actively competing in the capital markets . . . are, and should be, free to trade, to innovate, to invest—and to fail'. As he continues, 'Managements, stockholders or partners would be at risk, able to profit handsomely or to fail entirely, as appropriate in a competitive free enterprise system'. Not dissimilarly, for HM Treasury and the Department of Business, Innovation and Skills (2012: 4), 'A zero-failure financial system is not our aim, nor should it be. We want a dynamic financial system that is stable over time'.

The point of the activist regulations that are applied to commercial and investment banking is thus to advance the resilience of each of the main modules of finance, and the resilience of commercial banking in particular. Disciplinary regulation sought to prevent financial failure in a precautionary manner, and carefully and conservatively prescribed the obligatory practices of banking in support of the national economy. Market-based, invisible-hand regulation placed its faith in mechanisms that supposedly controlled the future threats posed by uncertain financial circulations in a pre-emptive manner, as exemplified by insuring and hedging default risks through the derivative products that completed and perfected the markets. Activist, market-based regulation, in contrast, seeks to mitigate those same threats by advancing preparedness for their crisis-laden eventualities.

Revealing in this respect are the origins of the ring-fencing technique which was brought forward in UK banking by the Vickers report, and the way in which ring-fenced banks are singled out for particular regulatory treatment. According to a brief section in the Bank of England's (2009b: 55–6) *Financial Stability Report* of December 2009, 'ring-fencing' is a 'regulatory tool' designed to ensure the supply of ' "essential" services to the public' that was first developed for the privatized utilities industries (e.g. water, electricity, gas). Specifically, ring-fencing is said to be written into 'operator licences' in order 'to prevent cross-subsidy of non-regulated activities either by financial transfers from or risk transfers to regulated activities'. In the terms of Haldane and May (2011) discussed earlier in this chapter, ring-fencing advances the 'modularity' of a system or network. The ring-fencing regulatory technique travelled to the financial domain as one of the 'lessons' available 'for how banking regulation could address network risk and the too important to fail problem' (Bank of England 2009b: 55). As it rejected calls for structural regulation that would create narrow, utility banks, the Vickers report and subsequent legislation enrolled a sovereign regulatory technique initially designed to secure the marketized circulations of the utilities sector.

Once certain banking entities were placed inside the ring-fence, then, their preparedness and resilience for the potentially damaging eventualities of the future could become the focus of particular regulatory attention. So, while it was said to be the case that 'All institutions require robust and rigorous supervision', a ring-fenced bank was nonetheless required to have risk management processes that are distinct from those of the universal bank holding company of which it is part (HM Treasury and Department of Business, Innovation and Skills 2012: 11). Although banks operating inside the ring-fence were required to 'meet capital and liquidity requirements on a standalone basis' (2013: 26), capital requirements were also higher for ring-fenced banks which were placed on the same regulatory footing as 'UK-headquartered global systemically important banks' (2013: 33). Making ring-fenced banks more resilient was thus deemed to require not only that they are institutionally separated from certain wholesale financial market circulations—*a la* Volcker—but also that their 'primary loss-absorbing capacity' was greater (2013: 33). Indeed, alongside the broad implementation of the Basel III capital adequacy standards at the national level, ring-fenced banks in the UK were required to hold a further 3 percent 'ring-fence buffer' of equity capital. This was said to be 'a proportionate measure to ensure that these firms, which provide vital services to the UK economy, are more resilient to shocks' (2013: 34). A large, ring-fenced bank was thus envisaged as holding 10 percent of equity capital to risk-weighted assets. No additional requirements were placed on ring-fenced banks, over and above Basel III standards, for either liquidity or leverage ratios.

Conclusions

No adequate account of the governance of the global financial crisis can be offered which does not consider the ways in which the crisis was rendered manageable as a problem of regulation. Although regulatory interventions were not the immediate focus for crisis governance actions—problems of liquidity, toxicity, and solvency appeared, in particular, to be more pressing—diagnoses of the crisis as a regulatory issue were present from the outset. Indeed, leaving aside specific points of analytical disagreement and differing prescriptions for change, a concern with the failings of the pre-crisis regulatory regime was one of the main points of intersection between official and critical academic explanations of the crisis. This attention to regulatory questions was, in our terms, a corollary of the consensus over crisis governance that is rooted in the deeply engrained and shared assumptions of economics and political economy about financial crisis management. Once the sovereign state is positioned as the agent of crisis governance that seeks to restore the circulations of banking, the markets, and finance capital, then it is only a short step to asking whether the state was successfully undertaking its regulatory responsibilities prior to the crisis, how the state might better discharge those responsibilities in the wake of the crisis, what form banking and financial market regulation by the state should take, and so on. Such deliberations serve to reproduce the distribution of the sensible that, in Rancière's (2010) terms, reduces the crisis and its aftermath to technical questions over the proper role of the state and to liberal pluralist questions over the adjustment of competing societal interests.

Contributing to the book's critical encounter with the consensus on the governance of the global financial crisis, this chapter's analysis of the apparatus that rendered the crisis manageable as a problem of regulation is especially significant in two crucial respects. First, it has been shown here how the more extensive and activist regulation that was put in place by way of crisis governance cannot be simply explained as a return of the state and emboldening of public authority. That this holds for the structural regulations of Volcker and Vickers—which were contentious precisely because, unlike other regulatory interventions, they expressly targeted and sought to frame the purpose of too-big-to-fail banking—is highly revealing. Even when enacting structural regulation, state institutions were incorporated into a distributed and relational apparatus of crisis governance in such a way that sovereign regulatory techniques were redesigned. Second, and related, what emerged from the apparatus that governed the crisis as a problem of structural regulation was a particular technical fix to the destructive forces of uncertain financial circulations. The purpose of sovereign regulatory techniques was not to prohibit those wholesale market circulations deemed to be speculative and destabilizing, but to position them at one remove from the ostensibly essential and vital circulations of deposit-taking, ring-fenced banking. Moreover, as Volcker and Vickers erected new regulatory lines between domains of financial circulation, the point was not to enclose each in order to subject them to the standardizations of disciplinary and precautionary regulation, something that the constant comparison of the Volcker rule to the Glass–Steagall Act of 1933 would suggest. Instead, and for the sphere of commercial banking circulations in particular, sovereign regulatory techniques were restyled to advance preparedness, resilience, and, by extension, the financialized security of the population.

Notes

1. Turner's remarks were made in the interview, entitled 'How to Tame Global Finance', which he gave to *Prospect Magazine*. The format of the interview was such that Turner responded to the questions and provocations offered by John Gieve (former Deputy Governor of the Bank of England), Jonathan Ford (an associate editor of *Prospect*), Gillian Tett of the *Financial Times*, and Paul Woolley of the London School of Economics. A number of contributors also provided online responses to the interview. The original interview and online responses are available at: <http://www.prospectmagazine.co.uk/magazine/how-to-tame-global-finance/#. UtPTm8hFAcA> (accessed June 2014).

2. This separation of commercial from investment banking was formally brought to an end in 1999 by the Financial Services Modernization Act (Gramm–Leach–Bliley Act). The provisions of Glass–Steagall had, however, been gradually eroded from the mid-1980s by a range of decisions taken by the Federal Reserve Board in relation to individual cases as both investment and commercial banks sought to extend their businesses in such a way as to encroach on the turf of the other (Crawford 2011).

3. Given the focus here on the governance of the global financial crisis in its Anglo-American heartland, the Liikanen Report lies beyond the remit of this chapter. It is available at: <http://ec.europa.eu/internal_market/bank/structural-reform/index_en.htm> (accessed June 2014).

4. This description is taken from the PERAB webpages, which are available at: <http://www.whitehouse.gov/administration/eop/perab/about> (accessed June 2014). PERAB was replaced, from February 2011, by the President's Council on Jobs and Competitiveness.

5. The Dodd–Frank Act is truly vast. As Myron Scholes (2011: xiii) summarizes it in his 'Foreword' to Acharya et al.'s (2011) edited volume devoted to the Act, 'At 2,319 pages, the Act requires that 243 new formal rules be adopted by eleven different regulatory agencies, all within a year and a half of its passage. This is a massive undertaking'.

6. Federal Reserve Board Press Releases, 10 December 2013. Available at: <http://www.federalreserve.gov/newsevents/press/bcreg/20131210a.htm>; and <http://www.federalreserve.gov/aboutthefed/boardmeetings/20131210openmaterials.htm> (accessed June 2014).

7. The quotation is taken from the terms of reference section of the ICB website. Available at: <http://www.bankingcommission.independent.gov.uk/terms-of-reference/> (accessed June 2014).

8. The full version of the Financial Services (Banking Reform) Act is available at: <http://webarchive.nationalarchives.gov.uk/+/bankingcommission.independent.gov.uk> (accessed June 2014).

9. Given impetus by the Pecora Hearings, the Banking Act of 1933 is known as the Glass–Steagall Act because it was carried through Congress by former Treasury Secretary, Carter Glass, and the then Chairman of the House Banking and Currency Committee, Henry B. Steagall. The legislation separated deposit-taking commercial banks from investment banks, and created the FDIC to guarantee bank deposits and

prevent bank runs. During the period between 1930 and 1933, when forty per cent of US banks failed, Glass became the spokesman for a period in popular culture marked by chastening revulsion at the 'madhouse' of speculation during the roaring twenties (Fraser 2005: 367–90). As the new President Franklin D. Roosevelt famously put it at his inauguration speech in March 1933, 'Practices of the unscrupulous money changers stand indicted in the court of public opinion, rejected by the hearts and minds of men' (in Chancellor 2000: 220).

8

Debt

Introduction: 'a sovereign debt crisis'

> there is a well trodden path that has led, in different times of history and different places in the world, from a banking crisis to a sovereign debt crisis. For the rapid and unsustainable increase in private sector debt that precipitated our current problems has not, for the large part, been eliminated. Instead much of it has been shifted from private sector balance sheets to the public sector. . . . Dealing with this inheritance from its predecessor is the single greatest economic challenge the new Government faces. For what business will invest with confidence if they fear ever higher deficits will lead to ever higher taxes? What family will spend with confidence if they fear ever higher debts mean ever higher interest rates?
>
> > George Osborne, Speech at the Lord Mayor's Dinner for Bankers and Merchants of the City of London, Mansion House, 10 June 2010.

Delivering the first of his annual speeches at the Mansion House in the City of London—one month after he became Chancellor of the Exchequer, and a week before his first budget—George Osborne was clear that the governance of the global financial crisis was not over. For Osborne (2010), this was because the 'rapid and unsustainable increase in private sector debt' that had 'precipitated our current problems' had passed to 'the public sector'. What was more, HM Treasury was being whipsawed by contending pressures and demands. The crisis and its accompanying recession produced a sharp contraction in total tax revenues, roughly one-quarter of which had been collected from the financial sector in 2007. Yet, there had also been a step-wise increase in government expenditure due to the costs of bank bailouts, growing welfare payments, and the brief rediscovery of Keynesian deficit spending by the predecessor government. The 'banking crisis' had become a looming 'sovereign debt crisis', then, as evidenced by a spike in the government's fiscal deficit and thus in aggregate public borrowing.[1] There was, for Osborne, something inevitable about the problem-object that now presented itself. He also held it to be demonstrable by the punishment that was being meted out to Greece, at the time of the speech, by bond markets which had discovered disarray in the public accounts of this profligate member of the Eurozone. Moreover, in Osborne's view, a view that had also recently come to prevail across the governments of the EU and G-20 (Blyth 2013: 59–62), there was only one feasible solution to this problem: cuts in public expenditure that would reduce the fiscal deficit and slow the rate of increase in sovereign indebtedness. The 'challenge', in short, was to adopt a governmental programme of fiscal austerity.[2]

Although the state of US sovereign finances broadly paralleled those of the UK by 2010,[3] the Obama administration certainly did not adopt fiscal retrenchment with the same zeal as Osborne's Conservative–Liberal Coalition Government. Especially after the Republican Party came to hold a majority in the House of Representatives following the midterm elections of November 2010, deficit reduction through budgetary legislation in the US became mired in fundamental disagreements over the best way to proceed. For the Obama administration, fiscal deficit reduction was to be best achieved through a combination of tax increases and benefit reductions targeted at the wealthy, and relatively shallow and gradual cuts in expenditure that sheltered key budget lines deemed necessary for future economic competitiveness and basic social welfare. It was a matter of deploying 'a scalpel and not a machete to reduce the deficit', as President Obama (2011) memorably put it. This agenda stood in tension with Republican preferences for tax cuts, and for deep reductions in welfare spending that typically required the radical reform of healthcare provision and the retirement insurance provided by Social Security. Locked into these disagreements, the fiscal austerity of the Federal government in the US was thus relatively less extensive by comparison with that of the Coalition Government in UK. That said, once the expansionary Federal deficit spending of 2009 had waned, swingeing cuts in expenditure began in earnest at the state, local, and municipal levels of government which were typically experiencing their own vicious combinations of shrinking sales and property tax receipts and growing spending commitments.

Despite these differences, there were broad and important similarities in how the global financial crisis was governed on both sides of the Atlantic from 2010. In the UK and the US, policies of fiscal expansion, which briefly sought to provide a solution to the crisis-induced recession, were quickly curtailed as a new will to govern the crisis emerged. The crisis was reproblematized as one of excessive sovereign indebtedness, prompting an about turn in fiscal policy that aimed to reduce the budget deficits of the central governments. More-over, the results of public spending cuts on either side of the Atlantic also had a strong resemblance, especially given that the UK central government's austerity programme explicitly targeted the funding of various local government expenditures. The consequences of austerity had an unequal and uneven socio-spatial distribution, and continue to be experienced most acutely by those individuals, households, and communities that rely greatly upon public or quasi-public sector employment, transfer payments, services, and so on. In the US, the effects of austerity were disproportionately felt in cities that were already struggling with big bureaucratic budgets, huge public sector pension liabilities, and large, economically marginalized populations in need of social assistance (Peck 2012, 2013b). In the UK, the distributional costs of austerity had class (Atkinson et al. 2012), race (Sandhu et al. 2013), and gender dynamics (MacLeavy 2011), all of which were compounded by geographical disparities which weigh heavily on urban areas outside of the southeast of England (Beatty and Fothergill 2013; Hamnett 2014).

Continuing this book's analysis of the management of the global financial crisis, the focus here is upon the emergence and consolidation of the security apparatus that, in Anglo-America through 2010 and 2011, rendered the crisis governable as a problem of sovereign debt, and which prescribed fiscal austerity by way of solution. The opening section of the chapter provides an overview of the main governance interventions during this period that sought to act upon fiscal deficits and to reduce the rate of increase in public indebtedness. These interventions include the sweeping austerity programme of the Coalition Government in the UK, and the relatively limited measures undertaken in the US amid the deadlock between the Obama administration and Congress over Federal budgets. In the second section, the chapter asks how the crisis was abstracted as a problem of sovereign debt. Attention is drawn to the narratives and concepts from liberal economic theory that position public borrowing, by its very nature, as interrupting the vital market circulations of investment and exchange, and to how these narratives and concepts were mustered in relation with economic discourses and devices that presented the growth of sovereign debt as an urgent and pressing problem that inevitably and necessarily had to be addressed. The third and final section of the chapter turns its attention to consider how the apparatus began to enact fiscal austerity by way of a crisis governance solution. The focus here is upon the mobilization of the juridical and legislative authorization and budgetary techniques of the fiscal sovereigns, the enrolment of the public through austerity's intuitive and moral appeal, and the eliciting of an affective atmosphere of confidence among investors, entrepreneurs, and consumers in the search for so-called 'growth-friendly fiscal consolidation'. As George Osborne (2010) put it in his Mansion House speech of June 2010, businesses and families could not be expected to confidently invest and consume in the face of fears that deficits and debts would lead to 'ever higher taxes' and 'ever higher interest rates'.

Austerity Measures

The austerity measures that were introduced by the UK and US governments from 2010 were in stark contrast with the explicit fiscal stimulus that each undertook during the preceding year. As was detailed in Chapter 5, the fiscal machinery of the state was committed to crisis management at the height of the tumult, corralled as a relational element in the bailout apparatus. Continuing into 2009, however, and despite monetary policies that had enacted historically unprecedented cuts to interest rates, the financial crisis ripped through the 'real' economy of production and consumption, generating sharp contractions in output, rising unemployment, and accelerating foreclosure rates. Indeed, such was the severity and potential global reach of the crisis that the initial fiscal policy response to its deleterious socio-economic impacts was, to some degree at least, agreed and coordinated internationally as a 'global Keynesianism' (Blyth 2013: 54–6; see BIS 2009: 56–114). Leading Keynesian economists on both sides of the Atlantic breathed a very public sigh of relief (e.g. Skidelsky 2009; Krugman 2009). This was because governments had apparently zeroed in on the critical problem of economic output and growth, and had begun to enact demand-restoring measures by way of response (e.g. tax cuts targeted at restoring consumption, increased government deficit spending on infrastructure investments). Keynesians remained cautious, however. They were concerned that the fiscal stimulus was not of a sufficient size to restore the economy to full capacity, and that the crisis had not yet provoked the kind of reregulation of banking which they deemed necessary to form circuits of productive economic investment.

The Keynesian deficit spending of the US fiscal stimulus came largely through the American Recovery and Reinvestment Act. This $787 billion package of measures combined over $500 billion of additional public spending programmes with tax cuts. The latter, targeted at small businesses and middle- and low-income Americans, were projected to be worth $276 billion (Blinder and Zandi 2010; Coates 2012; Pollin 2012). Meanwhile, in the UK in November 2008 the Labour government reduced value-added tax (VAT) from 17.5 per cent to fifteen per cent, and brought forward plans for £3 billion worth of capital spending. Rather than additional, 'discretionary' public expenditure during 2009, what the UK fiscal stimulus largely amounted to was the maintenance of existing spending commitments which were financed through increased counter-cyclical borrowing and the operation of so-called 'automatic stabilizers' (Sawyer 2012).[4] However, the Brown administration was alone among the governments of the major economies when it combined fiscal stimulus in 2009 with a plan to reduce the UK fiscal deficit during 2010 (BIS 2009: 111). This was a commitment that the government also extended into the future when it passed the Fiscal Responsibility Act of 2010, and made more than a parting nod to the remnants of Brown's famous mantra of 'prudence with a purpose'.

The turn away from Keynesian deficit spending in the UK gained impetus, however, once the Conservative–Liberal Coalition Government came to power in May 2010. Austerity was a binding commitment in the Coalition Agreement that obliged the new government to 'significantly accelerate the reduction of the structural deficit over the course of a Parliament, with the main burden of deficit reduction borne by reduced spending rather than increased taxes' (HM Government 2010: 15). This was confirmed by David Cameron (2010a) in the first major speech that he gave as Prime Minister, and put into effect by the so-called 'emergency budget' of June 2010. While containing some tax increases (e.g. sales and capital gains taxes) and also introducing a bank levy designed to raise £2 billion per annum, the focus for the budget was upon achieving a £32 billion annual cut in government outlays by 2014/15, £11 billion of which was to be achieved through 'welfare reform savings' (HM Treasury 2010b: 2). Planned reductions in spending included a two-year public sector pay freeze, the reindexation of welfare payments to consumer prices rather than retail prices, new restrictions on housing benefits (christened 'the bedroom tax' by opponents), and a clamp-down upon the rules governing Disability Living Allowance payments. The extent of the austerity programme that was envisaged was unparalleled in British history, save for the infamous 'Geddes Axe' of 1921, which cut government spending by eleven per cent across two years.

The headline objective of the emergency budget of 2010 was not actually to reduce sovereign indebtedness, but to achieve 'a forward-looking fiscal mandate to achieve cyclically-adjusted current balance by the end of the rolling, five-year forecast period' (HM Treasury 2010b: 1). It set what was called a 'pathway' to fiscal rectitude (2010b: 16). The impact of the financial crisis on the state's finances was of such magnitude that it was typically explained by the drawing of an analogy with the fiscal legacies of the World Wars of the twentieth century (e.g. Cameron 2010a; Osborne 2010). In this context, what the Coalition Government's plan for extensive deficit cuts entailed was a real-term increase in public spending compared with 2007; that is, a return to the levels of public spending that prevailed at that time and when a booming financial sector was providing roughly one-quarter of tax revenues. Lower than expected rates of economic growth and taxation revenues after 2010 forced some budgetary recalculations, and the government also rowed-back from some of its more politically contentious and unworkable measures (Gamble 2012). Planned spending cuts were deepened in an attempt to achieve revised targets for deficit reduction which were now also projected forward over a longer time horizon (HM Treasury 2013).

As in the UK, there were already strong indications in 2009 that the US fiscal stimulus was envisaged as something of a passing moment. As the 'President's Message' that accompanied the budgetary plans for this bout of Keynesian deficit spending put it, 'we must begin the process of making the tough choices necessary to restore fiscal discipline, cut the deficit in half by the end of my first term in office, and put our Nation on sound fiscal footing' (Office of Management and Budget 2009: 3). Accordingly, the 2011 budget (for the fiscal year, October 2010 to September 2011), submitted for Congressional approval in February 2010, proposed a three-year freeze in non-security discretionary spending,[5] and a commitment was also made to 'establish a bipartisan fiscal commission charged with identifying additional policies to put our country on a fiscally sustainable path—balancing the Budget, excluding interest payments on the debt, by 2015' (Office of Management and Budget 2010: 4). Under the intense glare of the media spotlight, the National Commission on Fiscal Responsibility and Reform (2010) reported before the end of the year on a range of medium-term measures that, if introduced, were held to be capable of closing the gap between the projected revenues and expenditures of the Federal government. The recommendations of the Commission included: further cuts to discretionary spending; a mixture of reduced rates and reform in relation to taxation; the further containment of health care costs, to which the Affordable Care Act ('Obamacare') of March 2010 was already expected to contribute; and the reform of the Social Security system of public retirement insurance.

The 2011 budget was not agreed upon by Congress before the deadline of 30 September 2010. Financing of the Federal government over the following six months relied upon a series of continuing resolutions that maintained funding at or near 2010 levels. With the shutdown of the Federal government just hours away, the 2011 budget was finally agreed upon in April 2011. The minimal spending reductions and taxation changes that this agreement entailed meant that the 2011 budget, approving a total of around $3.5 trillion of annual expenditure, had very little impact on the fiscal deficit. In the meantime, the Obama administration had proposed a 2012 budget that, including a number of the recommendations made by the National Commission, would trim the deficit by around $1 trillion over ten years (Office of Management and Budget 2011). If fully implemented by Congress, the 2012 budget certainly did not seek to reduce sovereign indebtedness as such, but rather to reduce fiscal deficits to around three per cent of GDP by the middle of the decade, and to thereby put 'the Nation on a fiscally responsible path' (2011: 20).

However, buoyed by the Tea Party movement and victories in the November 2010 midterm elections, the House Republicans led by Paul Ryan put forward their own budget proposals in early April 2011 (House of Representatives Committee on the Budget 2011). Aimed at preventing 'the nation' from moving 'ever-faster toward a debt-fuelled economic crisis' (2011: 58), the proposals were passed by the House, but were rejected by the Senate. The Ryan budget called for fiscal expenditure cuts that primarily targeted mandatory spending on Medicare, Medicaid, and Social Security programmes. These reductions were roughly five-fold those proposed by the Obama administration. The Ryan budget also set out a programme of tax cuts that would reduce projected fiscal revenues by approximately $4 trillion over the coming decade. With the Congressional budgetary process in deadlock and disarray, President Obama (2011) responded by offering a compromise budget proposal that would reduce the deficit by $4 trillion over twelve years, a projected figure that was to be achieved through approximately $2 trillion of spending cuts, $1 trillion of tax revenue increases, and $1 trillion of savings on the interest payable on the ever-rising stock of US sovereign debt.

Congressional and political debates over the 2012 Federal budget were brought to a head by a related but separate legislative process: the requirement that Congress authorize any increase of the statutory maximum that the US Treasury is permitted to borrow from global markets. Without the raising of the so-called 'debt ceiling' by the first few days of August 2011, there was the spectre of a default on the interest payable on US sovereign debt, and of the crisis that this would have presumably generated in global financial markets (e.g. Dash and Schwartz 2011). In return for agreeing to raise the ceiling, the Republican-led House of Representatives demanded a binding commitment to fiscal austerity. The eventual result—the Budget Control Act of 2011—was an agreement between President and Congress that traded a debt ceiling increase of around $900 billion for fiscal retrenchment of similar magnitude over ten years. Also included in the trade was the creation of a Congressional Joint Select Committee that was authorized to produce detailed legislation that would generate a further $1.5 trillion reduction in the deficit across the coming decade.[6]

The bipartisan Committee failed to agree their legislative programme by the November deadline, however. This set in motion an automatic clause in the Budget Control Act, known as 'the sequester', which instituted $1.2 trillion worth of projected, across-the-board cuts to government spending which were due to come into effect from 1 January 2013. That the sequester cuts were to coincide with the end of the 2001 and 2003 tax cuts made by the Bush administration gave rise to what became known as the 'fiscal cliff', a simultaneous contraction of government spending and tax increases which was widely predicted to lead to recession (Congressional Budget Office 2012). Although the passage of the frantically put together American Taxpayer Relief Act of 2012 reduced the scale of the tax increases, the sequester cuts were only postponed and the deadlock over the debt ceiling and deficit reduction continued throughout 2013 (FSOC 2013).

The Debt Dilemma

As the previous chapters of this book have shown, the apparatuses of global financial crisis governance consistently sought to restore the uncertain circulations of the markets and banking, thereby securing the apparently productive force of those circulations for wealth and well-being in a valued form of liberal life. Crucial in this respect was how the ostensibly vital and routine relations and flows of credit-debt (e.g. mortgages, consumer credit, car loans, bank loans) were positioned as intimately bound up with the restarting of global financial circulations. Whatever the immediate aims of crisis management—returning liquidity to global money and capital markets that were free from toxic assets, for instance, or repairing a banking system such that it was sufficiently capitalized, able to deal with default risk, and effectively regulated—the perpetuation of everyday forms of debt deemed essential to the financialized security of the population was a strategic consideration across apparatuses of crisis governance. Save for the need for some deleveraging of banking and the quelling of certain debt-fuelled speculative excesses, indebtedness and its accompanying transferable and derivative claims were not questioned in the course of crisis governance. Exception was to be made, however, when the debt obligations in question were those of the sovereign state.

The apparatus that rendered the crisis as a problem of sovereign debt mobilized the long tradition of classical economic thinking that, positing the natural laws and truths of the market, creates limits on the role of the state which are internal to liberal government (Foucault 2008: 10–11; Terranova 2009). As the market operates as 'a site of veridiction' that 'good government' has to abide by, the result is 'the intensive and extensive development of governmental practice' which is 'nevertheless supposed to be frugal' (Foucault 2008: 28–33). Such ontological limits are especially apparent in the more recent, neo-liberal form of governmental practice that has developed since the economic crises of the 1970s. As it extends an 'economic grid' to explain social processes, neo-liberalism also features the permanent 'criticism and appraisal of the action of public authorities in market terms' (2008: 246–8; Collier 2011). For neo-liberalism, moreover, Keynesian policies and economic planning—such as the deficit spending pursued on both sides of the Atlantic in 2009—are a crucial 'adversary and target', 'something extraneous and threatening' that pushes up against the internal limits of liberal government (Foucault 2008: 218–19).

In relation with liberal and neo-liberal narratives of frugal government, three specific orthodox economic concepts were enrolled such that the apparatus could govern the crisis as a problem of sovereign debt. All three concepts regard sovereign debt as a universal problem, and together and in combination they provided a conceptual armoury that could be called upon to justify fiscal retrenchment (see Boyer 2012). The first concept, dating from the turn of the nineteenth century, is 'Say's law'. This holds that supply creates its own demand, as products and money necessarily circulate at their maximum rate in markets. It follows that Keynesian deficit financing and the accumulation of public debt to stoke-up demand is unnecessary and unhelpful, as it is not possible for an economy to have capacity that is underemployed. Second, and as initially developed in an 1820 essay by David Ricardo that considered the differences between sovereign taxation and debt issue in the financing of warfare, the notion of 'Ricardian equivalence' was mustered by the apparatus. This is the idea that firms, households, and individuals understand increased public borrowing to be deferred taxation. Households will therefore respond to increased sovereign debt and government spending by reducing their consumption in advance of anticipated future tax increases. Conversely, should spending be reduced, this creates an expectation of lower taxation in the future, leading to more spending and investment in the present. Again, contrary to Keynesianism, it follows that cutting sovereign debt and public spending will actually boost demand, as cuts will be offset by the response of the private sector. Third, the idea of 'crowding out' suggests that an increase in sovereign debt reduces private investment, capital formation, and spending because it makes credit scarce and leads the market to raise interest rates. Again, the concept of crowding out has a long historical lineage (Blyth 2013: 107–9, 113–14). It stretches back to the eighteenth century, to the critique of public debt as enfeebling the British merchant class that was offered by David Hume, and to Adam Smith's view that sovereign indebtedness interferes with the link between parsimonious saving and investment that generates market dynamism.

Implicitly or otherwise—and the often conflated together in different ways—the concepts of Say's Law, Ricardian equivalence, and crowding out were at work, for example, in the framing of the fiscal objectives of the US and UK governments. Here the concepts were arranged to establish the actuality of the debt dilemma, making future threats to valued life actionable in the present. As President Obama (2011) sought to move away from his administration's previously more limited approach to fiscal retrenchment, for instance, he warned that 'ultimately, all this rising debt will cost us jobs and damage our economy'. This was because:

> Businesses will be less likely to invest and open shop in a country that seems unwilling or unable to balance its books. And if our creditors start worrying that we may be unable to pay back our debts, that could drive up interest rates for

everybody who borrows money—making it harder for businesses to expand and hire, or families to take out a mortgage.

Similarly, in HM Treasury's (2010b: 11) emergency budget of June 2010, the new government's 'fiscal policy framework' and commitment to 'reducing public sector borrowing' was justified on the grounds that it will 'reduce competition for funds for private sector investment'—'failure to address rising public sector debt in the UK' is said to risk 'pushing up long-term interest rates, which would affect not just the Government, but also families and businesses through the higher costs of loans and mortgages'. To support this view, HM Treasury (2010b: 11) approvingly cites some IMF research that quantifies the costs of crowding out. What the research is said to show is that for every ten per cent increase in sovereign debt (measured as a proportion of GDP) the results will be: a 0.5 per cent increase on the interest rates payable on all forms of credit denominated in the sovereign currency, and an annual reduction in 'long-term economic growth' of 0.25 per cent.

The deployment of such figures and calculations in HM Treasury's (2010b) emergency budget also begins to illustrate a further element which was arranged in the governance apparatus: the macroeconomic, budgetary metrics that provided various measures of the material givens of the sovereign debt problem. The principal measures in this respect were ratios that set a range of numerators against the denominator of GDP. Such numerators included present government spending, the net fiscal deficit, annual debt interest payments, and total aggregate debt. So, for example, the Coalition Government's emergency budget set a target for reducing government spending from 48 to forty per cent of GDP by 2015/16 (HM Treasury 2010b: 16). More specifically, and in terms of attempts to calculate crowding out, one notable way in which these material givens were marshalled was through the suggestion that it was possible to identify a threshold beyond which sovereign debt became especially dangerous to economic life (e.g. House of Representatives Committee on the Budget 2011: 20–1; Osborne 2011; Trichet 2010). For instance, through Congressional testimony and a paper that was widely cited in policymaking circles, Carmen Reinhart (2011; Reinhart and Rogoff 2010) of Harvard University propounded the argument that ninety per cent of GDP was indeed a tipping point beyond which the threats posed by sovereign debt could be expected to materialize into a significant drag on economic growth.

A further and notable feature of the budgetary material givens of the debt dilemma was that they were often deployed to show the worsening of fiscal balances into the future, and thereby rested on fiscal forecasting techniques that are notoriously inaccurate, at best. The main indicators of sovereign finances going forward were thus necessarily subject to continual updates and revised projections, all of which were contested and debated. Revealing in this respect was the move by the Coalition Government in the UK, undertaken upon taking office, to create the newly independent Office for Budget Responsibility (OBR). The design of the OBR largely mirrored the Congressional Budget Office (CBO) in the US, and signalled a move to the model of fiscal policymaking advocated by the IMF (HM Treasury 2010b: 12). It was said, by Chancellor George Osborne (2010), to be 'an independent body immune to the temptations of the political cycle'. Taking responsibility for the forecasting of economic growth and fiscal budgets from HM Treasury, the creation of the OBR thus gave the diagnosis of the material givens of the UK's sovereign debt problem an additional veneer of expert objectivity, transparency, and vigilance.

Although liberal and neo-liberal economic narratives, orthodox economic concepts, and a number of national budgetary devices all contributed to the rendering of the crisis as a problem of sovereign debt, additional discursive and calculative-material elements were essential to establishing that problem as urgent in 2010. The debt dilemma was thus abstracted as not merely a perpetual and nagging fiscal issue that, arguably, is a more-or-less permanent tension in the workings of the contemporary liberal states of the Global North (O'Connor 1973; Pierson 2001; Schäfer and Streeck 2013).[7] Rather, the apparatus that governed the crisis as one of sovereign debt made that problem appear as an object of immediate and pressing concern; that is, as a sovereign debt crisis. To paraphrase from Derek McCormack's (2012: 1539) research into the liberal government of inflation, fiscal deficits and sovereign debt were effectively transformed from 'one of those little dangers containing the germinal threat of systemic disruption' into an ostensibly real and burning systemic threat. This also made it possible for the deficit to appear as a technical and depoliticized object. In the words of David Cameron (2010b), for example, his government's plan for 'unavoidable deficit reduction' was not being 'driven by theory or ideology', but was 'driven by the urgent truth'. Identifying and acting on the problem of public debt thus seemed to be an emergency pragmatism, rather than the enactment of a political programme.

Significant to establishing the urgency of the sovereign debt dilemma was the comparative historical discourse which held that financial crises inevitably lead to fiscal crises. A key contributor to this discourse was Reinhart and Rogoff's hugely influential book, *This Time is Different*. As they put it (2009: 231):

> Declining revenues and higher expenditures, owing to a combination of bailout costs and higher transfer payments and debt servicing costs, lead to a rapid and marked worsening of the fiscal balance.... a build-up in government debt has been a defining characteristic of the aftermath of banking crises for over a century.

On average, across thirteen national cases since 1977, Reinhart and Rogoff calculate that, three years after the onset of a banking crisis, outstanding public debt is eighty six per cent higher. Placed in the comparative historical context provided by *This Time is Different* and similar analyses, by 2010 the fiscal consequences of the contemporary crisis thus appeared to follow the pattern of previous crises, and they necessarily had to be confronted. More-over, as Cecchetti et al. (2010) of the BIS stressed, the fiscal consequences of the contemporary global crisis were greater for the US and the UK than was typically the case in previous, national crises. And, for Niall Ferguson (2010) writing in *Foreign Affairs*, the dangers that these consequences posed for US power were especially pressing, if the contribution of fiscal crises to the decline of previous empires was taken as a guide.

The financial tumult in the Eurozone—initially centred upon Greek government bonds in 2010—provided the basis for a further comparative discourse that was of particular import to establishing the debt dilemma as an immediate problem in Anglo-America.[8] Comparison here was cross-national rather than historical, but again the result was to generalize a systemic and pressing problem on the basis of quite specific and distinct cases. On both sides of the Atlantic, the Greek sovereign debt crisis appeared as a warning of that which would necessarily and shortly befall all governments who failed sufficiently to recognize and act upon their own excessive debts. In the US, for example, consider the following from the opening pages of *The Moment of Truth*, the report of the National Commission on Fiscal Responsibility and Reform (2010: 6–7):

> The contagion of debt that began in Greece and continues to sweep through Europe shows us clearly that no economy will be immune. If the U.S. does not put its house in order, the reckoning will be sure and the devastation severe.... After all the talk about debt and deficits, it is long past time for America's leaders to put up or shut up. The era of debt denial is over, and there can be no turning back.

Similarly, and by way of illustration from the UK, an early Prime Ministerial speech by David Cameron (2010b) acknowledged that 'Our debts are not as bad as Greece' because 'Our underlying economic position is stronger'. Nonetheless, for Cameron, it remained the case that:

> Greece stands as a warning of what happens to countries that lose their credibility, or whose Governments pretend that difficult decisions can be avoided. Thankfully this is a warning that has now focused the attention of the international community. This is why we believe there is only one option in front of us: to take immediate and decisive action.

That the Eurozone had institutionalized discrete monetary and fiscal arrangements—wherein national governments, such as Greece, were unable to monetize their public debts through the creation of central bank reserves, or to devalue their currency to improve the competitiveness of their export sector—was seemingly of little consequence as comparisons between the US, UK, and Greece were readily drawn. As it was constantly reiterated on both sides of the Atlantic, all governments were confronting the pressing problem of a sovereign debt crisis.

As the rupture in Greek and Eurozone sovereign debt markets seemingly provided a live scenario of how the debt dilemma could crystalize for all (e.g. House of Representatives Committee on the Budget 2011: 19–20), it also drew nervous attention to a set of real-time material givens. The immediate indicators of the sovereign debt crisis were thus the fluctuations in the interest rates payable on public debt instruments that were constantly being calculated on global markets, and the judgements delivered on of those instruments by the principal bond rating agencies. Indeed, keeping interest rates down and bond ratings up seemingly became the very purpose of crisis management in the short term (e.g. Osborne 2010; House of Representatives Committee on the Budget 2011). Should the cost of servicing the national debt exceed the underlying trend in economic growth rate for a prolonged period, then governments were reminded that this was a sign of their likely insolvency (Cecchetti et al. 2010). The spectre of a bond rating downgrade loomed large. This was assumed to automatically result in an increase in the interest that investors would demand in return for holding government debt, and therefore to lead to a worsening of deficits and debts.

On the evening of Friday 8 August 2011, and in a historically unprecedented move, Standard & Poor's downgraded long-term US sovereign debt (from AAA to AA+). That the downgrade did not result in an increase in the interest rates payable on US sovereign debt, either at the time or subsequently (FSOC 2013: 30–1), did not interrupt the consolidation of the sovereign debt crisis apparatus, however. To justify the downgrade, and in relation to the Budget Control Act specifically, Standard & Poor's offered the following explanation:

> The downgrade reflects our opinion that the fiscal consolidation plan that Congress and the Administration recently agreed to falls short of what, in our view, would be necessary to stabilize the government's medium-term debt dynamics.[9]

The downgrade also came with the following threat:

> The outlook on the long-term rating is negative. We could lower the long-term rating to 'AA' within the next two years if we see that less reduction in spending than agreed to, higher interest rates, or new fiscal pressures during the period result in a higher general government debt trajectory than we currently assume in our base case.

So, while the downgrade may not have caused 'Black Monday'—the sixth largest single-day loss on the Dow Jones Industrial Average that followed it (Blyth 2013: 1–3)—this precipitous fall in the stock prices of major US corporations nonetheless seemed to reinforce the bleak outlook on the US economy offered by Standard & Poor's. As such, despite having a negligible impact on the rates for US T-bonds and T-bills, the downgrade served to increase the pressure to act upon the problem of sovereign debt. The February 2013 downgrade of UK government gilts by Moody's, who cited the 'sluggish growth' of the UK economy as the main 'driver' impacting their judgement,[10] similarly provoked the Coalition government to assert a redoubling of the efforts to address their own sovereign debt dilemma.

Austerity, Redemption, and Confidence

As it emerged and consolidated during 2010 and 2011, the apparatus that governed the global financial crisis as a problem of sovereign debt held out fiscal retrenchment as the principal solution. Managing the sovereign debt crisis appeared to require the intensified frugality of austerity governance. Acting upon the crisis in this way, and through what Jamie Peck (2013b: 742) aptly calls 'necessitarian budget cutting', required the enlistment of sovereign fiscal techniques and budgetary procedures. This went beyond the contribution made by the macroeconomic, budgetary metrics of the treasury institutions, CBO, and OBR to the forging of the material givens of the problem upon which the apparatus was supposed to act. Once again, and as was stressed in Chapters 4 and 5, the mustering of the fiscal rights of the sovereign and incorporation of treasury institutions into the apparatuses that governed the global financial crisis entailed specific juridical and legislative provisions. Just as public spending support for crisis governance interventions that purchased toxic assets and recapitalized banking was contingent upon such provisions, so too was acting on the crisis through the making of public spending cuts.

Activating the sovereign authority to reduce the US fiscal deficit and slow the increase in public indebtedness was a difficult proposition. The separation of powers between President and Congress is built into the budget process by Article I of the US Constitution. It is Congress, and not the Presidential administration, that is ultimately responsible for writing the laws which raise revenues and appropriate funds for each of the requests that are included in the President's budget (House of Representatives Committee on the Budget 2011). In the midst of the disagreements in Washington over how best to act upon the sovereign debt problem, this juridical configuration of US fiscal sovereignty ensured that the austerity cutbacks of the Federal government remained limited relative to those achieved in the UK and to those underway across state, municipal, and local government in the US (Peck 2012, 2013b). The will to govern the problem of sovereign debt through austerity measures was certainly present in the US, but the precise legislative form to be taken by those measures could not be consistently established at the Federal level.

At the same time, however, and as was also discussed in Chapter 4, the US Federal government continued to enjoy the unique fiscal flexibility and 'exorbitant privilege' (Eichengreen 2011) bestowed by the dollar's status as global money. As fiscal deficits remained relatively untouched and the volume of outstanding US sovereign debt continued to grow, US Treasury instruments also remained the safe haven for global investors (Stokes 2014). Indeed, domestic and foreign institutional investors (e.g. pension funds, sovereign wealth funds) had increasingly switched to US Treasuries from Agency MBS during 2009, and the central banks of China, Japan, and South Korea also added huge volumes of Treasuries to their burgeoning foreign exchange reserves. For a brief period during 2011, and taking into account inflation, the yields on US T-bills in secondary markets actually dipped to negative rates in real terms. Investors were willing to pay the US Treasury for the privilege of holding its short-term sovereign debts. Moreover, by dint of the massive liquidity injections provided by the Fed's OMOs and, especially, its QE2 programme, roughly ten per cent of total US sovereign debt now came to be held by its very own central bank (Federal Reserve Bank of New York 2013). In short, Federal fiscal retrenchment, such as it was, was accompanied by a massive monetization of US sovereign debt.

Meanwhile, in the UK, Parliamentary statutes, the majority enjoyed by the Coalition Government in the House of Commons, and the centralized authority of HM Treasury in the budgetary process all served to authorize the sovereign decisions of austerity governance. Once the emergency budget of 2010 was passed by Parliament, HM Treasury (2010c) was able to undertake a *Spending Review* which established and enforced spending cuts on various government departments that, for the first time, were instituted over a longer, four-year period. Leaving aside the Department of Health and the budget for overseas aid, both of which were ring-fenced, the average cumulative cuts in spending across government departments were planned to be nineteen per cent in real terms and by 2014–2015. Despite the implementation of these and further swingeing cuts in an attempt to reduce the deficit in the years that followed, the level of outstanding UK public debt continued to rise. The total value of UK government gilts in circulation, at the end of March 2013, reached in excess of £1.25 trillion. Between one-quarter and one-third of that debt (£375 billion) was held by the APF, and as a result of the Bank of England's QE programme.[11]

Enacting austerity, then, was not simply a matter of deploying sovereign fiscal techniques to implement change in fiscal policymaking. Action required that the governance apparatus arranged a number of distributed elements in relation. Also significant in this regard was the idea of 'austerity', which was itself important to establishing the appeal of fiscal rectitude. As Mark Blyth (2013: 98–9) has shown, the 'intellectual history' of austerity is 'both short and shallow', and there is 'no well worked out "theory of austerity"'. For Blyth, the idea of austerity is thus most appropriately understood as 'a sensibility', and as 'a derivative consequence of other shared beliefs' (2013: 100). Such an understanding of austerity also helps to explain how fiscal rectitude holds such deep-seated lustre in the US, despite the term austerity itself lacking popular currency and appeal (Peck 2013b: 741). Austerity is derived, then, from the broad trajectory of liberal and neo-liberal economic thought that, developing as 'the intellectual and institutional antidote to the confiscatory politics of the king', regards 'the government, and its debt' as 'deeply problematic' (Blyth 2013: 100). Austerity, as Blyth documents it, can be traced to John Locke, and especially to David Hume and Adam Smith. It also has multiple manifestations and expressions in subsequent liberal and neo-liberal economics and governmental practice, such as post-1945 German *ordoliberalism*. Aspects of these theoretical and conceptual features of the sensibility of austerity were noted above, as they were present in the framing of the contemporary financial crisis as a problem of sovereign debt. Further theoretical and conceptual aspects will also be highlighted below, especially as they find their voice in the explicitly positive case for fiscal retrenchment and sovereign debt reduction that was made on either side of the Atlantic.

As Blyth (2013: 7–10) is also keen to stress, the sensibility of austerity also draws sustenance from an intuitive and morally laden understanding of what should be done in the face of excessive indebtedness of any form: reduce spending and pare down the debt. In liberal society, the finances of the sovereign, and the question of how to best address a problem of sovereign debt, are thus essentially of the same logical and moral regulatory order as addressing the debt of a household or an individual. This was not always so. Prior to the 'financial revolution' in Britain during the late seventeenth and early eighteenth centuries, 'public credit' was somewhat exceptional because sovereigns often reneged on their debt obligations (Dickson 1967). As modern finance developed, however, frugality, thrift, and prudence began to appear as virtuous for all debtors—including the sovereign—and calculative planning and financial self-discipline came to be seen as necessary to ensuring that borrowers always met outstanding debt obligations in full. For example, juridical enforcement mechanisms, such as bankruptcy and foreclosure procedures, policed the rationality and morality of debt repayment by individuals and households (Driver 1993; Langley 2009). Not only did these assembled arrangements of modern debt sustain the unequal power relations of credit-debt, they also came to hold such force when conditioning states, households, and individuals alike that, for Maurizio Lazzarato (2012: 11), it is credit-debt (and not exchange) that provides 'the paradigm of the social' in liberal society. The idea of austerity as fiscal rectitude held a distinctive intuitive and moral capacity that was critical, then, to the attachment of US and UK publics to policies of deficit reduction.

Consider, for example, the appeal that was made to the innate logic and morality of austerity by David Cameron (2011), in a speech he delivered to the Conservative Party Conference of October 2011. As he put it:

> The only way out of a debt crisis is to deal with your debts. That's why households are paying down their credit card and store card bills. It means banks getting their books in order. And it means governments—all over the world—cutting spending and living within their means.

In this instance, however, the analogy that Cameron drew between acting on household and sovereign debt proved to be particularly controversial. At a briefing on the evening before the speech, the media were informed by the Prime Minister's staff that he would echo Margaret Thatcher, who often compared the nation's public finances to household bills. The intention was that Cameron's speech would include the following lines: 'The only way out of a debt crisis is to deal with your debts. That means households—all of us—paying off the credit card and store card bills' (in Watt 2011). This instruction to the population was quickly seized upon by the media as likely to impact negatively on already weak levels of aggregate consumer spending. Some, such as Larry Elliott (2011) of the *Guardian* newspaper, were also quick to point towards the Keynesian notions of 'fallacy of composition' and 'paradox of thrift' in order to explain why the Prime Minister's directive to 'all of us' was misguided. The precise words included in the speech were thus rapidly revised, but the analogy between public and household finances and the intuitive and moral appeal to austerity was nonetheless retained.

In order for the problem of sovereign debt to be acted upon through austerity measures, the moral responsibilizations of debt were also significant to luring the public to fiscal retrenchment in other, related ways. The enactment of austerity was certainly subject to continuous challenge and moments of intense contestation (Bramall 2012), such as the UK public sector pension strike of 30 June 2011. What is of interest here, however, are the strategies employed to create a morally infused cultural space in which the public could be enrolled in the will to govern the crisis through fiscal austerity. With the consequences of fiscal austerity measures most acutely 'visited on the dispossessed, the disenfranchised and the disempowered' (Peck 2012: 632), fiscal austerity positioned households and individuals in a relation of 'cruel optimism' to its measures and sacrifices (Berlant 2010). As the austerity apparatus featured optimistic and hopeful appeals to an idealized and righteous pathway to the future 'good life', it 'bound' the publics on either side of the Atlantic 'to a situation of profound threat' which actually made 'it impossible to attain the expansive transformation' for which they were striving (2010: 2).

In the early months of the Coalition Government's fiscal austerity in the UK, for example, 'fairness' was said to be a guiding principle, and it was oft-repeated that 'we're all in this together' (e.g. Cameron 2010b; see Atkinson et al. 2012: 4–5). Alongside the tendency to draw parallels with the state of the public finances in the wake of World War II, such a message invoked the spirit of austerity from the immediate post-war years (Kynaston 2007). However, it also figured fiscal austerity as a kind of collective penance for the excesses of the debt-fuelled boom years (Blyth 2013: 13). If this penance was paid and excesses were atoned for, society would emerge out of the dark days of debt and into the light. Not dissimilarly, in the US fiscal austerity was presented in the populist messages of the Republican party as a 'redemptive promise', an opportunity to renew the spiritual health of the nation and 'redress its perversion by the permissiveness and paternalism of progressive liberalism' (Konings 2013: 128). As Konings (2013) shows, by reading austerity in the US through Agamben's (2011) work on the infusion of *oikonomia* with divinity, it played on the summoning-up of 'believers' who 'prove their faithfulness by displaying the correct, non-idolatrous attitude' towards credit money (2011: 122). While austerity entailed 'discipline in the sense of internalised market norms', it also stood for 'self-control that is motivated by the anticipation of its purifying effects, driven by the prospect of something that remains elusive and lies beyond the norms and signs of the market' (2011: 124).

The apparent promises of redemption were not available, of course, to those Americans who failed to return to the righteous and austere path, and to stop worshipping the debt-fuelled excesses of consumptive materialism. This more divisive moral message was also explicitly communicated in the UK, where a virtue was made of targeting spending cuts at those households and individuals who were receiving welfare payments and entitlements of one form or another (MacLeavy 2011). It appeared to be right and proper, then, that those who had apparently benefitted most from public spending that the state could ill-afford would now endure the costs of the spending cuts. If the feckless and 'work-shy' would not redeem themselves and join the collective effort of austerity, then they would be forced to do so. After all, it seemed as though the bloated welfare system had created a situation in which, for some at least, it paid not to work (see Department of Work and Pensions 2010). This was clearly unfair on 'hard working families' who were 'striving to succeed' while feeling the brunt of real-terms wage cuts and recession. As David Cameron

(2010a) put it in his first major speech as Prime Minister, for example, 'Our huge deficit and rapidly growing public debt are the clearest manifestations of our economic mistakes—the glaring warning sign overhead telling us we have taken the wrong route'. This was a path that was said to have 'become over-reliant on welfare, with mass worklessness accepted as a fact of life'. For Cameron's Conservatives, as for the Republicans in the US, austerity was not only a crisis management solution to the problem of sovereign debt. It was also teeming with the morality of indebtedness, and presented a political opportunity to re-establish the credentials of a particular liberal imaginary of the good life. Playing on the popular sensibilities and redemptive promises of austerity was important, then, as the governance apparatus attempted to cut borrowing and pare down the debt.

The strategic actions of the austerity apparatus also explicitly targeted, and attempted to work on and through, the affective conditions of confidence. This cajoling of an atmosphere of confidence took two main forms. First, austerity measures sought to prompt the confidences animating the sovereign debt markets specifically, luring a professional market public of investors to newly prescribed governmental commitments and policies aimed at deficit reduction. Holders and would-be holders of Treasuries and government gilts were supposed to feel reassured and comforted, for example, by medium- and long-term fiscal imaginaries of 'a fiscally sustainable path' (Office of Management and Budget 2010: 4) and a 'forward-looking fiscal mandate' (HM Treasury 2010b: 1). As with the apparatuses of global financial crisis governance already analysed in this book, 'confidence' was thus envisaged as 'an affective orientation in which the future is relatively stable', but which also entails 'faith in the capacities and willingness of government to act decisively' (McCormack 2012: 1550). Fiscal austerity sought to reflect back to bond market investors their own vision of the future of sovereign debt, and to convey intensive activity and binding commitments in the present that appeared as necessary to securing that future.

Second, eliciting an atmosphere of confidence was also a key concern as the apparatus made an explicit positive economic case for deficit reduction, and charted a future trajectory of so-called 'growth-friendly' or 'expansionary fiscal consolidation'. Here austerity was presented as a supply-side measure that potentially fed economic growth and expansion because it provided the 'fiscal space' for confidence-inspiring tax cuts and lower interest rates. Although the conceptual groundings of such a view stretch back to the notions of Say's Law, Ricardian equivalence, and the crowding out of Smithian 'productive parsimony', its most immediate source of academic legitimacy was provided by a body of research undertaken over a number of recent decades by Italian economists trained at the Bocconi University of Milan (Blyth 2013: 165–76). To be clear, this was not simply a matter of occasioning the conditions of confidence necessary to generating economic growth and thus tax revenues that would ultimately pare down the sovereign debt. This would have been to imbue economic confidences with a Keynesian emphasis on consumer demand and national economic management, something that tended to be foregrounded in the budget plans and proposals of the Obama administration. However, neither was this the adoption of the 'implicit growth model' of 'fiscal conservatism' (Gamble 2012: 46), and of the laissez-faire that was at the heart of the 'liquidationism' of the Hoover administration in the late 1920s and the UK 'Treasury view' of the 1930s, for instance (Blyth 2013: 119–25). Rather, for the contemporary Republicans in the US and the Coalition Government in the UK, expansionary fiscal austerity sought to provoke an affective atmosphere of confidence among investors and entrepreneurs in the face of an uncertain future.

The investors and entrepreneurs called up by expansionary fiscal consolidation were imagined and notional figures, the meta-subjects of desire that feature in liberal and neo-liberal economics. Restoring confidence through austerity measures was thus a matter of 'unleashing the genius of America's workers, investors, and entrepreneurs' (House of Representatives Committee on the Budget 2011: 10), or of moving 'from an economy built on debt and borrowing to one built on saving and investment' by creating 'the space for private sector investment' (Cameron 2010a). As HM Treasury's (2010b: 9) emergency budget framed the issue, for instance:

> Accelerated fiscal consolidation will help keep market interest rates lower for longer, supporting economic recovery and lowering the proportion of tax revenues devoted to debt service payments. The Government has set out a credible deficit reduction plan that should provide businesses with the confidence they need to plan and invest, supporting the necessary recovery in business investment.

Accordingly, what HM Treasury and Department of Business, Innovation and Skills (2011: 5) termed *The Plan for Growth* was one in which 'economic stability is not in itself sufficient to put the UK on track to deliver long-term growth'. Rather, 'For sustainable growth to be driven by private sector investment and enterprise, the Government needs to act in a way that supports growth rather than hampers it'. The key priorities for such action were: to create the most competitive tax system in the G-20 (including, for example, the tax cuts for the highest earners which were announced in the 2012 budget); to improve the conditions and financing arrangements for new business start-ups; to encourage the competitiveness of certain sectors in order to promote export-led economic growth; and to produce a more educated and highly skilled workforce that nonetheless remained the most flexible in Europe.

What the targeting and cajoling of a climate of investor and entrepreneurial confidence underscores, moreover, it that the austerity apparatus did not regard the future financial viability of the sovereign as its principle rationale. The point of austerity governance was not primarily to stabilize what Berlant (2011) terms the 'Austerity State', 'an attempt to reattach collective fantasy to the state's aura as sovereign actor'. Rather, the return to frugal governmental practice was held to be but a first step to recovering the desires of the population, a move to begin to create the right conditions (i.e. low tax, low and stable interest rates, high confidence) in which that dynamism would be released. Put another way, the problem of sovereign debt was certainly urgent and pressing, but it did not require action because of the threat that it posed to the security of the state. It was the securing of a valued form of life—a mode of existence in which the opportunities for wealth and well-being, apparently afforded by uncertain circulations, are embraced by investors and entrepreneurs—that was being 'crowded out' by the excessive indebtedness of the sovereign and the attendant threats of high interest rates and burdensome levels of taxation.

Conclusion

Bringing the book's concrete analysis of the governance of the global financial crisis to a close, this chapter has focused upon the emergence and consolidation during 2010 and 2011 of a governance apparatus that, at the time of writing in early 2014, remains largely intact. To say nothing of the ongoing travails and torments in the Eurozone, the problem of public indebtedness presently continues to preoccupy governmental practice on both sides of the Atlantic. Representations of sovereign debt as an urgent crisis may have faded, but concerns with the problem-object of fiscal retrenchment continue to prevail. Moreover, given the way in which the apparent solution of fiscal austerity creates an aversion to alternative policies that could potentially attend to the issue—including, for example, tax increases targeted at the wealthy, mild inflation, currency devaluation, sovereign default, and Keynesian deficit spending to create short-term growth and increase medium- and long-term tax revenues—the relation of cruel optimism that austerity creates for the majority of the population continues to hold. Originally envisaged as necessary in the UK until around 2015, for instance, an already deepened programme of fiscal austerity is now projected to continue through to 2018 at the earliest (Stewart and Inman 2012). Even then, such projections assume that fiscal austerity is capable of producing the outcomes that it seeks, an assumption that is questionable at best (Blyth 2013).

Set alongside the previous chapters which have also elaborated upon the problem-orientated security apparatuses that governed the global financial crisis, three features of the austerity assemblage stand out. First, one of the main proclivities that has been shown to be common across all crisis governance apparatuses is the way in which they are governed by and through economy. The austerity apparatus is, in this respect, somewhat different from the others, save for the assemblage which sought to manage the crisis as a problem of toxic assets. While the crisis governance apparatuses were typically relational arrangements in which there was a resonance between liberal, Keynesian, and other heterodox theorizations of economy, this was not the case with the austerity apparatus. The making up and management of the crisis as a problem of sovereign debt featured an array of theoretical ideas and concepts, but all were taken from within the liberal tradition. Second, although the cajoling of an affective atmosphere of confidence has been shown to have been a feature of crisis governance, the austerity apparatus was notable for targeting the confidences of an imagined population of investors and entrepreneurs. Crisis governance apparatuses typically sought to restore financial stability through the confidences of a professional market public. Expansionary fiscal consolidation, meanwhile, sought to attach newly confident and would-be investors and entrepreneurs to a broader vision of the economic future. Third, as has been shown across Chapters 5, 6, and 7 in particular, crisis governance apparatuses provided intermediary diagrams for post-crisis governance. The legacy of the governance of the global financial crisis was thus the emergence of new technical fixes that seek to further the resilience of banking, advance the management of financial risk, and ensure more effective means of macroprudential regulation. However, these technical legacies have been joined by a further inheritance of crisis governance—a governmental commitment to a grinding and seemingly unending fiscal austerity.

Notes

1. Expressed as a percentage of GDP, and calculated by the OECD in 2009, the UK's fiscal balance was projected to reach minus 13.3 per cent in 2010, up from minus 2.7 per cent in 2007, before falling back slightly to minus 12.5 per cent in 2011. Similarly expressed, general government debt was projected to rise from forty three per cent in 2007 to eighty three per cent in 2010 and ninety four per cent in 2011 (in Cecchetti et al. 2010).
2. Strictly speaking, as Blyth (2013: 2) defines it, 'austerity' refers to a broader economic programme than reducing sovereign debt by fiscal retrenchment: 'Austerity is a form of voluntary deflation in which the economy adjusts through the reduction of wages, prices, and public spending to restore competitiveness, which is (supposedly) best achieved by cutting the state's budget, debts, and deficits'.

3. Expressed as a percentage of GDP, and calculated by the OECD in 2009, the US's fiscal balance was projected to reach minus 10.7 per cent in 2010, up from minus 2.8 per cent in 2007, before falling back slightly to minus 9.4 per cent in 2011. Similarly expressed, general government debt was projected to rise from sixty two per cent in 2007 to ninety two per cent in 2010 and 100 per cent in 2011 (in Cecchetti et al. 2010).

4. Unlike the household, fiscal treasuries enjoy considerable options for issuing debt in order to address a present mismatch between income/revenues and expenditure. The use of such tools is widely regarded as essential to 'smoothing' economic cycles. As such, and written into the fiscal rules adopted by the Labour government headed by Tony Blair and, subsequently, by Gordon Brown, 'automatic stabilizers' permitted the movement of the budget into deficit as the economy slowed down.

5. In broad terms, government expenditure under the US budget is divided between 'mandatory' and 'discretionary spending'. The former includes spending commitments that are not typically debated by Congress in the budgetary process, such as interest payments on outstanding sovereign debt and so-called 'entitlement programmes' (including Social Security and the Medicare and Medicaid health programmes). 'Discretionary spending' features the costs of government bureaucracy (e.g. pay to Federal officials) and spending on defence.

6. White House Press Release, 31 July 2011. Available at: <http://www.whitehouse.gov/the-press-office/2011/07/31/remarks-president> (accessed June 2014).

7. Over the last four decades, limits to fiscal expansion would seem to impose themselves as a consequence of the combination of global financial market pressures, slower economic growth, static and reduced real wages, democratic disaffection, and corporate tax avoidance on the one hand, and the increased welfare costs of an underemployed and ageing population on the other. In the absence of fiscal expenditures and in the run up to the crisis at least, household and individual debt thus funded consumption and welfare through the 'privatized Keynesianism' of the 'debtfare state' (Crouch 2011; Soederberg 2013).

8. As noted at the very outset of this book, the governance of the crisis as a specific issue of sovereign debt in the Eurozone lies beyond our scope here. What is of particular interest, however, is how the initial tumult in the Eurozone that was centred on Greek sovereign debt instruments was mobilized in the emergence and consolidation of an apparatus of Anglo-American global financial crisis governance. For analyses offering different perspectives on how the sovereign debt issue ricocheted throughout the Eurozone and on how it was governed, see Blyth (2013) and Lapavitsas (2012).

9. Available at: <http://www.standardandpoors.com/ratings/articles/en/us/?assetID=1245316529563> (accessed June 2014).

10. Available at: <http://www.moodys.com/research/Moodys-downgrades-UKs-government-bond-rating-to-Aa1-from-Aaa–PR_266844> (accessed June 2014).

11. Data from the Debt Management Office and the Bank of England. Available at: <http://www.dmo.gov.uk/index.aspx?page=Gilts/Portfolio_Statistics> and <www.bankofengland.co.uk/statistics/Pages/bankstats/2014/jan.aspx> (accessed June 2014).

9

Conclusion

> [W]hen turbulence in US housing markets metastasized into the worst global financial crisis in more than seventy five years, he conjured up trillions of new dollars and blasted them into the economy; engineered massive public rescues of failing private companies; ratcheted down interest rates to zero; lent to mutual funds, hedge funds, foreign banks, investment banks, manufacturers, insurers and other borrowers who had never dreamed of receiving Fed cash; jump-started stalled credit markets in everything from car loans to corporate paper; revolutionized housing finance with a breathtaking shopping spree for mortgage bonds; blew up the Fed's balance sheet to three times its previous size; and generally transformed the staid arena of central banking into a stage for desperate improvisation. He didn't just reshape US monetary policy; he led an effort to save the world economy
>
> Michael Grunwald, *Time Magazine*, 16 December 2009

Time Magazine's decision to name Ben Bernanke as Person of the Year 2009 provides an illustrative reminder of the consensus on the governance of the contemporary global financial crisis, and of the motivations of this book's challenge to that consensus. Official, popular, and academic explanations of crisis governance—both during the crisis and subsequently—are typically much less impressed than *Time Magazine* with the leadership and crisis management skills of any one individual (cf. Irwin 2013). Yet, the image of the Federal Reserve Chairman—sheltered 'inside his marble fortress', acting as conjurer, engineer, lender, revolutionary, improviser, and, above all, as the saviour of 'the world economy' (Grunwald 2009)—sits quite comfortably with the prevailing perception. Understood through the binaries employed by the consensus, the actions that attempted to control the crisis are firmly centred upon the agency of the sovereign state, and especially the central banks, treasuries, and regulatory institutions in the US and UK. The intention of those actions is said to have been to restore the circulations of the markets, banking, and finance capital. Put in the slightly different terms favoured by some political economy accounts in particular, crisis governance was the public socialization of private losses.

When seeking an alternative account of how the global financial crisis was governed, the analytical motivations of this book have certainly not been to downplay the significance of the Federal Reserve, Bank of England, US Treasury, HM Treasury, and so on. Indeed, when detailing the experimental and unprecedented nature of governmental interventions, the transformation of sovereign techniques has been stressed here as one of the key tendencies of crisis management. As was shown in Chapter 3, for instance, the LOLR techniques of the Federal Reserve and Bank of England were radically reworked, such that liquidity could be pumped into money and capital markets in new ways and on a scale that was previously unimaginable. However, a core feature of the book's analysis has also been to decentre crisis governance, to refuse to equate crisis management actions with sovereign power and the apparent agency of state officials and institutions. Crisis governance has been shown to have been strategically enacted through the distributed and relational agency of a number of discrete 'apparatuses of security' (Foucault 2007), apparatuses that, at once, mobilized and continually questioned sovereign power, institutions, and techniques.

Time Magazine's portrayal of the award-winning Ben Bernanke as 'professorial'—his 'arguments aren't partisan or ideological; they're methodical, grounded in data and the latest academic literature' (Grunwald 2009)—draws attention to the founding of the consensus in entrenched frameworks of academic thought and their accompanying debates. For Bernanke, the Fed had been insufficiently active on the previous occasion when it had been confronted by a complete meltdown of US banking and finance (see Bernanke 2000). In the contemporary crisis, he was thus committed to ensuring that the Fed stepped up in such a way that the worst eventualities of the tumult might be averted. Bernanke, in effect, took a position in debates in economics and political economy over whether public interventions in financial crises can and should be avoided. For him, it was highly likely that crisis management would be both necessary and critical in the course of a crisis (see Bernanke 2012). As Chapter 2 detailed, it is these academic fields and their debates—including the more radical positions held by Marxist political economists—which provide the intellectual coordinates for the consensus on crisis governance. Despite sharp differences within and across economics and political economy, these fields provide strikingly similar accounts of crisis management wherein sovereign states can, and typically do, restart and reset the circulations of capitalist banking and financial markets.

Taking forward this book's analytical aspirations entailed, then, a set of methodological and conceptual moves that situated the analysis of contemporary financial crisis governance in cultural economy and SSF, and not in economics and political economy. In effect, the book has asked what the interdisciplinary fields of cultural economy and SSF can bring to the task of thinking anew about how the contemporary global financial crisis was governed. To date, SSF has largely been content to leave questions of government and governance to political sociologists, political geographers, political scientists, and political economists. However, as has been shown here, SSF and the broader field of cultural economy have much to offer in this respect. Specifically, and on the basis of the account of crisis governance provided by this book, there would seem to be considerable analytical potential in mapping the topologies of problem-based governmental assemblages (also Collier 2009), and in re-engaging with the Foucauldian and Deleuzean roots of debates over agency and action that tend to preoccupy cultural economy. SSF has become adept at providing detailed and decentred accounts of the market agency of firms, traders, consumers, and so on. However, infusing SSF with the broader concerns of cultural economy can also provide conceptual tools that, when carefully deployed, are capable of generating revealing relational accounts of the achievement of governmental actions that figure and reconfigure markets.

The limits that the consensus placed (and continues to place) upon the politicization of crisis governance is also highlighted by *Time Magazine*'s decision to name Ben Bernanke as Person of the Year 2009. As Michael Grunwald (2009) justifies the magazine's choice, he makes it plain that not all will agree that 'Bailout Ben' is worthy of such an award. However, such disagreement is necessarily confined to narrow debates over the principles and practicalities of state action: were the interventions of the Federal Reserve an unnecessary abuse of monetary power and, if they were indeed necessary, what form should those interventions have taken? Once sovereign state officials and institutions appeared to be in the unique and powerful position to choose whether to save the markets from themselves, then politics was (and continues to be) a question of what the state should or should not do. Related and more significant debates follow about the distributional politics of the public socialization of private losses, but, ultimately, they do not challenge the perceived parameters within which political debate takes place.

When pursuing its analytical and conceptual motivations, this book thus also explicitly acknowledged that the consensus, by contributing to what Rancière (2010) terms 'the distribution of the sensible', depoliticized crisis governance. The expert, technical solutions of crisis management certainly served to close down alternative approaches. For instance, the governance of the crisis as a problem of toxicity—a virulent infection of the lifeblood of capital market circulations which was traced to transferable claims on subprime mortgage debts—had the effect of sidelining a contending agenda for action that focused on the underlying credit-debt relations of sub-prime mortgages themselves (Barofsky 2012; Blackburn 2011; Langley 2009). However, these disagreements over the most appropriate form to be taken by crisis governance necessarily remained debates over what was the most appropriate form of state action. In this context, then, the book has sought to contribute towards a redistribution of the sensible. In early 2014, when so much political disagreement presently concentrates on the benefits or otherwise of state policies of fiscal austerity, provocations such as those made by this book would seem to be necessary steps to opening up new political possibilities and emancipatory prospects. Austerity should be opposed, but the politicization of post-crisis governmental practices must also move beyond questions about state actions and their distributional consequences.

Growing out of the book's underlying motivations, three principal sets of analytical claims have also been advanced about how the contemporary global financial crisis was governed. The first set of claims have been concerned with how the will to govern the crisis did not take the form of a confrontation with given and materially evident developments in the circulations of markets, banking, and capitalism. As has been shown, the crisis literally had to be made up such that it could be managed. Drawing on Michel Foucault's (2003a) method of problems and problematization, and mapped from Chapter 3 through to Chapter 8, the crisis has been shown to have been rendered governable in a highly contingent manner and as a series of six problem-objects: the liquidity of global money and capital markets; the toxicity of assets poisoning global capital markets; the solvency of global banks and banking; the deficiencies of probabilistic and micro-prudential risk management employed by the major banks; the inadequacies of a limited, 'light touch' form of market-reinforcing regulation in the main centres of global finance; and the excesses of national budgetary deficits and sovereign indebtedness that followed as the global financial crisis became a fiscal crisis. Accordingly, the interventions of crisis management sought to treat these specific problems, rather than offer a solution to the tumult of global finance as such.

The second set of analytical claims made by this book focused on how crisis governance was enacted through the distributed and relational agency of apparatuses of security. The emphasis placed here on the achievement of discrete, multiple, and, at times, highly experimental attempts to govern the crisis is clearly very different to the somewhat structural-functional account provided by the state-centric consensus. Each apparatus has been shown to have mobilized and arranged a number of specific elements, all of which took part in the action of crisis governance. The relational coming together of these elements was necessary such that each apparatus framed a problem-object to be addressed, and acted on that problem by way of solution. As was illustrated in Chapter 4 with particular reference to the reverse auction element of the TARP, the failure to muster any one necessary element undermined the apparatus in question. That said—and as the concept of security *dispositif* explicitly underscores—the relational assemblages of crisis governance were strategic in orientation. Produced amid the power relations which provided their common conditions of possibility, the governance apparatuses were urgent responses to the disorder and insecurity that was engendered by the crisis.

A third and final set of analytical claims have also been advanced here which are more extensive and wide reaching in nature. Certain tendencies have been pinpointed and elaborated upon that, to a greater or lesser degree, were common to each of the discrete crisis governance apparatuses. Such tendencies are obscured by the consensus view that reduces processes of crisis management to the sovereign state bailing out banking, and to the public socialization of private losses. For the book's analysis, however, it is the tendencies shared by the discrete apparatuses that gave contemporary crisis governance its distinctive content and character. By way of bringing the book to a close, then, I want to revisit the commonalities that marked the crisis governance apparatuses, and briefly touch upon their implications for a range of post-crisis academic research agendas.

Modes of Power and Sovereign Techniques

One of the tendencies present within crisis governance that has been emphasized by this book has already been briefly noted in this conclusion: in the problem space of each apparatus, sovereign techniques were transformed and put to work in new ways. Given the severity of the crisis, a quite remarkable feature of crisis governance was that monetary, fiscal, and regulatory techniques were not reworked to facilitate the prohibition, prevention, or synchronization of those practices that were implicated in causing the tumult. The juridical, centralizing, and territorial modality of sovereign power did not provide the guiding rationality of crisis governance. Neither were disciplinary grammars to the fore. Rather, state institutions and sovereign techniques were mobilized and transformed in the specific relational configurations of governance apparatuses, and amid the contemporary correlation of the sovereign, disciplinary, and biopolitical modalities of power.

Consider again, for example, the transformation of the LOLR techniques of the Federal Reserve and Bank of England that were highlighted in Chapter 3. The central bank's unprecedented liquidity operations—grounded in the minting of fiat, base money on a massive scale—followed from an already established monetary policy rationale. In the crisis, the conventional 'modulation' of market circulations through a combination of interest rate decisions, routine OMOs, and open mouth operations by the central banks was no longer deemed to be sufficient (Deleuze 1992). Inciting and accelerating money and capital market circulations that had 'dried up' apparently required that monetary techniques became 'unconventional', a change that emerged in a relational manner as the elements comprising the apparatus were mobilized. The central banks' balance sheets, for instance, did not merely record this change, but were an active element in an apparatus that transformed the techniques of the monetary sovereigns.

Similarly, Chapters 4, 5, and 7 teased out how sovereign fiscal and regulatory techniques were transformed in the course of crisis governance. Fiscal techniques were modified such that toxic assets could be temporarily purchased by the TARP bad bank and, ultimately, such that insolvent banking could be recapitalized rather than nationalized. Here, again, the bailout of banking by taxpayers was the result of the relational arrangement of the elements of an apparatus that featured the performative power of the balance sheet, and of a productive interplay between different modalities of power in which the biopolitical rationality prevailed. Meanwhile, and with particular reference to the structural regulation of the Volcker rule and Vickers' ring-fence, Chapter 7 highlighted how sovereign regulatory techniques were transformed in a crisis governance apparatus that did not seek to outlaw those wholesale market circulations deemed to be speculative and destabilizing. Rather, new activist regulatory techniques attempted to differentiate between financial circulations; volatile wholesale market movements were placed at one remove from ostensibly vital retail banking circulations, and the latter were subjected to additional supervisory scrutiny in order to further their resilience.

The stress placed by this book upon the transformation of sovereign techniques in crisis governance has implications for a number of post-crisis research agendas. It opens up a new line of inquiry, for example, within work that seeks to go beyond the 'balance' between state and market institutions in order to comprehend the configuration of contemporary regulation (e.g. Levi-Faur and Parker 2010; Vogel 2010). It also gives further impetus to recent calls to explore the post-crisis period as one of 'central bank-led capitalism' (Bowman et al. 2013; Thompson 2013), calls which are especially pertinent given the way in which the 'unconventional monetary policy' of QE has ossified and become difficult to reverse. What the book's analysis suggests in this regard, however, is that research needs to extend to the interplay of modalities of power that monetary policy entails (cf. Mann 2010a), and also to how the sovereign monetary techniques of central banking are assembled from both within and without (Holmes 2013).

Economy and Economics at Large

Alongside the transformation of sovereign techniques, attention has also been drawn here to the various ways in which the knowledges and calculative devices of economics were immanent to crisis governance. This was the tendency for apparatuses to govern the crisis by and through economy, rather than to govern over a financial economy in disarray. Crisis governance by economy was shown not to amount to the implementation of a coherent neo-liberal theory and political programme. There were, of course, particular apparatuses wherein the governance of the crisis was largely foregrounded through liberal and neo-liberal ideas. The designation of certain assets as abnormal and 'toxic' drew heavily, for instance, on classical liberal conceptions of the norms of liquid markets (Chapter 4). Liberal and neo-liberal concepts were especially prevalent in the apparatus that governed the crisis as an issue of sovereign debt, and which prescribed fiscal austerity by way of response (Chapter 8). Even here, however, the definition of the debt problem and the preferred solution of austerity did not simply emerge from orthodox economics, as the apparatus also mobilized a discourse on the moral responsibilizations of debt that envisages a redemptive, righteous, and entrepreneurial pathway in the face of an uncertain future.

What crisis management by economy tended to amount to in the first instance, then, were specific resonances that folded economic narratives and notions together within particular problem-orientated and practical governance apparatuses. Take, for example, the apparatus that abstracted the crisis as a problem of risk. As Chapter 6 has shown, a seemingly contradictory array of economic theories and concepts were blended together, both in the critique of probabilistic, micro-prudential risk management and the embrace of anticipatory, macro-prudential techniques. As the apparatus moved to recognize and manage the fundamental uncertainty of credit-debt relations and global financial market circulations, it brought together elements of liberal and neo-liberal thought with Keynesianism and complex adaptive systems theory. Moreover, what the tendency to govern the crisis by economy has also been shown to have entailed was the mobilization of devices that were already at large in markets and their accounting practices. Each of the six governance apparatuses analysed by this book enrolled the calculations of specific market devices and tools. From the LIBOR-OIS spread as an indicator of money market liquidity, to the various ratios of sovereign indebtedness measured as a percentage of GDP, these devices did not merely provide indicators of the scale of the problems at hand. Rather, they contributed, materially, to making up the givens of the problem-objects to be acted on, and typically provided real-time reference points through which the success or otherwise of particular interventions were assessed.

Such analytical claims about crisis governance by economy have particular implications for a lively debate, presently underway in critical academic and political circles, about how the power of neo-liberal economics seemingly emerged from the crisis largely unscathed (e.g. Collier 2012; Dean 2012; Gamble 2009; Hall 2011; Harvey 2010; Mirowski 2013). As Jamie Peck (2013a: 132) has it, for example, in an article that summarizes and reflects upon this debate, 'the global crisis—far from marking an inauspicious end to the regime of market rule—seems to have brought about something like a redoubling of its intensity and reach'. The analytical styles adopted in the debate are multiple, and there is clearly not scope to rehearse them here. Nonetheless, it is important to note that what this book's analysis provides, in part at least, is support for a cultural economy approach to 'finding and placing neo-liberalism in muddy hybrids, in fraught and often frustrated forms of partial or distorted realization' (2013a: 142; see Collier 2012). For Peck, such an approach is said to be limited because it does not recognize 'how family resemblances connect hybrid formulations' with the 'more abstract and/or macro formulations' of neo-liberalism (2013a: 143). For this book, in contrast, the neo-liberal ideas and concepts present in discrete crisis governance apparatuses have been 'connected', so to speak, not to broader currents of neo-liberal thought and practice, but with the power of economics as a means of administration.

Affect and an Atmosphere of Confidence

As elaborated by this book, a further proclivity shared by the apparatuses of crisis governance was the eliciting of an affective atmosphere of confidence. The 'confidences' at stake were often ill-defined, and were certainly not the same for each of the apparatuses. Reading across Chapters 3, 5, 6, and 8, confidence can be seen to have been variously understood in crisis governance. It was, for example: synonymous with the liquid circulations of money and capital markets; that which sustains the solvency of fractional reserve banking by preventing bank runs by creditors; crucial to the practicability of calculations of risk and the management of uncertainty; and that which is crowded out of the private sector when public indebtedness threatens higher rates of taxation and higher interest rates for all. That said, the significance that provoking confidence had across these different crisis governance apparatuses also reveals something important about how each sought to act, strategically, in order to stabilize finance. Rather than intervening directly in banks and other market institutions, crisis governance targeted the atmospheric conditions of banking and markets in order to re-energize the affectively charged and uncertain circulations of finance.

Cajoling confidence in crisis governance was thus shown here to have been something of a marketing exercise: the success or otherwise of this or that intervention appeared to turn on whether market publics could be attached to it, and thus enrolled in the apparatus in question. When seeking to restore liquidity, for example, it was noted in Chapter 3 that central banking practice was premised on the assumption that, as a confidence-restoring measure, a pledge to act was likely to be just as effective as actually undertaking an injection of liquidity. Promises made in the present and with regard to future action were also shown to have been a feature of the confidence-inspiring, fiscal imaginaries of austerity covered by Chapter 8. It mattered little, then, that even the swingeing deficit cuts of the Coalition Government in the UK had no immediate impact on outstanding sovereign indebtedness, so long as the confidences of investors and entrepreneurs could be said to have been reignited. Not dissimilarly, in Chapter 5 crisis management was shown to have sought to restore confidence in the solvency and stability of banking through sovereign fiscal and monetary pledges, assurances which committed vast sums to recapitalization drives and debt guarantee programmes that went far beyond market expectations. In the terms of a brief but highly revealing description of the BRF package offered by the Bank of England (2008: 29, original emphasis), for instance, it *'was scaled to remove solvency fears'*. In Chapter 6, meanwhile, attaching a market public to the SCAP's attempt to restore confidence in US banking was shown to hinge upon the 'precision' of the anticipatory risk management techniques that were deployed (Daston 1995). The markets, in short, had to feel confident in the capacity of macro-prudential, stress testing techniques to manage risk if they were to feel differently about the future of US banking.

With reference to post-crisis research, this book's analysis certainly begins to address the pre-crisis neglect by SSF of the affective atmospheres which make wholesale financial market actions possible (Callon 2012; Zaloom 2008). In doing so, however, the book also forges a number of links with existing literatures that, taken together, suggest a particular trajectory for research. Cultural economy accounts which stress the mobilization of affective energies by marketing practices in consumer and retail financial markets have been extended here (Cochoy 2007; Deville 2012; McFall 2009), such that achieving market attachments via confidence-inspiring measures have also been shown to be of strategic importance to governmental practices. When furthering a research agenda that regards the manipulation of affective atmospheres as a leitmotif of neo-liberal governance (Anderson 2012; McCormack 2012; Massumi 2005), the book has drawn specific attention to the various forms that this can take in the context of a market panic. Indeed, and to this end, one further and notable feature of the analysis offered here has been consideration of the ways in which market devices and prices (e.g. LIBOR-OIS spreads, banks' share prices) provided the barometers through which the success or otherwise of confidence-restoring interventions was judged, both in real time and subsequently.

Uncertain Circulations and Financialized Security

As noted at the outset of this book and explored in Chapter 2, the consensus holds that the ends of financial crisis governance are to ensure the circulations of capitalist markets and banking. The apparatuses that were assembled in contemporary crisis governance have certainly been shown here to have sought to keep things in motion. However, what Chapters 4, 5, and 7 in particular have shown is that, especially at the height of the crisis, the 'option of circulation' (Foucault 2007: 49) was a key preference in crisis governance apparatuses because it was regarded as vital to opportunities for the future wealth and well-being of the population. Restoring the uncertain circulations of finance and banking was foregrounded, in short, as a matter of security, as an urgent need to refurbish the financialized security of a particular and valued form of Anglo-American, neo-liberal life. To paraphrase from David Harvey (2011: 7), it was not that 'everyone in power recognized' the crisis to be 'a matter of life and death for capital', but that there was a tendency for the crisis to be rationalized and strategized as a threat to the security of life itself.

What Chapter 4 has shown, for example, was that placing toxic assets in bad banks appeared to be essential to restoring the uncertain capital market circulations which potentially provide for retirement investment returns, mortgages, credit cards, student loans, and so on. Similarly, and in Chapter 5, the bailout of insolvent banking drew a tight and irrevocable relation of capital–confidence–life: recapitalization was positioned as providing the material resources necessary for the return of confidence in banking, and thus of the essential but uncertain circulations of life. To that end, taxpayers who picked up the tab for the bailouts were cast as temporary public investors in banking, and not as owners of nationalized assets. In the structural regulations that provided the focus for Chapter 7, moreover, deposit-taking and ring-fenced banks were consistently reiterated to be 'vital' and 'critical' to the routines and rhythms of everyday life. As such, regulation separated out the uncertain circulations of wholesale and retail finance such that the apparently productive opportunities for wealth and well-being afforded by each could be differentiated, and their destructive forces defused accordingly.

This book's analysis of the governance of the crisis as a dilemma of biopolitical security has taken its cue from a body of academic literature which concerns itself with the interstices of 'finance/security' (de Goede 2010, 2012; Amoore 2011; Boy et al. 2011; Lobo-Guerrero 2011; Martin 2007). While not uninterested in how sovereign money and finance relates to national security, and certainly not seeking to downplay how financial market circulations may actually produce considerable insecurity (Marazzi 2010; Lazzarato 2012), what primarily preoccupies this literature is how the logics, calculations, and techniques of finance relate to processes of securitization; that is, to the rendering and governing of social phenomena as security problems in an uncertain future (de Goede 2010). As it matures in a post-crisis setting, future research into finance/security could take a number of cues from this book's analysis. Most notably, and as has been stressed here, governmental practices that emerge at the intersection of finance/security could be explored in terms of the role of dynamic sovereign monetary, fiscal, and regulatory techniques; broader questions about the power of economics as a means of administration; and the strategic significance of the mobilization of 'the passions' through the cajoling of affective atmospheres. Such post-crisis research might also consider how governing at the intersection of finance/security also features the continual development of techniques designed to tame the destructive forces of the uncertain future, something to which we now turn.

Mechanisms of Modulation and Mitigation

Perhaps one of the most startling conclusions that can be reached on the basis of this book's analysis is that, for all the experimentation that governing the contemporary crisis entailed, there was no concerted attempt to redesign global finance in order to prevent the next crisis. Rather, the rationale which gradually surfaced in the course of crisis management was to govern through, as opposed to against, uncertainty; to accept that the destructive forces which crystalize during crises are inherent to global financial circulations, and that trying to thwart future crises threatens to destroy the ostensibly productive contribution of those labile circulations to securing a valued form of life. That said, what also emerged as a tendency that was shared by the crisis governance apparatuses were changes in the technical mechanisms designed to 'modulate' (Deleuze 1992) and to 'mitigate' (Collier 2008) the dangers of uncertain global financial circulations. Consolidating into reform agendas usually captured under the terminology of 'macro-prudentialism' and 'resilience', what these mechanisms seek to achieve is to minimize the extent of a future crisis, and to prepare as effectively as possible for its eventualities.

Specifically, and as was shown in Chapter 5, rendering the crisis governable as a problem of banking solvency mobilized a critical economic discourse on the Basel II capital adequacy standards. In doing so, it set a trajectory for the ongoing recapitalization of banking via the hastily updated Basel III. Making post-crisis banking better prepared and more resilient apparently turned, in the first instance, on mechanisms for making banks hold higher-quality capital in higher quantities. This dovetailed with elements of the apparatus that abstracted the crisis as one of micro-prudential, probabilistic risk management. It was thus found to be the case that banking had not only been undercapitalized prior to the crisis, but that it was necessarily hamstrung by the fundamental incapacity of VaR to calculate and manage future uncertainties. As Chapter 6 made plain, the turn to macro-prudentialism led not just to the one-off stress testing of banking. Rather, these anticipatory techniques became incorporated into a broader, post-crisis agenda focused on the 'counter-cyclical' provisioning of capital which is supposed to modulate the circulations of national banking systems in aggregate terms. In sum, in the wake of crisis governance, micro-prudential risk management and the market price modulations of derivatives markets alone came to be deemed insufficient to the ongoing task of stabilizing finance. Furthermore, as was shown in Chapter 7, what also emerged from the governance of the crisis as a problem of structural regulation was an allied macro-prudential commitment: mechanisms for mitigating and modulating destructive uncertainties were to be applied, in particular, to the vital and newly demarcated circulations of retail banking.

The book's analysis of the tendency for post-crisis blueprints to emerge from the contingent and multiple apparatuses that managed the crisis has a number of implications for academic research going forward. This aspect of the book's analysis stands in contrast, for instance, to political economy research into governance and regulation which suggests that relatively little has changed to date as a consequence of the crisis—a point that is typically made through recourse to historical comparison which suggests that it takes a decade or so for such post-crisis change to materialize anyway (e.g. Blyth 2013; Hay 2011; Helleiner 2014). The stress placed here on the emergence of new technical fixes for global finance would also seem to open up a promising avenue for research in SSF, assuming that the field accepts this book's call to address the questions of governance which it has tended to neglect in the past, but which it presently shows signs of beginning to consider (e.g. MacKenzie 2013). Infused with cultural economy insights into the 'eternally optimistic' and 'congenitally failing' qualities of liberal governmental practices (Miller and Rose 1990: 10–11), SSF would seem especially well placed to map and critically interrogate the development of these ostensible technical fixes. It remains to be seen, for example, how macro-prudential techniques will modulate in counter-cyclical terms, and whether they will throw sufficient sand into the wheels of runaway global finance to ensure that it will not lurch quite so violently out of control once again. What also remains to be seen, moreover, is how effective or ineffective attempts to advance the resilience of banking will prove to be. It is on such questions that the struggle to secure a financialized way of life will be likely to continue to turn, at least until the next time that liquidity is lost.

Bibliography

Abolafia, M. (2012) 'Central banking and the triumph of technical rationality', in K. Knorr Cetina and A. Preda (eds.) *The Oxford Handbook of the Sociology of Finance*, Oxford, UK: Oxford University Press, 94–112.

Acharya, V.V., Cooley, T.F., Richardson, M., Sylla, R., and Walter, I. (2011) 'Prologue: A bird's eye view—The Dodd-Frank Wall Street Reform and Consumer Protection Act', in V.V. Acharya, T.F. Cooley, M.P. Richardson, and I. Walter (eds) *Regulating Wall Street: The Dodd-Frank Act and the New Architecture of Global Finance*, Hoboken, NJ: John Wiley & Sons, pp. 1–32.

Admati, A. and Hellwig, M. (2013) *The Bankers' New Clothes*, Princeton, NJ: Princeton University Press.

Agamben, G. (2011) *The Kingdom and the Glory: For a Theological Genealogy of Economy and Government*, Stanford, CA: Stanford University Press.

Agamben, G. (2005) *State of Exception*, Chicago, IL: University of Chicago Press.

Agamben, G. (2009) *What is an Apparatus? And Other Essays*, Stanford, CA: Stanford University Press.

Ahmed, S. (2010) *The Promise of Happiness*, Durham, NC: Duke University Press.

Aitken, R. (2007) *Performing Capital: Toward a Cultural Economy of Popular and Global Finance*, Basingstoke: Palgrave Macmillan.

Akerlof, G. and Shiller, R.J. (2009) *Animal Spirits: How Human Psychology Drives the Markets and Why it Matters for Global Capitalism*, Princeton, NJ: Princeton University Press.

Albo, G., Gindin, S., and Panitch, L. (2010) *In and Out of Crisis: The Global Financial Meltdown and Left Alternatives*, Oakland, CA: PM Press.

Allen, F., Carletti, E., Krahnen, J.P., and Tyrell, M. (eds) (2011) *Liquidity and Crises*, New York: Oxford University Press.

Allen, J. and Pryke, M. (1999) 'Money cultures after Georg Simmel: Mobility, movement, and identity', *Environment and Planning D: Society and Space*, 17, 1: 51–68.

Allen, W.A. and Moessner, R. (2010) 'Central bank co-operation and international liquidity in the financial crisis of 2008-9', BIS Working Paper No. 310. Available at: <http://www.bis.org/publ/work310.htm> (accessed June 2014).

Allesandri, P. and Haldane, A.G. (2009) 'Banking on the state', Federal Reserve Bank of Chicago 12th Annual International Banking Conference, September. Available at: <http://www.bankofengland.co.uk/archive/Pages/digitalcontent/historicpubs/speeches.aspx> (accessed June 2014).

Amato, M. and Fantacci, L. (2012) *The End of Finance*, Cambridge: Polity Press.

Amin, A. and Thrift, N. (2004) 'Introduction', in A.Amin and N.Thrift (eds) *The Blackwell Cultural Economy Reader*, Oxford: Blackwell, pp. x–xxx.

Amoore, L. (2011) 'Data derivatives: On the emergence of a security risk calculus for our times', *Theory, Culture & Society*, 28, 1: 24–43.

Amoore, L. (2013) *The Politics of Possibility: Risk and Security Beyond Probability*, Durham, NC: Duke University Press.

Anderson, B. (2012) 'Affect and biopower: Towards a politics of life', *Transactions of the Institute of British Geographers*, 37, 1: 28–43.

Anderson, B. (2009) 'Affective atmospheres', *Emotion, Space and Society*, 2, 1: 77–81.

Anderson, B. (2010) 'Preemption, precaution, preparedness: Anticipatory action and future geographies', *Progress in Human Geography*, 34, 6: 777–98.

Anderson, B. and McFarlane, C. (2011) 'Assemblage and geography', *Area*, 43, 2: 124–7.

Andrews, E.L. (2009) 'Rescue of banks hints at nationalization', *New York Times*, online edition, 16 January. Available at: <http://www.nytimes.com/2009/01/16/business/16banking.html?pagewanted=all&_r=0> (accessed June 2014).

Andrews, E.L. (2007) 'Treasury chief aims to stabilize credit markets', *New York Times*, online edition, 16 October. Available at: <http://www.nytimes.com/2007/10/16/business/16rescue.html?adxnnl=1&fta=y&adxnnlx=1402661630-BsPzTu42tvPB5jVZJWvV7A> (accessed June 2014).

Andrews, E.L., de la Merced, M.J., and Williams Walsh, M. (2008) 'Fed's $85 billion loan rescues insurer', *New York Times*, online edition, 16 September. Available at: <http://www.nytimes.com/2008/09/17/business/17insure.html?pagewanted=all&_r=0> (accessed June 2014).

Aragones, J.R., Blanco, C., and Dowd, K. (2001) 'Incorporating stress testing into market risk modelling', *Institutional Investor*, Spring, 44–9. Available at: <http://www.fea.com/resources/a_stresstest.pdf> (accessed June 2014).

Ashton, P. (2009) 'An appetite for yield: The anatomy of the subprime mortgage crisis', *Environment & Planning A*, 41, 6: 1420–41.

Atkinson, W., Roberts, S., and Savage, M. (2012) 'Introduction: A critical sociology of the age of austerity', in W. Atkinson, S. Roberts, and M. Savage (eds) *Class Inequality in Austerity Britain*, Basingstoke: Palgrave Macmillan, 1–12.

Bagehot, W. (2008) *Lombard Street: A Description of the Money Market*, Sioux Falls, SD: NuVision Publications.

Bajaj, V. (2008) 'Plan's mystery: What's all this stuff worth?', *New York Times*, online edition, 25 September. Available at: <http://www.nytimes.com/2008/09/25/business/25value.html?pagewanted=all> (accessed June 2014).

Baker, A. (2013) 'The new political economy of the macroprudential ideational shift', *New Political Economy*, 18, 1: 112–39.

Baker, T. and Simon, J. (2002) 'Embracing risk', in T. Baker and J. Simon (eds) *Embracing Risk: The Changing Culture of Insurance and Responsibility*, Chicago, IL: University of Chicago Press, pp. 1–26.

Bank of England (2012a) 'The distributional effects of quantitative easing', *Bank of England Quarterly Bulletin*, Q3: 254–66. Available at: <http://www.bankofengland.co.uk/publications/Pages/quarterlybulletin/a12.aspx> (accessed June 2014).

Bank of England (2006) *Financial Stability Report*, July 2006, Issue No. 20. Available at: <http://www.bankofengland.co.uk/publications/Pages/fsr/2006/fsr20.aspx> (accessed June 2014).

Bank of England (2009a) *Financial Stability Report*, June 2009. Issue No. 25. Available at: <http://www.bankofengland.co.uk/publications/Pages/fsr/2009/fsr25.aspx> (accessed June 2014).

Bank of England (2013) *Financial Stability Report*, June 2013. Issue No. 33. Available at: <http://www.bankofengland.co.uk/publications/Pages/fsr/2013/fsr33.aspx> (accessed June 2014).

Bank of England (2008) *Financial Stability Report*, October 2008, Issue No. 24. Available at: <http://www.bankofengland.co.uk/publications/Pages/fsr/2008/fsr24.aspx> (accessed June 2014).

Bank of England (2009b) *Financial Stability Report*, December 2009. Issue No. 26. Available at: <http://www.bankofengland.co.uk/publications/Pages/fsr/2009/fsr26.aspx> (accessed June 2014).

Bank of England (2012b) 'The Funding for Lending Scheme', *Bank of England Quarterly Bulletin*, Q4: 306–20. Available at: <http://www.bankofengland.co.uk/publications/Documents/quarterlybulletin/qb120401.pdf> (accessed June 2014).

Barofsky, N. (2012) *Bailout: An Inside Account of How Washington Abandoned Main Street While Rescuing Wall Street*, New York: Free Press.

BCBS, Basel Committee on Banking Supervision (2010) *Basel III: A Global Regulatory Framework for More Resilient Banks and Banking Systems*, Basel: Bank of International Settlements, December. Available at: <http://www.bis.org/publ/bcbs189.htm> (accessed June 2014).

BCBS, Basel Committee on Banking Supervision (2013) *Basel III: The Liquidity Coverage Ratio and Liquidity Risk Monitoring Tools*, Basel: Bank of International Settlement, January. Available at: <http://www.bis.org/publ/bcbs238.htm> (accessed June 2014).

BCBS (2011) *Global Systemically Important Banks: Assessment Methodology and the Additional Loss Absorbency Requirement—Rules Text*, Basel: Bank of International Settlements, June. Available at: <http://www.bis.org/publ/bcbs207.pdf> (accessed June 2014).

BCBS, Basel Committee on Banking Supervision (2008) *Principles for Sound Liquidity Risk Management and Supervision*, Basel: Bank of International Settlements, September. Available at: <http://www.bis.org/publ/bcbs144.htm> (accessed June 2014).

Beatty, C. and Fothergill, S. (2013) *Hitting the Poorest Places Hardest: The Local and Regional Impact of Welfare Reform*, Sheffield: Centre for Regional Economic and Social Research, Sheffield Hallam University.

Beck, U. (1992) *Risk Society: Towards a New Modernity*. London: Sage.

Bennett, T., McFall, L., and Pryke, M. (2008) 'Editorial: Culture/economy/social', *Journal of Cultural Economy*, 1, 1: 1–7.

Berezin, M. (2009) 'Exploring emotions and the economy: New contributions from sociological theory', *Theory and Society*, 38, 4: 335–46.

Berlant, L. (2011) 'Austerity, precarity, awkwardness', November 2011. Available at: <http://www.supervalentthought.com> (accessed June 2014).

Berlant, L. (2010) *Cruel Optimism*, Durham, NC: Duke University Press.

Bernanke, B. (2008c) 'Developments in the financial markets', Committee on Banking, Housing, and Urban Affairs, US Senate, 3 April 3. Available at: <http://www.federalreserve.gov/newsevents/testimony/bernanke20080403a.htm> (accessed June 2014).

Bernanke, B. (2000) *Essays on the Great Depression*, Princeton, NJ: Princeton University Press.

Bernanke, B. (2012) *The Federal Reserve and the Financial Crisis*, Princeton, NJ: Princeton University Press.

Bernanke, B. (2007) 'Financial regulation and the invisible hand', New York University Law School, New York, 11 April. Available at: <http://www.federalreserve.gov/newsevents/speech/bernanke20070411a.htm> (accessed June 2014).

Bernanke, B. (2004) 'The Great Moderation', Eastern Economic Association, Washington, DC, February. Available at: <http://www.federalreserve.gov/boarddocs/speeches/2004/20040220/default.htm> (accessed June 2014).

Bernanke, B. (2008b) 'Liquidity provision by the Federal Reserve', Federal Reserve Bank of Atlanta Financial Markets Conference, Sea Island, Georgia, 13 May. Available at: <http://fraser.stlouisfed.org/publication/?pid=453> (accessed June 2014).

Bernanke, B. (2009) 'Reflections on a year of crisis', Federal Reserve Bank of Kansas City, Jackson Hole, Wyoming, 21–23 August. Available at: <http://fraser.stlouisfed.org/publication/?pid=453> (accessed June 2014).

Bernanke, B. (2010b) 'The Supervisory Capital Assessment Program—one year later', Federal Reserve Bank of Chicago 46th Annual Conference on Bank Structure and Competition, 6 May. Available at: <http://www.federalreserve.gov/newsevents/speech/bernanke20100506a.pdf> (accessed June 2014).

Bernanke, B. (2010a) 'Testimony to the Financial Crisis Inquiry Commission', Washington, DC, 2 September. Available at: <http://www.federalreserve.gov/newsevents/testimony/bernanke20100902a.htm> (accessed June 2014).

Bernanke, B. (2008a) 'U.S. financial markets', Committee on Banking, Housing, and Urban Affairs, US Senate, 23 September. Available at: <http://www.federalreserve.gov/newsevents/testimony/bernanke20080923a1.htm> (accessed June 2014).

Best, J. (2005) *The Limits of Transparency: Ambiguity and the History of International Finance*, Ithaca, NY: Cornell University Press.

Best, J. (2007) 'Why the economy is often the exception to politics as usual', *Theory, Culture & Society*, 24, 4: 87–109.

Beuneza, D., Hardie, I., and MacKenzie, D. (2006) 'A Price is a social thing: Towards a material sociology of arbitrage', *Organization Studies*, 27, 4: 745–69.

BIS, Bank for International Settlements (2008) *78th Annual Report*, Basel: Bank of International Settlements, June. Available at: <http://www.bis.org/publ/arpdf/ar2008e.htm> (accessed June 2014).

BIS, Bank for International Settlements (2009) *79th Annual Report*, Basel: Bank of International Settlements, June. Available at: <http://www.bis.org/publ/arpdf/ar2009e.htm> (accessed June 2014).

BIS, Bank for International Settlements (2010) *80th Annual Report*, Basel: Bank of International Settlements, June. Available at: <http://www.bis.org/publ/arpdf/ar2010e.htm> (accessed June 2014).

BIS, Bank for International Settlements (2013) *83rd Annual Report*, Basel: Bank of International Settlements, June. Available at: <http://www.bis.org/publ/arpdf/ar2013e.htm> (accessed June 2014).

Bischoff, W. (2009) *UK International Financial Services—The Future*, London: The Stationery Office. Available at: <http://webarchive.nationalarchives.gov.uk/20100407010852/http:/www.hm-treasury.gov.uk/ukinternational_financialservices.htm> (accessed June 2014).

Blackburn, R. (2011) 'Crisis 2.0', *New Left Review*, 72: 33–62.

Blackburn, R. (2006) 'Finance and the fourth dimension', *New Left Review*, 39, 39–70.

Blinder, A.S. (2013) *After the Music Stopped: The Financial Crisis, the Response, and the Work Ahead*, New York: Penguin.

Blinder, A.S. and Zandi, M. (2010) How the Great Recession was brought to an end', Washington, DC, 27 July. Available at: <http://www.economy.com/mark-zandi/documents/End-of-Great-Recession.pdf> (accessed June 2014).

Blyth, M. (2013) *Austerity: The History of a Dangerous Idea*, Oxford: Oxford University Press.

Blyth, M. (2002) *Great Transformations: Economic Ideas and Political Change in the Twentieth Century*, Cambridge: Cambridge University Press.

Board of Governors of the Federal Reserve System (2011) *Comprehensive Capital Analysis and Review: Objectives and Overview*, 18 March. Available at: <http://www.federalreserve.gov/newsevents/press/bcreg/bcreg20110318a1.pdf> (accessed June 2014).

Board of Governors of the Federal Reserve System (2009a) *The Supervisory Capital Assessment Program: Design and Implementation*, 24 April. Available at: <http://www.federalreserve.gov/bankinforeg/bcreg20090424a1.pdf> (accessed June 2014).

Board of Governors of the Federal Reserve System (2009b) *The Supervisory Capital Assessment Program: Overview of Results*, 7 May 7. Available at: <http://www.federalreserve.gov/newsevents/press/bcreg/bcreg20090507a1.pdf> (accessed June 2014).

Boldizzoni, F. (2008) *Means and Ends: The Idea of Capital in the West, 1500–1970*, New York: Palgrave Macmillan.

Borio, C. (2010) 'Ten propositions about liquidity crises', *CESifo Economic Studies*, 56, 1: 70–95.

Bowman, A., Erturk, I., Froud, J., Johal, S., Leaver, A., Moran, M., and Williams, K. (2013) 'Central bank-led capitalism?', *Seattle University Law Review*, 36, 2: 455–87.

Boy, N., Burgess, J.P., and Leander, A. (2011) 'The global governance of security and finance', *Security Dialogue*, 42, 2: 115–22.

Boyer, R. (2012) 'The four fallacies of contemporary austerity policies: The lost Keynesian legacy', *Cambridge Journal of Economics*, 36, 2: 283–312.

Brady, N.F., Ludwig, E.A., and Volcker, P.A. (2009) 'Resurrect the Resolution Trust Corp.', *Wall Street Journal*, online edition, September 17. Available at: <http://online.wsj.com/news/articles/SB122161086005145779> (accessed June 2014).

Braithwaite, T. and Jenkins, P. (2013) 'Analysis: Balance sheet battle', *Financial Times*, August 15, 5.

Bramall, R. (2012) 'Popular culture and anti-austerity protest', *Journal of European Popular Culture*, 3, 1: 9–22.

Brassett, J. and Vaughan-Williams, N. (2012) 'Crisis is governance: Sub-prime, the traumatic event, and bare life', *Global Society*, 26, 1: 19–42.

Brown, G. (2008) 'The Global Economy', Reuters Building, London, October 13. Available at: <http://image.guardian.co.uk/sys-files/Politics/documents/2008/10/13/reutersspeech13102008.pdf?> (accessed June 2014).

Brunnermeier, M.K. (2008) 'Deciphering the liquidity and credit crunch, 2007–8', National Bureau of Economic Research Working Paper No. 14612, December. Available at: <http://www.nber.org/papers/w14612.pdf> (accessed June 2014).

Brunnermeier, M.K. (2009) 'Deciphering the liquidity and credit crunch 2007–2008', *Journal of Economic Perspectives*, 23, 1: 77–100.

Bryan, D. and Rafferty, M. (2013) 'Fundamental value: A category in transformation', *Economy and Society*, 42, 1: 130–53.

Buck-Morss, S. (1995) 'Envisioning capital: Political economy on display', *Critical Inquiry*, 21, 2: 434–67.

Buiter, W. (2008) 'Can central banks go broke?', *CEPR Policy Insight*, 24: 1–24. Available at: <http://www.cepr.org/sites/default/files/policy_insights/PolicyInsight 24.pdf> (accessed June 2014).

Bush, G.W. (2008) 'Transcript: President Bush's speech to the nation on the economic crisis', *New York Times*, online edition, 24 September. Available at: <http://www.nytimes.com/2008/09/24/business/economy/24text-bush.html> (accessed June 2014).

Calişkan, K. and Callon, M. (2009) 'Economization, part 1: Shifting attention from the economy to processes of economization', *Economy and Society*, 38, 3: 369–98.

Calişkan, K. and Callon, M. (2010) 'Economization, part 2: A research programme for the study of markets', *Economy and Society*, 39, 1: 1–32.

Calleo, D. (2009) *Follies of Power: America's Unipolar Fantasy*, Cambridge: Cambridge University Press.

Callinicos, A. (2012) 'Contradictions of austerity', *Cambridge Journal of Economics*, 36, 1: 65–77.

Callon, M. (2008) 'Economic markets and the rise of interactive *agencements*: From prosthetic agencies to habilitated agencies', in T. Pinch and R. Swedberg (eds) *Living in a Material World: Economic Sociology Meets Science and Technology Studies*, Cambridge, MA: MIT Press, 29–56.

Callon, M. (2012) 'For an anthropology of atmospheric markets: The exemplary case of financial markets', *Cultural Anthropology Online*, 15 May 15. Available at: <http://culanth.org/fieldsights/334-for-an-anthropology-of-atmospheric-markets-the-exemplary-case-of-financial-markets> (accessed June 2014).

Callon. M. (1998) 'Introduction: The embeddedness of economic markets in economics', in M. Callon (ed.) *The Laws of Markets*, Oxford: Blackwell, 1–57.

Callon, M. (1986) 'Some elements of a sociology of translation: Domestication of the scallops and the fishermen of St Brieuc Bay', in J. Law (ed.) *Power, Action and Belief: A New Sociology of Knowledge?*, London: Routledge, 196–223.

Callon, M. (2007) 'What does it mean to say that economics is performative?', in D. MacKenzie, F. Muniesa, and L. Siu (eds) *Do Economists Make Markets? On the Performativity of Economics*, Princeton, NJ: Princeton University Press, 311–57.

Callon, M. (2005) 'Why virtualism paves the way to political impotence', *Economic Sociology*, 6, 2: 3–20.

Callon, M. and Muniesa, F. (2005) 'Economic markets as calculative collective devices', *Organization Studies*, 26, 8: 1229–50.

Cameron, D. (2011) 'Leadership for a better Britain', Conservative Party Conference Speech, 5 October. Available at: <http://www.conservatives.com/News/Speeches/2011/10/David_Cameron_Leadership_for_a_better_Britain.aspx> (accessed June 2014).

Cameron, D. (2010a) 'Transforming the British economy: Coalition strategy for economic growth', 28 May. Available at: <https://www.gov.uk/government/speeches/transforming-the-british-economy-coalition-strategy-for-economic-growth> (accessed June 2014).

Cameron, D. (2010b) 'We must tackle Britain's massive deficit and growing debt', 7 June. Available at: <http://www.conservatives.com/News/Speeches/2010/06/David_Cameron_We_must_tackle_Britains_massive_deficit_and_growing_debt.aspx> (accessed June 2014).

Cameron, A., Nesvetailova, A., and Palan, R. (2011) 'Wages of sin? Crisis and the libidinal economy', *Journal of Cultural Economy*, 4, 2: 117–35.

Carruthers, B. (1996) *City of Capital: Politics and Markets in the English Financial Revolution*, Princeton, NJ: Princeton University Press.

Carruthers, B. and Espeland, W. (1991) 'Accounting for rationality: Double-entry bookkeeping and the rhetoric of economic rationality', *American Journal of Sociology*, 97, 1: 31–69.

Carruthers, B.G. and Stinchcombe, A.L. (1999) 'The social structure of liquidity: Flexibility, markets, and states', *Theory and Society*, 28, 3: 353–82.

Cassidy, J. (2008) 'The Minsky moment', *The New Yorker*, 4 February. Available at: <http://www.newyorker.com/talk/comment/2008/02/04/080204taco_talk_cassidy> (accessed June 2014).

Castells, M., Caraça, J., and Cardosa, G. (2012) 'The cultures of the economic crisis: An introduction', in M. Castells, J. Caraça, and G. Cardosa (eds) *Aftermath: The Cultures of the Economic Crisis*, Oxford: Oxford University Press, 1–16.

Catapano, P. (2011) 'Can you hear them now?', *New York Times*, Opinionator blog post, 30 September. Available at: <http://opinionator.blogs.nytimes.com/2011/09/30/can-you-hear-them-now-3/?ref=occupywallstreet> (accessed June 2014).

CEBS, Committee of European Banking Supervisors (2010) *Aggregate Outcome of the 2010 EU Wide Stress Test Exercise Coordinated by CEBS in Cooperation with the ECB*, 23 July. Available at: <https://www.rte.ie/news/2010/0723/cebs_summaryreport.pdf> (accessed June 2014).

Cecchetti, S.G. (2009) 'Crisis and responses: The Federal Reserve in the early stages of the financial crisis', *Journal of Economic Perspectives*, 23, 1: 51–75.

Cecchetti, S.G., Mohanty, M.S., and Zampolli, F. (2010) 'The future of public debt: Prospects and implications', BIS Working Paper No. 300, March. Available at: <http://www.bis.org/publ/othp09.htm> (accessed June 2014).

Chancellor, E. (2000) *Devil Take the Hindmost: A History of Financial Speculation*, Basingstoke: Macmillan.

Chiapello, E. (2007) 'Accounting and the birth of the notion of capitalism', *Critical Perspectives on Accounting*, 18, 2: 263–96.

Chinloy, P. and MacDonald, N. (2005) 'Subprime lenders and mortgage market completion', *The Journal of Real Estate Finance and Economics*, 30, 2: 153–65.

Christophers, B. (2013) *Banking across Boundaries: Placing Finance in Capitalism*, Chichester: John Wiley & Sons Ltd.

Clark, G.L. (2005) 'Money flows like mercury: The geography of global finance', *Geografiska Annaler*, 87B, 2: 99–112.

Clarke, C. (2012) 'Financial engineering, not economic photography: Popular discourses of finance and the layered performances of the sub-prime crisis', *Journal of Cultural Economy*, 5, 3: 261–78.

Coates, D. (2012) 'Dire consequences: The conservative recapture of America's political narrative?', *Cambridge Journal of Economics*, 36, 2: 145–53.

Cochoy, F. (2007) 'A brief theory of the "captation" of publics: Understanding the market with Little Red Riding Hood', *Theory, Culture & Society*, 24, 7–8: 203–23.

Collier, S.J. (2008) 'Enacting catastrophe: Preparedness, insurance, budgetary rationalization', *Economy and Society*, 37, 2: 224–50.

Collier, S.J. (2012) 'Neoliberalism as big Leviathan, or . . . ? A response to Wacquant and Hilgers', *Social Anthropology*, 20, 2: 186–95.

Collier, S.J. (2011) *Post-Soviet Social: Neoliberalism, Social Modernity, Biopolitics*, Princeton, NJ: Princeton University Press.

Collier, S.J. (2009) 'Topologies of power: Foucault's analysis of political government beyond "governmentality"', *Theory, Culture & Society*, 26, 6: 78–108.

Congressional Budget Office (2012) *Economic Effects of Policies Contributing to Fiscal Tightening in 2013*, Washington, DC: Congress of the United States, November. Available at: <http://www.cbo.gov/publication/43694> (accessed June 2014).

Congressional Oversight Panel (2009) *Accountability for the Troubled Asset Relief Program: The Second Report of the Congressional Oversight Panel*. January. Available at: <http://cybercemetery.unt.edu/archive/cop/20110401232106/http://cop.senate.gov/reports/library/report-010909-cop.cfm> (accessed June 2014).

Congressional Oversight Panel (2011) *The Final Report of the Congressional Oversight Panel*, March. Available at: <http://cybercemetery.unt.edu/archive/cop/20110401223133/http://cop.senate.gov/reports/library/report-031611-cop.cfm> (accessed June 2014).

Connolly, W.E. (2008) *Capitalism and Christianity, American Style*, Durham, N.C.: Duke University Press.

Connolly, W.E. (2004) 'The complexity of sovereignty', in J. Edkins, V. Pin-Fat, and M.J. Shapiro (eds) *Sovereign Lives: Power in Global Politics*, London: Routledge, 23–40.

Cooley, T.F., Schoenholtz, K., Smith, D.G., Sylla, R., and Wachtel, P. (2011) 'The power of central banks and the future of the Federal Reserve System', in V.V. Acharya, T.F. Cooley, M.P. Richardson, and I. Walter (eds) *Regulating Wall Street: The Dodd–Frank Act and the New Architecture of Global Finance*, Hoboken, NJ: John Wiley & Sons, 51–72.

Cooper, M. (2014) 'The strategy of default: Liquid foundations in the house of finance', *Polygraph: An International Journal of Culture and Politics*, 23/24: 79–96.

Cooper, M. (2010) 'Turbulent worlds: Financial markets and environmental crisis', *Theory, Culture & Society*, 27, 2–3: 167–90.

Cox, C. (2008) 'Role of Federal regulators: Lessons from the credit crisis for the future of regulation', Committee on Oversight and Government Reform, US House of Representatives, 23 October. Available at: <http://www.sec.gov/news/testimony/2008/ts102308cc.htm> (accessed June 2014).

Crawford, C. (2011) 'The repeal of the Glass–Steagall Act and the current financial crisis', *Journal of Business and Economics Research*, 9, 1: 127–33.

Cross, M., Fisher, P., and Weeken, O. (2010) 'The Bank's balance sheet during the crisis', *Bank of England Quarterly Bulletin*, Q1: 34–42.

Crouch, C. (2011) *The Strange Non-Death of Neoliberalism*, Cambridge: Polity Press.

Curry, T. and Shibut, L. (2000) 'The cost of the Savings and Loan crisis: Truth and consequences', *FDIC Banking Review*, 13, 2: 26–35.

Dabrowski, W. (2008) 'Buffett: Bank woes are "poetic justice"', *Reuters*, US Edition, 7 February. Available at: <http://www.reuters.com/article/2008/02/07/us-buffett-economy-idUSN0631767220080207> (accessed June 2014).

Darling, A. (2009) *Back from the Brink: 1,000 Days at Number 11*, London: Atlantic Books.

Darling, A. (2008c) 'Mais Lecture on Maintaining stability in a global economy', Cass Business School, London, 29 October. Available at: <http://webarchive.nationalarchives.gov.uk/20100407175625/http://www.hm-treasury.gov.uk/press_110_08.htm> (accessed June 2014).

Darling, A. (2008d) 'Statement by the Chancellor on the Bank Recapitalisation Scheme', 18 November. Available at: <http://webarchive.nationalarchives.gov.uk/20100407175639/http://www.hm-treasury.gov.uk/statement_chx_181108.htm> (accessed June 2014).

Darling, A. (2008b) 'Statement by the Chancellor on financial markets', 13 October. Available at: <http://webarchive.nationalarchives.gov.uk/20100407175639/http://www.hm-treasury.gov.uk/statement_chx_13_10_08.htm> (accessed June 2014).

Darling, A. (2008a) 'Statement by the Chancellor on financial stability', 8 October. Available at: <http://webarchive.nationalarchives.gov.uk/20100407175639/http://www.hm-treasury.gov.uk/statement_chx_081008.htm> (accessed June 2014).

Dash, E. (2009) '10 large banks allowed to exit U.S. aid program', *New York Times*, online edition, 10 June. Available at: <http://www.nytimes.com/2009/06/10/business/economy/10tarp.html> (accessed June 2014).

Dash, E. and Schwartz, N.D. (2011) 'Investors, worried about debt talks, look for havens', *New York Times*, online edition, 28 July. Available at: <http://www.nytimes.com/2011/07/28/business/economy/investors-worried-about-debt-talks-look-for-havens.html> (accessed June 2014).

Daston, L. (1995) 'The moral economy of science', *Osiris*, 10, 2–24.

Datz, C. (2013) 'The narrative of complexity in the crisis of finance: Epistemological challenge and macroprudential policy response', *New Political Economy*, 18, 4: 459–79.

Davies, H. and Green, D. (2010) *Banking on the Future: The Fall and Rise of Central Banking*, Princeton, NJ: Princeton University Press.

Dean, M. (2012) 'Free economy, strong state', in D. Cahill, L. Edwards, and F. Stilwell (eds) *Neoliberalism: Beyond the Free Market*, Cheltenham: Edward Elgar, 69–89.

Debt Management Office (2009) *DMO Annual Review, 2008–09*, August. Available at: <http://www.dmo.gov.uk/index.aspx?page=publications/annual_reviews> (accessed June 2014).

de Goede, M. (2001) 'Discourses of scientific finance and the failure of Long-Term Capital Management', *New Political Economy*, 6, 2: 149–70.

de Goede, M. (2009) 'Finance and the excess: The politics of visibility in the credit crisis', *Zeitschrift fur InternaionaleBeziehungen*, 16: 299–310.

de Goede, M. (2010) 'Financial security', in J.P.Burgess (ed.) *The Routledge Handbook of the New Security Studies*, London and New York: Routledge, 100–9.

de Goede, M. (2012) *Speculative Security: The Politics of Pursuing Terrorist Monies*, Minneapolis: University of Minnesota Press.

de Goede, M. (2005) *Virtue, Fortune and Faith: A Genealogy of Finance*, Minneapolis: University of Minnesota Press.

Deleuze, G. (1999) *Foucault*, London: Continuum.

Deleuze, G. (1992) 'Postscript on the societies of control', *October*, 59: 3–7.

Deleuze, G. and Guattari, F. (1983) *Anti-Oedipus: Capitalism and Schizophrenia*, Minneapolis: University of Minnesota Press.

Deleuze, G. and Guattari, F. (1987) *A Thousand Plateaus: Capitalism and Schizophrenia*, Minneapolis: University of Minnesota Press.

Deleuze, G. (2006) 'What is a *dispositif*?', in G. Deleuze, *Two Regimes of Madness: Texts and Interviews 1975–1995*, New York: Semiotext(e), 338–48.

Department of Work and Pensions (2010) *21st Century Welfare*, London: Stationery Office, July. Available at: <http://www.dwp.gov.uk/docs/21st-century-welfare.pdf> (accessed June 2014).

Deville, J. (2012) 'Regenerating market attachments: Consumer credit debt collection and the capture of affect', *Journal of Cultural Economy*, 5, 4: 423–39.

Diamond, D.W. and Dybvig, P.H. (2002) 'Bank runs, deposit insurance, and liquidity', in C. Goodhart and G. Illing (eds) *Financial Crises, Contagion, and the Lender of Last Resort: A Reader*, Oxford: Oxford University Press, 299–314.

Dickson, P.G.M. (1967) *The Financial Revolution in England: A Study in the Development of Public Credit, 1688–1756*, London: Macmillan.

Dillon, M. (2004) 'Correlating sovereign and biopower', in J. Edkins, V. Pin-Fat, and M.J. Shapiro (eds) *Sovereign Lives: Power in Global Politics*, London: Routledge, 41–60.

Dillon, M. (2007) 'Governing through contingency: The security of biopolitical governance', *Political Geography*, 26, 1: 41–7.

Dillon, M. and Lobo-Guerrero, L. (2008) 'Biopolitics of security in the 21st century: An introduction', *Review of International Studies*, 34, 2: 265–92.

Donelson, D. and Zaring, D. (2011) 'Requiem for a regulator: The Office of Thrift Supervision's performance during the financial crisis', *North Carolina Law Review*, 89, 4: 1777–812.

Douzinas, C. (2013) *Philosophy and Resistance in the Crisis*, Cambridge: Polity Press.

Dowd, K. and Hutchinson, M. (2010) *Alchemists of Loss: How Modern Finance and Government Intervention Crashed the Financial System*, New York: John Wiley & Sons.

Dowd, K. and Timberlake, R.H. (eds) (1997) *Money and the Nation-State: The Financial Revolution, Government and the World Monetary System*, New Brunswick, NJ: Transaction Publishers.

Driver F. (1993) *Power and Pauperism: The Workhouse System, 1834–1884*, Cambridge: Cambridge University Press.

du Gay, P. and Pryke, M. (eds.) (2002) *Cultural Economy: Cultural Analysis and Commercial Life*, London: Sage.

Duménil, G. and Levy, D. (2011) *The Crisis of Neoliberalism*, Cambridge, MA: Harvard University Press.

EBA, European Banking Authority (2011b) *2011 EU-Wide Stress Test Aggregate Report.* July 15. Available at: <https://www.eba.europa.eu/risk-analysis-and-data/eu-wide-stress-testing/2011/results> (accessed June 2014).

EBA, European Banking Authority (2011a) *2011 EU-Wide Stress Test: Methodological Note—Additional Guidance*, 9 June. Available at: <https://www.eba.europa.eu/risk-analysis-and-data/eu-wide-stress-testing/2011/results> (accessed June 2014).

Economist (2008b) 'All's fair', online edition, 18 September. Available at: <http://ww2.cfo.com/accounting-tax/2008/09/alls-fair/> (accessed June 2014).

Economist (2009a) 'Buttonwood: Minsky's moment', online edition 2 April. Available at: <http://www.economist.com/node/13415233> (accessed June 2014).

Economist (2010b) 'Crash-test dummies: The tortuous process of "stress testing" Europe's wobbly banks', online edition, 25 June. Available at: <http://www.economist.com/node/16438831> (accessed June 2014).

Economist (2008c) 'Credit derivatives: The great untangling', online edition, 6 November. Available at: <http://www.economist.com/node/12552204> (accessed June 2014).

Economist (2009f) 'Dashed expectations', online edition, 12 February. Available at: <http://www.economist.com/node/13110554> (accessed June 2014).

Economist (2008d) 'The doctors' bill', 27 September, 92–4.

Economist (2010a) 'The gods strike back: Special report on financial risk', online edition, 13 February. Available at: <http://www.economist.com/node/15474137> (accessed June 2014).

Economist (2009c) 'Hauled to safety', online edition, 11 June. Available at: <http://www.economist.com/node/13832261> (accessed June 2014).

Economist (2009e) 'The Obama rescue: This week marked a huge wasted opportunity in the economic crisis', online edition, 12 February. Available at: <http://www.economist.com/node/13108724?Story_ID=13108724> (accessed June 2014).

Economist (2013) 'Onshore financial centres: Not a palm tree in sight—Special report: Offshore finance', online edition, 16 February. Available at: <http://www.economist.com/news/special-report/21571554-some-onshore-jurisdictions-can-be-laxer-offshore-sort-not-palm-tree-sight> (accessed June 2014).

Economist (2008a) 'Paradise lost: A special report on international banking', online edition, 17 May. Available at: <http://www.economist.com/node/11325347> (accessed June 2014).

Economist (2009b) 'What went wrong with economics', 16 July, 4.

Economist (2009d) 'Rebuilding the banks: A special report on international banking', online edition, 16 May. Available at: <http://www.economist.com/node/13604663> (accessed June 2014).

Edkins, J. and Pin-Fat, V. (2004) 'Introduction: Life, power, resistance', in J. Edkins, V. Pin-Fat, and M.J. Shapiro (eds) *Sovereign Lives: Power in Global Politics*, London: Routledge, 1–22.

Eichengreen, B. (2011) *Exorbitant Privilege: The Rise and Fall of the Dollar and the Future of the International Monetary System*, New York: Oxford University Press.

Elliott, L. (2009) 'David Cameron is gaining ground even though Labour handled the crisis well', *The Guardian*, online edition, 12 October. Available at: <http://www.guardian.co.uk/business/2009/oct/12/cameron-outflanking-labour> (accessed June 2014).

Elliott, L. (2011) 'Paying off your debts hits the economy, stupid', *Guardian*, online edition, 5 October. Available at: <http://www.theguardian.com/business/2011/oct/05/david-cameron-paradox-of-thrift?guni=Article:in%20body%20link> (accessed June 2014).

Engelen, E., Ertürk, I., Froud, J., Sukhdev, J., Leaver, A., Moran, M., Nilsson, A., and Williams, K. (2011) *After the Great Complacence: Financial Crisis and the Politics of Reform*, Oxford: Oxford University Press.

Eppler, E. (2009) *The Return of the State?*, London: Forum Press.

Epstein, G.A. and Wolfson, M.H. (2013) 'Introduction: The political economy of financial crises', in M.H. Wolfson and G.A. Epstein (eds) *The Handbook of the Political Economy of Financial Crises*, Oxford: Oxford University Press, 1–20.

Ericson, R., Barry, D., and Doyle, A. (2000) 'The moral hazards of neo-liberalism: Lessons from the private insurance industry', *Economy and Society*, 29, 4: 532–58.

Erturk, I. and Solari, S. (2007) 'Banks as continuous reinvention', *New Political Economy*, 12, 3: 369–88.

Ewald, F. (1991) 'Insurance and risk', in G. Burchell, C. Gordon, and P. Miller (eds.) *The Foucault Effect: Studies in Governmentality*, London: Harvester Wheatsheaf, 197–210.

Faucette, D., Cunningham, T., and Loegering, J. (2009) 'Good bank/bad bank', *Banking Law Journal*, 126, 4: 291–8.

FCIC, Financial Crisis Inquiry Commission (2011) *The Financial Crisis Inquiry Report: Final Report of the National Commission on the Causes of the Financial and Economic Crisis in the United States*, Washington, DC: US Government Printing Office. Available at: <http://fcic.law.stanford.edu/report> (accessed June 2014).

Federal Reserve Bank of New York (2013) 'Domestic open market operations during 2012', report presented to the Federal Open Market Committee, April. Available at: <http://www.newyorkfed.org/markets/annual_reports.html> (accessed June 2014).

Felsted, A. and Burgess, K. (2008) 'AIG forms keystone of financial system', *Financial Times*, 16 September, 5.

Ferguson, N. (2010) 'Complexity and collapse: Empires on the edge of chaos', *Foreign Affairs*, March/April. Available at: <http://www.foreignaffairs.com/articles/65987/niall-ferguson/complexity-and-collapse> (accessed June 2014).

Financial Stability Board (2011) *Key Attributes of Effective Resolution Regimes for Financial Institutions*, October. Available at: <http://www.financialstabilityboard.org/publications/r_111104cc.htm> (accessed June 2014).

Fine, B. and Milonakis, D. (2011) '"Useless but true": Economic crisis and the peculiarities of economic science', *Historical Materialism*, 19, 2: 3–31.

Financial Times (2008) 'In depth: The big freeze', online edition, 8 August. Available at: <http://www.ft.com/indepth/creditsqueezeanniversary> (accessed June 2014).

Fisher, P. (2012) 'Liquidity support from the Bank of England: The Discount Window Facility', National Asset-Liability Management Global Conference, London, March. Available at: <http://www.bankofengland.co.uk/publications/Pages/speeches/2012/561.aspx> (accessed June 2014).

Foucault, M. (1972) *The Archaeology of Knowledge*, London: Tavistock.

Foucault, M. (2008) *The Birth of Biopolitics, Lectures at the Collège de France, 1978–1979*, ed. M. Senellart, trans. G. Burchell, Basingstoke: Palgrave Macmillan.

Foucault, M. (1980) '"The Confession of the Flesh"', in C.Gordon (ed.) *Power/Knowledge: Selected Interviews and Other Writings*, New York: Pantheon Books, 194–228.

Foucault, M. (1977) *Discipline and Punish: The Birth of the Prison*, London: Allen Lane.

Foucualt, M. (1991) 'Governmentality', in G. Burchell, C. Gordon, and P. Miller (eds) *The Foucault Effect: Studies in Governmentality*, Chicago, IL: University of Chicago Press, 87–104.

Foucault, M. (2003a) 'Polemics, politics, and problematizations: An interview with Michel Foucault', in P. Rabinow and N. Rose (eds) *The Essential Foucault*, New York and London: The New Press, 18–24.

Foucault, M. (2003b) 'Nietzsche, genealogy, history', in P. Rabinow and N. Rose (eds) *The Essential Foucault*, New York and London: The New Press, 351–69.

Foucault, M. (2007) *Security, Territory, Population, Lectures at the Collège de France, 1977–1978*, trans. G. Burchell, Basingstoke: Palgrave Macmillan.

Foucault, M. (2003c) *Society Must Be Defended*, London: Penguin.

Fraser, S. (2005) *Wall Street: A Cultural History*, London: Faber & Faber.

FRB Markets Group (2008) 'Domestic open market operations during 2007', report prepared for the Federal Open Market Committee by the Markets Group of the Federal Reserve Bank of New York, February. Available at: <http://www.newyorkfed.org/markets/omo/omo2007.pdf> (accessed June 2014).

FRB Markets Group (2009) 'Domestic open market operations during 2008', report prepared for the Federal Open Market Committee by the Markets Group of the Federal Reserve Bank of New York, January. Available at: <http://www.newyorkfed.org/markets/omo/omo2008.pdf> (accessed June 2014).

Freixas, X., Giannini, C., Hoggarth, G., and Soussa, F. (2002) 'Lender of last resort: A review of the literature', in C. Goodhart and G. Illing (eds) *Financial Crises, Contagion, and the Lender of Last Resort: A Reader*, Oxford: Oxford University Press, 27–56.

French, S. and Kneale, J. (2012) 'Speculating on careless lives: Annuitising the biofinancial subject', *Journal of Cultural Economy*, 5, 4: 391–406.

French, S. and Leyshon, A. (2010) '"These f@#king guys": The terrible waste of a good crisis', *Environment and Planning A*, 42, 11: 2549–59.

Froud, J., Moran, M., Nilsson, A., and Williams, K. (2010) 'Wasting a crisis? Democracy and markets in Britain after 2007', *Political Quarterly*, 81, 1: 25–38.

FSA, Financial Services Authority (2011) *The Failure of the Royal Bank of Scotland: Financial Services Authority Board Report*, December. Available at: <http://www.fsa.gov.uk/pubs/other/rbs.pdf> (accessed June 2014).

FSOC, Financial Stability Oversight Counsel (2013) *2013 Annual Report*, April. Available at: <http://www.treasury.gov/initiatives/fsoc/studies-reports/Pages/2013-Annual-Report.aspx> (accessed June 2014).

FSOC, Financial Stability Oversight Counsel (2011) *Study and Recommendations on Prohibitions on Proprietary Trading and Certain Relationships with Hedge Funds and Private Equity Funds*, January. Available at <http://www.treasury.gov/initiatives/fsoc/studies-reports/Pages/default.aspx> (accessed June 2014).

FT Reporters (2010) 'Banks find exercise relatively painless'. *Financial Times*, 24–5 July, 16.

Funnell, W.N. (2001) 'Distortions of history: Accounting and the paradox of Werner Sombart', *Abacus*, 12, 1: 55–78.

Gabor, D. (2012) 'The power of collateral: The ECB and geographies of bank funding', *Social Science Research Network*. Available at: <http://papers.ssrn.com/sol3/papers.cfm?abstract_id=2062315> (accessed June 2014).

Gamble, A. (2009) *The Spectre at the Feast: Capitalist Crisis and the Politics of Recession*, Basingstoke: Palgrave Macmillan.

Gamble, A. (2012) 'The United Kingdom: The triumph of fiscal realism', in W. Grant and G.K. Wilson (eds) *The Consequences of the Global Financial Crisis: The Rhetoric of Reform and Regulation*, Oxford: Oxford University Press, 34–50.

Geithner, T. (2008) 'Actions by the New York Fed in response to liquidity pressures in financial markets', Committee on Banking, Housing and Urban Affairs, US Senate, Washington, DC, 3April. Available at: <http://www.newyorkfed.org/newsevents/speeches/2008/gei080403.html> (accessed June 2014).

Geithner, T. (2009) 'My plan for bad bank assets', *Wall Street Journal*, online edition, 23 March. Available at: <http://online.wsj.com/article/SB123776536222709061.html> (accessed June 2014).

Germain, R.D. (2010) *Global Politics and Financial Governance*, Basingstoke: Palgrave Macmillan.

Germain, R.D. (2012) 'Governing global finance and banking', *Review of International Political Economy*, 19, 4: 530–5.

Germain, R.D. (1997) *The International Organization of Credit: States and Global Finance in the World-Economy*, Cambridge: Cambridge University Press.

Gilbert, E. (2005) 'Common cents: Situating money in time and place', *Economy and Society*, 34, 3: 357–88.

Gilbert, E. and Helleiner, E. (eds) (1999) *Nation-States and Money: The Past, Present and Future of National Currencies*, London: Routledge.

Goodhart, C. (2002) 'Myths about the lender of last resort', in C. Goodhart and G. Illing (eds) *Financial Crises, Contagion, and the Lender of Last Resort: A Reader*, Oxford: Oxford University Press, 227–45.

Goodhart, C. (2009) *The Regulatory Response to the Financial Crisis*, Cheltenham: Edward Elgar.

Goodhart, C. and Illing, G. (2002) 'Introduction', in C. Goodhart and G. Illing (eds) *Financial Crises, Contagion, and the Lender of Last Resort: A Reader*, Oxford: Oxford University Press, 1–26.

Gordon, C. (1991) 'Governmental rationality: An introduction', in G. Burchell, C. Gordon, and P. Miller (eds) *The Foucault Effect: Studies in Governmentality*, Chicago, IL: University of Chicago Press, 1–52.

Graeber, D. (2012) *Debt: The First 5000 Years*, Brooklyn, NY: Melville House.

Greenspan, A. (1997) 'Maintaining financial stability in a global economy', Federal Reserve Bank of Kansas City Economic Symposium, 29 August. Available at: <http://www.minneapolisfed.org/publications_papers/pub_display.cfm?id=3629> (accessed June 2014).

Greenspan, A. (2008) 'Testimony of Alan Greenspan', Committee of Government Oversight and Reform, US House of Representatives, 23 October. Available at: <http://clipsandcomment.com/wp-content/uploads/2008/10/greenspan-testimony-20081023.pdf> (accessed June 2014).

Grewal, D. (2010) 'The return of the state', *Harvard International Review*, 31, 4, online edition. Available at: <http://hir.harvard.edu/big-ideas/the-return-of-the-state> (accessed June 2014).

Griffith-Jones, S., Ocampo, J.A., and Stiglitz, J.E. (eds) (2010) *Time for a Visible Hand: Lessons from the 2008 World Financial Crisis*, Oxford: Oxford University Press.

Group of 7 Finance Ministers and Central Bankers (2008) 'G7 finance ministers and central bank governors: Plan of action', 10 October. Available at: <http://www.g8.utoronto.ca/finance/fm081010.htm> (accessed June 2014).

G-30, Group of 30 (2009) *Financial Reform: A Framework for Financial Stability*, Washington, DC: Group of 30. Available at: <http://www.group30.org/rpt_03.shtml> (accessed June 2014).

Grunwald, M. (2009) 'Person of the Year 2009: Ben Bernanke', *Time Magazine*, online edition, 16 December. Available at: <http://content.time.com/time/specials/packages/article/0,28804,1946375_1947251,00.html> (accessed June 2014).

Grynbaum, M.M. (2008) 'On Wall Street, eyes turn to the Fear Index', *New York Times*, online edition, 20 October. Available at: <http://www.nytimes.com/2008/10/20/business/20vix.html?pagewanted=all&_r=0> (accessed June 2014).

Guardian (2010) 'Barclays' Bob Diamond hits out at criticism of "casino banks"', *Guardian*, 12 September. Available at: <http://www.theguardian.com/business/2010/sep/12/barclays-bob-diamond-casino-banks> (accessed June 2014).

Haldane, A.G. (2011) 'Capital discipline', American Economic Association, Denver, January. Available at: <http://www.bis.org/review/r110325a.pdf> (accessed June 2014).

Haldane, A.G. (2012) 'On being the right size', The 2012 Beesley Lecture, Institute of Directors, London, October. Available at: <http://www.bankofengland.co.uk/publications/Pages/speeches/2012/615.aspx> (accessed June 2014).

Haldane, A.G. (2009b) 'Rethinking the financial network', Financial Student Association, Amsterdam, April. Available at: <http://www.bankofengland.co.uk/research/Pages/economists/staff/andy_haldane.aspx> (accessed June 2014).

Haldane, A.G. (2009a) 'Why banks failed the stress test', Marcus-Evans Conference on Stress Testing, February. Available at: <http://www.bankofengland.co.uk/archive/Documents/historicpubs/speeches/2009/speech374.pdf> (accessed June 2014).

Haldane, A.G. and May, R.M. (2011) 'Systemic risk in banking ecosystems', *Nature*, 469, 20 January, 351–5.

Hall, S. (2011) 'The neo-liberal revolution', *Cultural Studies*, 25, 6: 705–28.

Hamnett, C. (2014) 'Shrinking the welfare state: The structure, geography and impact of British government benefit cuts', *Transactions of the Institute of British Geographers*, DOI: 10.1111/tran.12049.

Harcourt, B.E. (2013) 'Political disobedience', in W.J.T. Mitchell, B.E. Harcourt, and M. Taussig *Occupy: Three Inquiries in Disobedience*, Chicago, IL: University of Chicago Press, 45–92.

Hardie, I. and MacKenzie, D. (2007) 'Assembling an economic actor: The *agencement* of a hedge fund', *Sociological Review*, 55, 1: 57–80.

Hardt, T. and Negri, T. (2000) *Empire*, Cambridge, MA: Harvard University Press.

Harvey, D. (2010) *The Enigma of Capital: And the Crises of Capitalism*, London: Profile Books.

Harvey, D. (1982) *The Limits to Capital*, Oxford: Blackwell.

Harvey, D. (2011) 'Roepke lecture in economic geography—Crises, geographic disruptions and the uneven development of political responses', *Economic Geography*, 87, 1: 1–22.

Harvey, D. (2001) *Spaces of Capital: Towards a Critical Geography*, Edinburgh: Edinburgh University Press.

Hay, C. (2011) 'The 2010 Leonard Schapiro lecture: Pathology without crisis? The strange demise of the Anglo-Liberal growth model', *Government & Opposition*, 46, 1: 1–31.

Helleiner, E. (1994) *States and the Re-emergence of Global Finance*. Ithaca, NY: Cornell University Press.

Helleiner, E. (2014) *The Status Quo Crisis? Global Financial Governance After the 2008 Meltdown*, Oxford: Oxford University Press.

Helleiner, E. (1993) 'When finance was the servant: International capital movements in the Bretton Woods order', in P.G. Cerny (ed.) *Finance and World Politics: Markets, Regimes and States in the Post-Hegemonic Era*, Aldershot: Edward Elgar, 20–48.

Helleiner, E., Pagliari, S., and Zimmermann, H. (eds) (2010) *Global Finance in Crisis: The Politics of International Regulatory Change*, London: Routledge.

Herszenhorn, D.M. (2008) 'Administration is seeking $700 billion for Wall Street', *New York Times*, online edition, 20 September. Available at: <http://www.nytimes.com/2008/09/21/business/21cong.html?pagewanted=all> (accessed June 2014).

Heukelom, F. and Sent, E-M. (2010) 'The economics of the crisis and the crisis of economics: Lessons from behavioral economics', *Krisis: Journal of Contemporary Philosophy*, 3: 26–37.

HM Treasury (2010b) *2010 Budget—Responsibility, Freedom, Fairness: A Five Year Plan to Re-build the Economy*, June, London: The Stationery Office. Available at: <http://www.official-documents.gov.uk/document/hc1011/hc00/0061/0061.asp> (accessed June 2014).

HM Treasury (2013) *2013 Budget*, March, London: The Stationery Office. Available at: <https://www.gov.uk/government/publications/budget-2013-documents> (accessed June 2014).

HM Government (2010) *The Coalition: Our Programme for Government*. London: Cabinet Office, 20 May. Available at: <https://www.gov.uk/government/uploads/system/uploads/attachment_data/file/78977/coalition_programme_for_government.pdf> (accessed June 2014).

HM Treasury (2010a) *A New Approach to Financial Regulation: Judgement, Focus, and Stability*, July, London: The Stationery Office. Available at: <https://docs.google.com/viewer?url=https://www.gov.uk/government/uploads/system/uploads/attachment_data/file/81389/consult_financial_regulation_condoc.pdf&chrome=true> (accessed June 2014).

HM Treasury (2012) *A New Approach to Financial Regulation: Securing Stability, Protecting Consumers*, January, London: The Stationery Office. Available at: <http://webarchive.nationalarchives.gov.uk/20130319161430/http://hm-treasury.gov.uk/fin_financial_services_bill.htm> (accessed June 2014).

HM Treasury (2010c) *Spending Review 2010*, October, London: The Stationery Office. Available at: <http://www.official-documents.gov.uk/document/cm79/7942/7942.asp> (accessed June 2014).

HM Treasury and Department of Business, Innovation and Skills (2012) *Banking Reform: Delivering Stability and Supporting a Sustainable Economy*, June, London: The Stationery Office. Available at: <http://www.hm-treasury.gov.uk/d/whitepaper_banking_reform_140512.pdf> (accessed June 2014).

HM Treasury and Department of Business, Innovation and Skills (2011) *The Plan for Growth*, March, London: The Stationery Office. Available at: <https://www.gov.uk/government/publications/plan-for-growth–5> (accessed June 2014).

Hobson, J.A. (1997) *The Wealth of States: A Comparative of International Economic and Political Change*, Cambridge: Cambridge University Press.

Holmes, D.R. (2009) 'Economy of words', *Cultural Anthropology*, 24, 3: 381–419.

Holmes, D.R. (2013) *Economy of Words: Communicative Imperatives in Central Banks*, Chicago, IL: University of Chicago Press.

House of Commons Treasury Select Committee (2009) *Banking Crisis: Regulation and Supervision, Fourteenth Report of Session 2008–09*. July. London: The Stationery Office. Available at: <http://www.publications.parliament.uk/pa/cm200809/cmselect/cmtreasy/cmtreasy.htm> (accessed June 2014).

House of Representatives Committee on the Budget (2011) *The Path to Prosperity: Restoring America's Promise*, 5 April. Available at: <http://paulryan.house.gov/news/documentsingle.aspx?DocumentID=234001#.UzCcJchFBlY> (accessed June 2014).

Humphrey, T.M. and Keleher, R.E. (2002) 'The lender of last resort: A historical perspective', in C. Goodhart and G. Illing (eds) *Financial Crises, Contagion, and the Lender of Last Resort: A Reader*, Oxford: Oxford University Press, 73–108.

ICB, Independent Commission on Banking (2011) *Independent Commission on Banking Final Report: Recommendations*, September, London: Domarn Group. Available at: <http://webarchive.nationalarchives.gov.uk/+/bankingcommission.independent.gov.uk> (accessed June 2014).

IMF, International Monetary Fund (2008) *Global Financial Stability Report. Financial Stress and Deleveraging: Macro-Financial Implications and Policy*, October, Washington, DC: International Monetary Fund. Available at: <http://www.imf.org/external/pubs/ft/gfsr/2008/02/index.htm> (accessed June 2014).

IMF, International Monetary Fund (2009) *Global Financial Stability Report: Navigating the Financial Challenges Ahead*, October, Washington, DC: International Monetary Fund. Available at: <http://www.imf.org/External/Pubs/FT/GFSR/2009/02/index.htm> (accessed June 2014).

Ingham, G. (2011) *Capitalism*, 2nd edition, Cambridge: Polity Press.

Ingham, G. (2004) *The Nature of Money*, Cambridge: Polity Press.

Irwin, N. (2013) *The Alchemists: Three Central Bankers and a World on Fire*, New York: Penguin.

Jenkins, P. and Masters, B. (2011) 'Analysis: Again under strain', *Financial Times*, 8 July, 11.

Jenkinson, N. (2008) 'Strengthening regimes for controlling liquidity risk: Some lessons from the recent turmoil', Euromoney Conference on Liquidity and Funding Risk Management, London, 24 April. Available at: <http://www.bankofengland.co.uk/archive/Documents/historicpubs/speeches/2008/speech345.pdf> (accessed June 2014).

Johnson, J. (1966) 'The money = blood metaphor, 1300–1800', *The Journal of Finance*, 21, 1: 119–22.

Johnson, T. (2010) 'Prohibiting certain high-risk investment activities by banks and bank holding companies', Committee on Banking, Housing and Urban Affairs, US Senate, 2 February. Available at: <http://banking.senate.gov/public/index.cfm?FuseAction=Hearings.Hearing&Hearing_ID=54b42cc0-7ecd-4c0d-88c0-65f7d2002061> (accessed June 2014).

Jorion, P. (2007) *Value at Risk: The New Benchmark for Managing Financial Risk*, New York: McGraw Hill.

Joyce, M., Tong, M., and Woods, R. (2011) 'The United Kingdom's quantitative easing policy: Design, operation and impact', *Bank of England Quarterly Bulletin*, Q3: 200–12.

Kalthoff, H. (2005) 'Practices of calculation: Economic representations and risk management', *Theory, Culture & Society*, 22, 2: 69–97.

Kapstein, E. (1994) *Governing Global Finance: International Finance and the State*, Cambridge, MA: Harvard University Press.

Kay, J. (2010) 'Should we have "narrow banking"?', in A. Turner, A.G. Haldane, and P. Woolley (eds) *The Future of Finance: The LSE Report*, London: London School of Economics and Political Science, 208–26.

Keynes, J.M. (1964) *The General Theory of Employment, Interest and Money*, New York: Harcourt Brace.

Kiff, J. and Mills, P.S. (2007) 'Money for nothing and checks for free: Recent developments in US subprime mortgage markets', International Monetary Fund Working

Paper, WP/07/188, July. Available at: <http://www.imf.org/external/pubs/cat/long res.aspx?sk=21200.0> (accessed June 2014).

Kindleberger, C.P. (1996) *Manias, Panics and Crashes: A History of Financial Crises*, 3rd edition, New York: John Wiley & Sons.

Kindleberger, C.P. (1986) *The World in Depression, 1929–1939*, Berkeley, CA: University of California Press.

King, M. (2010) 'Banking: From Bagehot to Basel, and back again', The Second Bagehot Lecture, Buttonwood Gathering, New York, 25 October. Available at: <http://www. bis.org/review/r101028a.pdf> (accessed June 2014).

King, M. (2009) 'Letter to the Chancellor of the Exchequer', 29 January. Available at: <http://www.bankofengland.co.uk/markets/Documents/apfgovletter090129.pdf> (accessed June 2014).

King, M. (2008) 'Speech to the CBI, Institute of Directors, Leeds Chamber of Commerce and Yorkshire Forward', Leeds, 21 October. Available at: <http://www.bank ofengland.co.uk/archive/Pages/digitalcontent/historicpubs/speeches.aspx> (accessed June 2014).

Knafo, S. (2013) *The Making of Modern Finance: Liberal Governance and the Gold Standard*, London: Routledge.

Knight, F.H. (1921) *Risk, Uncertainty, and Profit*, Boston, MA: Hart, Schaffner & Marx; Houghton Mifflin Co.

Knorr Cetina, K. and Breugger, U. (2000) 'The market as an object of attachment', *Canadian Journal of Sociology*, 25, 2: 141–68.

Knorr Cetina, K. and Preda, A. (eds) (2012) *The Oxford Handbook of the Sociology of Finance*, Oxford: Oxford University Press.

Knorr Cetina, K. and Preda, A. (eds) (2005) *The Sociology of Financial Markets*, Oxford: Oxford University Press.

Kohn, D.L. (2009) 'American International Group', Committee on Banking, Housing, and Urban Affairs, US Senate, Washington, DC, 5 March. Available at: <http://www. federalreserve.gov/newsevents/testimony/kohn20090305a.htm> (accessed June 2014).

Konings, M. (2013) 'Austerity's redemptive promise', in T. Bennett (ed.) *Challenging (the) Humanities*, Melbourne: The Australian Academy of the Humanities, 117–33.

Konings, M. (2010) 'Neoliberalism and the American state', *Critical Sociology*, 36, 5: 741–65.

Krippner, G. (2011) *Capitalizing on Crisis: The Political Origins of the Rise of Finance*, Cambridge, MA: Harvard University Press.

Krippner, G. (2007) 'The making of US monetary policy: Central bank transparency and the neoliberal dilemma', *Theory and Society*, 36, 6: 477–513.

Krugman, P. (2008) 'Cash for trash', *New York Times*, online edition, 21 September. Available at: <http://www.nytimes.com/2008/09/22/opinion/22krugman.html?ex= 1379736000&en=b7e661b6c4c8c1ea&ei=5124&partner=permalink&exprod=perma link&_r=0> (accessed June 2014).

Krugman, P. (2009) 'Failure to rise', *New York Times*, online edition, 12 February. Available at: <http://www.nytimes.com/2009/02/13/opinion/13krugman.html?ref= paulkrugman> (accessed June 2014).

Kynaston, D. (2007) *Austerity Britain, 1945–1951*, London: Bloomsbury.

Lahart, J. (2007) 'In time of tumult, obscure economist gains currency', *Wall Street Journal*, online edition, 18 August. Available at: <http://online.wsj.com/news/art icles/SB118736585456901047> (accessed June 2014).

Landler, M. (2008) 'U.S. investing $250 billion in banks', *New York Times*, online edition, 14 October. Available at: <http://www.nytimes.com/2008/10/14/business/ economy/14treasury.html> (accessed June 2014).

Landler, M. and Andrews, E.L. (2008) 'For Treasury Dept., now comes hard part of bailout', *New York Times*, online edition, 4 October. Available at: <http:// www.nytimes.com/2008/10/04/business/economy/04plan.html?pagewanted=all> (accessed June 2014).

Langley, P. (2009) 'Debt, discipline and government: Foreclosure and forbearance in the sub-prime mortgage crisis', *Environment and Planning A*, 41, 6: 1404–19.

Langley, P. (2014) 'Equipping entrepreneurs: Consuming credit and credit scores', *Consumption, Markets & Culture*, DOI:10.1080/10253866.2013.849592.

Langley, P. (2008b) *The Everyday Life of Global Finance: Saving and Borrowing in Anglo-America*, Oxford: Oxford University Press.

Langley, P. (2010) 'The performance of liquidity in the sub-prime mortgage crisis', *New Political Economy*, 15, 1: 71–89.

Langley, P. (2006) 'Securitising suburbia: The transformation of Anglo-American mortgage finance', *Competition & Change*, 10, 3: 283–99.

Langley, P. (2008a) 'Sub-prime mortgage lending: A cultural economy', *Economy and Society*, 37, 4: 469–94.

Langley, P. (2002) *World Financial Orders: An Historical International Political Economy*, London: Routledge.

Lapavitsas, C. (2012) *Crisis in the Eurozone*, London: Verso.

Lapavitsas, C. (2009) 'Financialised capitalism: Crisis and financial expropriation', *Historical Materialism*, 17, 2: 114–48.

Larsen, P. and Scholtes, S. (2008) 'Macabre game of prediction begins again', *Financial Times*, 16 September, 5.

Latour, B. (2005) 'From realpolitik to dingpolitik, or how to make things public', in B. Latour and P. Weibel (eds) *Making Things Public: Atmospheres of Democracy*, Cambridge, MA: MIT Press, 4–31.

Latour, B. (1988) 'Mixing humans and nonhumans together: The sociology of a door closer', *Social Problems*, 35, 3: 298–310.

Law, J. (2009) 'Actor network theory and material semiotics', in B.S. Turner (ed.) *The New Blackwell Companion to Social Theory*, Oxford: Blackwell Publishing, 141–8.

Law, J. and Hassard, J. (eds) (1999) *Actor Network Theory and After*, Oxford and Keele: Wiley-Blackwell and the Sociological Review.

Lazzarato, M. (2012) *The Making of the Indebted Man*, Los Angeles, CA: Semiotext(e).

Leaver, A. (2012) 'Moral hazard: A mutable mobile', unpublished paper, available from the author (adam.leaver@mbs.ac.uk).

Lemke, T. (2011) *Biopolitics: An Advanced Introduction*, New York: New York University Press.

Leonhardt, D. (2009) 'Test of banks may bring hope more than fear', *New York Times*, online edition, 4 May. Available at: <http://www.nytimes.com/2009/05/04/us/politics/04stress.html?pagewanted=all> (accessed June 2014).

Levi-Faur, D. and Parker, C. (2010) 'Three narratives of the global economic crisis', *Socio-Economic Review*, 8, 3: 547–53.

Lewis, M. (2008) 'The end', *Portfolio.com*, December. Available at: <http://www.portfolio.com/news-markets/national-news/portfolio/2008/11/11/The-End-of-Wall-Streets-Boom> (accessed June 2014).

Leyshon, A. and Thrift, N. (2007) 'The capitalization of almost everything: The future of finance and capitalism', *Theory, Culture & Society*, 24, 7–8: 97–115.

Lex Column (2007) 'Defining "liquidity"', *Financial Times*, 11 August, 12.

Lex Column (2011) 'Shale of the century', *Financial Times Weekend*, 16–17 July, 34.

Lobo-Guerrero, L. (2011) *Insuring Security: Biopolitics, Security and Risk*, London: Routledge.

Lohr, S. (2008) 'Intervention is bold, but has a basis in history', *New York Times*, online edition, 14 October. Available at: <http://www.nytimes.com/2008/10/14/business/economy/14nationalize.html> (accessed June 2014).

Lowenstein, R. (2010) *The End of Wall Street*, New York: Penguin Press.

Luce, E. and Guha, K. (2009) 'Analysis: Fumble to stumble', *Financial Times Weekend*, 14–15 February, 9.

Lury, C. (2009) 'Brand as assemblage', *Journal of Cultural Economy*, 2, 1–2: 67–82.

MacKenzie, D. (2011) 'The credit crisis as a problem in the sociology of knowledge', *American Journal of Sociology*, 116, 6: 1778–841.

MacKenzie, D. (2006) *An Engine, Not a Camera: How Financial Models Shape Markets*, Cambridge, MA: MIT Press.

MacKenzie, D. (2013) 'The magic lever', *London Review of Books*, 35, 9: 16–19.

MacKenzie, D. (2009) *Material Markets: How Economic Agents are Constructed*, Oxford: Oxford University Press.

MacKenzie, D. (2005) 'Opening the black boxes of global finance', *Review of International Political Economy*, 12, 4: 555–76.

MacKenzie, D., Muniesa, F., and Siu, L. (eds) (2007) *Do Economists Make Markets? On the Performativity of Economics*, Princeton, NJ: Princeton University Press.

Macleavy, J. (2011) A 'new politics' of austerity, workfare and gender? The UK coalition government's welfare reform proposals', *Cambridge Journal of Regions, Economy and Society*, 4, 3: 355–67.

Madigan, B.F. (2009) 'Bagehot's dictum in practice: Formulating and implementing policies to combat the financial crisis', Federal Reserve Bank of Kansas City's Annual Economic Symposium, Jackson Hole, Wyoming, 21 August. Available at: <http://www.federalreserve.gov/newsevents/speech/madigan20090821a.htm> (accessed June 2014).

Mann, G. (2010a) 'Hobbes' redoubt? Toward a geography of monetary policy', *Progress in Human Geography*, 34, 5: 601–25.

Mann, G. (2010b) 'Value after Lehman', *Historical Materialism*, 18, 4: 172–88.

Marazzi, C. (2010) *The Violence of Financial Capitalism*, Los Angeles, CA: Semiotext(e).

Marron, D. (2009) *Consumer Credit in the United States: A Sociological Perspective from the Nineteenth Century to the Present*, Basingstoke: Palgrave Macmillan.

Martin, R. (2007) *An Empire of Indifference: American War and the Financial Logic of Risk Management*, Durham, NC: Duke University Press.

Massumi, B. (2005) 'The future birth of the affective fact', Genealogies of Biopolitics Conference proceedings. Available at: <http://browse.reticular.info/text/collected/massumi.pdf> (accessed June 2014).

Massumi, B. (2002) *Parables of the Virtual: Movement, Affect, Sensation*, Durham, NC: Duke University Press.

Maurer, B. (2006) 'The anthropology of money', *Annual Review of Anthropology*, 35, 15–36.

Mayhew, A. (2011) 'Money as electricity', *Journal of Cultural Economy*, 4, 3: 245–53.

McCloskey, D.M. (1998) *The Rhetoric of Economics*, Madison: University of Wisconsin Press.

McCormack, D. (2012) 'Governing economic futures through the war on inflation', *Environment and Planning A*, 44, 7: 1536–53.

McDowell, D. (2012) 'The US as "sovereign international last-resort lender": The Fed's currency swap programme during the Great Panic of 2007–09', *New Political Economy*, 17, 2: 157–78.

McFall, L. (2008) 'Commentary—rethinking cultural economy: Pragmatics and politics?', *Journal of Cultural Economy*, 1, 2: 233–7.

McFall, L. (2009) 'Devices and desires: How useful is the "new" new economic sociology for understanding market attachment?', *Sociology Compass*, 3, 2: 267–82.

McKeen-Edwards, H. and Porter, T. (2013) *Transnational Financial Associations and the Governance of Global Finance: Assembling Wealth and Power*, London: Routledge.

McNay, L. (2009) 'Self as enterprise: Dilemmas of control and resistance in Foucault's *The Birth of Biopolitics*', *Theory, Culture & Society*, 26, 6: 55–77.

Mehrling, P. (2011) *The New Lombard Street: How the Fed Became the Dealer of Last Resort*, Princeton, NJ: Princeton University Press.

Mikes, A. (2011) 'From counting risk to making risk count: Boundary-work in risk management', *Accounting, Organizations and Society*, 36, 2: 226–45.

Miller, P. (1994) 'Accounting as a social and institutional practice: An introduction', in A.G. Hopwood and P. Miller (eds) *Accounting as Social and Institutional Practice*, Cambridge: Cambridge University Press, pp. 1–39.

Miller, P. and Napier, C. (1993) 'Genealogies of calculation', *Accounting, Organizations and Society*, 18, 7–8: 631–47.

Miller, P. and Rose, N. (1990) 'Governing economic life', *Economy and Society*, 19, 1: 1–31.

Millo, Y. and MacKenzie, D. (2009) 'The usefulness of inaccurate models: Towards an understanding of the emergence of financial risk management', *Accounting, Organizations and Society*, 34, 5: 638–53.

Minsky, H.P. (1982) 'The financial-instability hypothesis: Capitalist processes and the behavior of the economy', Hyman P. Minsky Archive, Paper 282. Available at: <http://digitalcommons.bard.edu/hm_archive/282> (accessed June 2014).

Minsky, H.P. (1986) *Stabilizing an Unstable Economy*, New Haven, CT: Yale University Press.

Mirowski, P. (2002) *Machine Dreams: Economics Becomes a Cyborg Science*, Cambridge, MA: Cambridge University Press.

Mirowski, P. (2013) *Never Let a Serious Crisis Go to Waste: How Neoliberalism Survived the Financial Meltdown*, London: Verso.

Mitchell, T. (2008) 'Rethinking economy', *Geoforum*, 39, 3: 1116–21.

Moseley, F. (2013) 'The bailout of the "too big to fail" banks: Never again', in M.H. Wolfson and G.A. Epstein (eds) *The Handbook of the Political Economy of Financial Crises*, Oxford: Oxford University Press, 644–56.

Muniesa, F. and Callon, M. (2007) 'Economic experiments and the construction of markets', in D. MacKenzie, F. Muniesa, and L. Siu (eds) *Do Economists Make Markets? On the Performativity of Economics*, Princeton, NJ: Princeton University Press, 163–89.

Muniesa, F., Millo, Y., and Callon, M. (2007) 'An introduction to market devices', in M. Callon, Y. Millo, and F. Muniesa (eds) *Market Devices*, Oxford: Blackwell, 1–12.

Nakamoto, M. and Wighton, D. (2007) 'Citygroup chief stays bullish on buy-outs', *Financial Times*, online edition, 9 July. Available at: <http://www.ft.com/cms/s/0/80e2987a-2e50-11dc-821c-0000779fd2ac.html#axzz2h7hKE61S> (accessed June 2014).

NAO, National Audit Office (2009a) *HM Treasury: The Nationalisation of Northern Rock*, London: The Stationery Office. Available at: <http://www.nao.org.uk/report/hm-treasury-the-nationalisation-of-northern-rock/> (accessed June 2014).

NAO, National Audit Office (2009b) *Maintaining Financial Stability Across the United Kingdom's Banking System*, London: The Stationery Office. Available at: <http://www.nao.org.uk/report/maintaining-financial-stability-across-the-united-kingdoms-banking-system/> (accessed June 2014).

National Commission on Fiscal Responsibility and Reform (2010) *The Moment of Truth: Report of the National Commission on Fiscal Responsibility and Reform*, December. Available at: <http://www.fiscalcommission.gov/news/moment-truth-report-national-commission-fiscal-responsibility-and-reform> (accessed June 2014).

Nesvetailova, A. (2010) *Financial Alchemy in Crisis: The Great Liquidity Illusion*, London: Pluto Press.

Nesvetailova, A. (2007) *Fragile Finance: Debt, Speculation and Crisis in the Age of Global Credit*, Basingstoke: Palgrave Macmillan.

Nocera, J. (1994) *A Piece of the Action: How the Middle Class Joined the Money Class*, New York: Simon & Schuster.

Nolke, A. and Perry, J. (2006) 'The political economy of international accounting standards', *Review of International Political Economy*, 13, 4: 559–86.

Obama, B. (2011) 'Remarks by the President on fiscal policy', George Washington University, 13 April. Available at: <http://www.whitehouse.gov/the-press-office/2011/04/13/remarks-president-fiscal-policy> (accessed June 2014).

Obama, B. (2010) 'The "Volcker Rule" for financial institutions: Remarks by the President on financial reform', 21 January. Available at: <http://www.whitehouse.gov/the-press-office/remarks-president-financial-reform> (accessed June 2014).

O'Brien, J. (2011) 'Insurance, risk and the limits of sentimental representation', *Journal of Cultural Economy*, 4, 3: 285–99.

O'Connor, J. (1973) *The Fiscal Crisis of the State*, New York: St. Martin's Press.

Office of Management and Budget (2010) *Budget of the US Government*, February, Washington, DC: US Government Printing Office. Available at: <http://www.gpo.gov/fdsys/browse/collection.action?collectionCode=BUDGET&bread=true> (accessed June 2014).

Office of Management and Budget (2011) *Living Within Our Means and Investing in the Future: The President's Plan for Economic Growth and Deficit Reduction*, September, Washington, DC: Office of Management and Budget. Available at: <http://www.gpo.gov/fdsys/browse/collection.action?collectionCode=BUDGET&bread=true> (accessed June 2014).

Office of Management and Budget (2009) *A New Era of Responsibility: Renewing America's Promise*, February, Washington, DC: US Government Printing Office. Available at: <http://www.gpo.gov/fdsys/browse/collection.action?collectionCode=BUDGET&bread=true> (accessed June 2014).

O'Malley, P. (2000) 'Uncertain subjects: Risks, liberalism and contract', *Economy and Society*, 29, 4: 460–84.

O'Malley, P. (2009) 'Uncertainty makes us free: Liberalism, risk and individual security', *Behemoth: A Journal of Civilization*, 2, 3: 24–38.

Ong, A. and Collier, S.J. (eds) (2004) *Global Assemblages: Technology, Politics, and Ethics as Anthropological Problems*, Oxford: Wiley-Blackwell.

Osborne, G. (2010) 'Speech at the Lord Mayor's dinner for bankers and merchants of the City of London', Mansion House, London, 16 June. Available at: <https://www.gov.uk/government/speeches/speech-by-the-chancellor-of-the-exchequer-rt-hon-george-osborne-mp-at-mansion-house> (accessed June 2014).

Osborne, G. (2011) 'Speech at the Lord Mayor's dinner for bankers and merchants of the City of London', Mansion House, London, 15 June. Available at: <http://webarchive.nationalarchives.gov.uk/20130319161430/http://hm-treasury.gov.uk/press_58_11.htm> (accessed June 2014).

Osborne, G. (2013) 'Speech at the Lord Mayor's dinner for bankers and merchants of the City of London', Mansion House, London, 19 June. Available at: <https://www.gov.uk/government/speeches/speech-by-chancellor-of-the-exchequer-rt-hon-george-osborne-mp-mansion-house-2013> (accessed June 2014).

Panetta, F., Faeh, T., Grande, G., Ho, C., King, M., Levy, A., Signoretti, F.M., Taboga, M., and Zaghini, A. (2009) *An Assessment of Financial Sector Rescue Programmes*, BIS Papers No. 48, July 2009. Available at: <http://www.bis.org/publ/bppdf/bispap48.pdf> (accessed June 2014).

Parliamentary Commission on Banking Standards (2013) *Changing Banking for Good—Report of the Parliamentary Commission on Banking Standards, Volume I: Summary, and Conclusions and recommendations*, June, London: The Stationery Office. Available at: <http://www.parliament.uk/business/committees/committees-a-z/joint-select/professional-standards-in-the-banking-industry/news/changing-banking-for-good-report/> (accessed June 2014).

Partnoy, F. (2004) *Infectious Greed: How Deceit and Risk Corrupted the Financial Markets*, London: Profile Books.

Pasanek, B. and Polillo, S. (2011) 'After the crash, beyond liquidity', *Journal of Cultural Economy*, 4, 3: 231–8.

Paulson, H. (2010) *On the Brink: Inside the Race to Stop the Collapse of the Global Financial System*, London: Headline Publishing Group.

Paulson, H. (2008b) 'Statement by U.S. Treasury Secretary Henry Paulson following the meeting of the G7 finance ministers and central bank governors', 10 October, Washington, DC. Available at: <http://www.g8.utoronto.ca/finance/fm081010-paulson. htm> (accessed June 2014).

Paulson, H. (2008c) 'Statement by Secretary Henry M. Paulson, Jr. on actions to protect the U.S. economy', 14 October. Available at: <http://www.treasury.gov/press-center/ press-releases/Pages/hp1205.aspx> (accessed June 2014).

Paulson, H. (2008a) 'Turmoil in US credit markets: Recent actions regarding government sponsored entities, investment banks and other financial institutions', Banking Committee, US Senate, 23 September. Available at: <http://www.treasury.gov/press-center/press-releases/Pages/hp1153.aspx> (accessed June 2014).

Peck, J. (2012) 'Austerity urbanism', *City: Analysis of Urban Trends, Culture, Theory, Policy, Action*, 16, 6: 626–55.

Peck, J. (2013a) 'Explaining (with) neoliberalism', *Territory, Politics, Governance*, 1, 2: 132–57.

Peck, J. (2013b) 'Pushing austerity: State failure, municipal bankruptcy and the crises of fiscal federalism in the USA', *Cambridge Journal of Regions, Economy and Society*, 7, 1: 17–44.

Peckham, R. (2013) 'Economies of contagion: Financial crisis and pandemic', *Economy and Society*, 42, 2: 226–48.

Pierson, P. (2001) 'Coping with permanent austerity: Welfare state restructuring in affluent democracies', in P. Pierson (ed.) *The New Politics of the Welfare State*, Oxford: Oxford University Press, 410–56.

Pinch, T. and Swedberg, R. (eds) (2008) *Living in a Material World: Economic Sociology Meets Science and Technology Studies*, Cambridge, MA: MIT Press.

Pixley, J. (ed.) (2012) *New Perspectives on Emotions in Finance: The Sociology of Confidence, Fear and Betrayal*, London: Routledge.

Plender, J. (2008) 'The return of the state: How government is back at the heart of economic life', *Financial Times*, online edition, 21 August. Available at: <http://www. ft.com/cms/s/0/73dfc892-6fb2-11dd-986f-0000779fd18c.html#axzz2sLoCJm2G> (accessed June 2014).

Politi, J. (2008) 'Senators promise action this week', *Financial Times*, 1 October, 8.

Pollin, R. (2012) 'US government deficits and debt amid the great recession: What the evidence shows', *Cambridge Journal of Economics*, 36, 2: 161–87.

Poon, M. (2009) 'From New Deal institutions to capital markets: Commercial consumer risk scores and the making of subprime mortgage finance', *Accounting, Organizations and Society*, 34, 5: 654–74.

Porter, T. (1986) *The Rise of Statistical Thinking 1820–1900*, Princeton, NJ: Princeton University Press.

Porter, T. (1993) *States, Markets and Regimes in Global Finance*, New York: St. Martin's Press.

Porter, T. (ed.) (2014) *Transnational Financial Regulation After the Crisis*, London: Routledge.

Power, M. (2005) 'Enterprise risk management and the organization of uncertainty in financial institutions', in K. Knorr Cetina and A. Preda (eds) *The Sociology of Financial Markets*, Oxford: Oxford University Press, 250–68.

Power, M. (2007) *Organized Uncertainty: Designing a World of Risk Management*, Oxford: Oxford University Press.

Preda, A. (2009) *Framing Finance: The Boundaries of Markets and Modern Capitalism*, Chicago, IL: University of Chicago Press.

President's Working Group on Financial Markets (2008) *Policy Statement on Financial Market Developments*, March. Available at: <http://www.treasury.gov/resource-center/fin-mkts/Pages/Financial-Market-Policy.aspx> (accessed June 2014).

Pryke, M. and du Gay, P. (2007) 'Take an issue: Cultural economy and finance', *Economy and Society*, 36, 3: 339–54.

Quaglia, L. (2009) 'The "British Plan" as a pace-setter: The Europeanization of banking rescue plans in the EU?', *Journal of Common Market Studies*, 47, 5: 1063–83.

Rabinow, P. and Rose, N. (2003) 'Introduction: Foucault today', in P. Rabinow and N. Rose (eds) *The Essential Foucault*, New York: The New Press, pp. vii–xxxv.

Rancière, J. (2010) *Dissensus: On Politics and Aesthetics*, London: Continuum.

Rancière, J. (2011) 'The thinking of dissensus: Politics and aesthetics', in P. Bowman and R. Stamp (eds) *Reading Rancière*, London and New York: Continuum, 1–17.

Rebonato, R. (2010) *Coherent Stress Testing: A Bayesian Approach to the Analysis of Financial Risk*, Chichester: John Wiley & Sons.

Reinhart, C.M. (2011) 'Lifting the crushing burden of debt', Committee on the Budget, US House of Representatives, 10 March. Available at: <http://budget.house.gov/hearingschedule/2011hearings.htm> (accessed June 2014).

Reinhart, C.M. and Belen Sbrancia, M. (2011) 'The liquidation of government debt', National Bureau of Economic Research Working Paper 16893, March. Available at: <http://www.nber.org/papers/w16893> (accessed June 2014).

Reinhart, C.M. and Rogoff, K.S. (2010) 'Growth in a time of debt', *American Economic Review*, 100, 2: 573–8. Available at: <http://www.aeaweb.org/articles.php?doi=10.1257/aer.100.2.573> (accessed June 2014).

Reinhart, C.M. and Rogoff, K.S. (2009) *This Time is Different: Eight Centuries of Financial Folly*, Princeton, NJ: Princeton University Press.

Reinhart, V. (2011) 'A year of living dangerously: The management of the financial crisis in 2008', *Journal of Economic Perspectives*, 25, 1: 71–90.

Rethel, L. and Sinclair, T. (2012) *The Problem with Banks*, London: Zed Books.

Richardson, M., Smith, R.C., and Walter, I. (2011) 'Large banks and the Volcker rule', in V.V. Acharaya, T.F. Cooley, M.P. Richardson, and I. Walter (eds) *Regulating Wall Street: The Dodd-Frank Act and the New Architecture of Global Finance*, Hoboken, NJ: John Wiley & Sons, 181–212.

Riles, A. (2011) *Collateral Knowledge: Legal Reasoning in the Global Financial Markets*, Chicago, IL: University of Chicago Press.

Rockoff, H. (2011) 'Parallel journeys', *Journal of Cultural Economy*, 4, 3: 255–83.

Rotman, B. (1987) *Signifying Nothing: The Semiotics of Zero*, Stanford, CA: Stanford University Press.

Rushton, E.W. (2007) 'Mortgage market turmoil: Causes and consequences', Committee on Banking, Housing, and Urban Affairs, US Senate, 22 March. Available at: <http://www.banking.senate.gov/public/index.cfm?FuseAction=Hearings.Testimony&Hearing_ID=4ccca4e6-b9dc-40b1-bab5-137b3a77364d&Witness_ID=851bc77b-51d6-4931-ade5-ccfc32d54c9b> (accessed June 2014).

Ryan, T. (2008) 'A lesson from the savings and loans rescue', *Financial Times*, 25 September, 19.

Sandhu, K., Stephenson, M., and Harrison, J. (2013) *Layers of Inequality: A Human Rights and Equality Impact Assessment of the Public Spending Cuts on Black Asian and Minority Ethnic Women in Coventry*, Coventry: University of Warwick.

Savat, D. (2009) 'Deleuze's objectile: From discipline to modulation', in M. Poster and D. Savat (eds) *Deleuze and New Technology*, Edinburgh: Edinburgh University Press, 45–62.

Sawyer, M. (2012) 'The tragedy of UK fiscal policy in the aftermath of the financial crisis', *Cambridge Journal of Economics*, 36, 2: 205–21.

Schäfer, A. and Streeck, W. (2013) 'Introduction: Politics in the age of austerity', in A. Schäfer and W. Streeck (eds) *Politics in the Age of Austerity*, Cambridge: Polity Press, 1–25.

Scholes, M.S. (2011) 'Foreword', in V.V. Acharaya, T.F. Cooley, M.P. Richardson, and I. Walter (eds) *Regulating Wall Street: The Dodd-Frank Act and the New Architecture of Global Finance*, Hoboken, NJ: John Wiley & Sons, xi–xvi.

Schumpeter, J. (1950) *Capitalism, Socialism and Democracy*, New York: Harper Torchbooks.

SEC, Securities and Exchange Commission (2008) 'SEC halts short selling of financial stocks to protect investors and markets', 19 September. Available at: <http://www.sec.gov/news/press/2008/2008-211.htm> (accessed June 2014).

Sengupta, R. and Tam, Y.M. (2008) 'The LIBOR-OIS spread as a summary indicator', *Federal Reserve Bank of St. Louis Economic Synopses*, Number 25. Available at <http://research.stlouisfed.org/publications/es/08/ES0825.pdf> (accessed June 2014).

Shiller, R. (2001) *Irrational Exuberance*, Princeton, NJ: Princeton University Press.

Shiller, R. (2008) *The Subprime Solution: How Today's Global Financial Crisis Happened, and What to Do About It*, Princeton, NJ: Princeton University Press.

Shin, H.S. (2010) *Risk and Liquidity (Clarendon Lectures in Finance)*, Oxford: Oxford University Press.

Simmel, G. (2004) *The Philosophy of Money*, 3rd edition, ed. D.Frisby, trans. T. Bottomore and D. Frisby, London: Routledge.

Skidelsky, R. (2009) 'Keynesian reforms could stop us falling into more economic foxholes', *The Sunday Telegraph*, 30 August, 15.

Skidelsky, R. (2011) 'The relevance of Keynes', *Cambridge Journal of Economics*, 35, 1: 1–13.

Smith, S.J. (2008) 'Owner occupation: At home with a hybrid of money and materials', *Environment and Planning A*, 40, 3: 520–35.

Soederberg, S. (2013) 'The US debtfare state and the credit card industry: Forging spaces of dispossession', *Antipode*, 45, 2: 493–512.

Sombart, W. (1967) *The Quintessence of Capitalism*, trans. M. Epstein, New York: Howard Fertig.

Sorge, M. (2004) 'Stress-testing financial systems: An overview of current methodologies', BIS Working Paper No. 165, December. Available at: <http://www.bis.org/publ/work165.pdf> (accessed June 2014).

Sorkin, A. (2010) *Too Big to Fail: Inside the Battle to Save Wall Street*, London: Penguin.

Sorkin, A. (2012) 'The Volker rule and the costs of good intentions', *New York Times*, 13 February, online edition. Available at: <http://dealbook.nytimes.com/2012/02/13/the-volcker-rule-and-the-costs-of-good-intentions/> (accessed June 2014).

Soros, G. (2008) 'Paulson cannot be allowed a blank cheque', *Financial Times*, 25 September, 19.

Stern, G.H. and Feldman, R.J. (2004) *Too Big to Fail: The Hazards of Bank Bailouts*, Washington, DC: Brookings Institution Press.

Stewart, H. and Inman, P. (2012) 'Autumn statement 2012: Austerity will last until 2018, admits George Osborne', *Guardian*, online edition, 5 December. Available at: <http://www.theguardian.com/uk/2012/dec/05/osborne-admits-austerity-until-2018> (accessed June 2014).

Stewart, J.B. (2011) 'Volcker rule, once simple, now boggles', *New York Times*, online edition, 21 October. Available at: <http://www.nytimes.com/2011/10/22/business/volcker-rule-grows-from-simple-to-complex.html?pagewanted=all&_r=0> (accessed June 2014).

Stiglitz, G. (2008b) 'A better bailout', *The Nation*, 26 September. Available at: <http://www.countercurrents.org/stiglitz270908.htm> (accessed June 2014).

Stiglitz, J.E. (2008a) 'The triumphant return of John Maynard Keynes', *Project Syndicate*, December. Available at: <http://www.project-syndicate.org/commentary/the-triumphant-return-of-john-maynard-keynes> (accessed June 2014).

Stokes, D. (2014) 'Achilles' deal: Dollar decline and US grand strategy after the crisis', *Review of International Political Economy*, DOI:10.1080/09692290.2013.779592.

Strange, S. (1986) *Casino Capitalism*, Oxford: Blackwell.

Swedberg, R. (2012) 'The role of confidence in finance', in K. Knorr Cetina and A. Preda (eds) *The Oxford Handbook of the Sociology of Finance*, Oxford: Oxford University Press, 529–43.

Taleb, N.N. (2007) *The Black Swan: The Impact of the Highly Improbable*, London: Penguin.

Taleb, N.N. (2009) 'The risks of financial modeling: VaR and the economic meltdown', Committee on Science, Space, and Technology, US House of Representatives, 10 September. Available at: <http://science.house.gov/hearing/subcommittee-investigations-and-oversight-hearing-risks-financial-modeling> (accessed June 2014).

Tarullo, D.K. (2009b) 'Confronting too big to fail', Exchequer Club, Washington, DC, 21 October. Available at: <http://www.federalreserve.gov/newsevents/speech/tarullo20091021a.htm> (accessed June 2014).

Tarullo, D.K. (2009a) 'In the wake of the crisis', Phoenix Metropolitan Area Community Leaders' Luncheon, Phoenix, Arizona, 8 October. Available at: <http://www.

federalreserve.gov/newsevents/speech/tarullo20091008a.htm> (accessed June 2014).

Tarullo, D.K. (2010) 'Lessons from the Crisis Stress Tests', Federal Reserve Board International Research Forum on Monetary Policy, Washington, DC, 26 March. Available at: <http://www.federalreserve.gov/newsevents/speech/tarullo20100326a.pdf> (accessed June 2014).

Tarullo, D.K. (2012) 'The Volcker rule', Subcommittee on Capital Markets and Government Sponsored Enterprises and the Subcommittee on Financial Institutions and Consumer Credit, Committee on Financial Services, US House of Representatives, Washington, DC, 18 January. Available at: <http://www.federalreserve.gov/newsevents/testimony/tarullo20120118a.htm> (accessed June 2014).

Taylor, J.B. (2009) *Getting Off Track: How Government Actions and Interventions Caused, Prolonged, and Worsened the Financial Crisis*. Stanford, CA: Hoover Institution.

Taylor, M.C. (2004) *Confidence Games: Money and Markets in a World Without Redemption*, Chicago, IL: University of Chicago Press.

Terranova, T. (2009) 'Another life: The nature of political economy in Foucault's genealogy of biopolitics', *Theory, Culture & Society*, 26, 6: 234–62.

Tett, G. (2009) *Fool's Gold: How Unrestrained Greed Corrupted a Dream, Shattered Global Markets and Unleashed a Catastrophe*, London: Little & Brown.

Tett, G. (2008) 'RTC repeat may not end the drama', *Financial Times*, 20–1 September, 2.

Thomas, L.B (2013) *The Financial Crisis and Federal Reserve Policy*, New York: Palgrave Macmillan.

Thompson, G. (2013) 'Activist central banking and its possible consequences', Copenhagen Business School Working Paper in Business and Politics, No. 80. Available at: <http://research.cbs.dk/en/publications/uuid(e41cdca5-fecb-40fa-ab55-8ac41b40f1bd).html> (accessed June 2014).

Thompson, J.B. (2012) 'The metamorphosis of a crisis', in M. Castells, J. Caraça, and G. Cardosa (eds) *Aftermath: The Cultures of the Economic Crisis*, Oxford: Oxford University Press, 59–81.

Thornhill, J. (2008) 'Sarkozy sets out bigger state role', *Financial Times*, online edition, 25 September. Available at: <http://www.ft.com/cms/s/0/58bc11e4-8b35-11dd-b634-0000779fd18c.html#axzz2XDsTbkxM> (accessed June 2014).

Thornton, H. (2002) 'An enquiry into the nature and effects of the paper credit of Great Britain' (excerpts), in C. Goodhart and G. Illing (eds) *Financial Crises, Contagion, and the Lender of Last Resort: A Reader*, Oxford: Oxford University Press, 57–66.

Thrift, N. (2008) *Non-representational Theory: Space, Politics, Affect*, London and New York: Routledge.

Triana, P. (2012) *The Number that Killed Us: A Story of Modern Banking, Flawed Mathematics, and a Big Financial Crisis*, Hoboken, NJ: John Wiley & Sons, Inc.

Trichet, J-C. (2010) 'Stimulate no more—it is now time for all to tighten', *Financial Times*, online edition, 22 July. Available at: <http://www.ft.com/cms/s/0/1b3ae97e-95c6-11df-b5ad-00144feab49a.html#axzz2vHnnPQSs> (accessed June 2014).

Tucker, P. (2009) 'The repertoire of official section interventions in the financial system: Last resort lending, market-making, and capital', 2009 International Conference: Financial System and Monetary Policy, Bank of Japan, 27–8 May. Available at:

<http://www.bankofengland.co.uk/archive/Pages/digitalcontent/historicpubs/speeches.aspx> (accessed June 2014).

Tucker, P., Hall, S., and Pattani, A. (2013) 'Macroprudential policy at the Bank of England', *Bank of England Quarterly Bulletin*, Q3: 192–200.

Turner, A. (2009c) 'How to tame global finance', *Prospect*. Available at: <http://www.prospectmagazine.co.uk/magazine/how-to-tame-global-finance/#.UtPTm8hFAcA> (accessed June 2014).

Turner, A. (2009b) 'Mansion House speech', The City Banquet, The Mansion House, London, 22 September. Available at: <http://www.fsa.gov.uk/pages/Library/Communication/Speeches/2009/0922_at.shtml> (accessed June 2014).

Turner, A. (2009a) *The Turner Review: A Regulatory Response to the Global Financial Crisis*, March, London: Financial Services Authority. Available at: <http://www.fsa.gov.uk/pages/Library/Corporate/turner/index.shtml> (accessed June 2014).

Turner, A. (2010) 'What do banks do, what should they do, and what public policies are needed to ensure best results for the real economy?', CASS Business School, 17 March. Available at: <http://www.fsa.gov.uk/library/communication/speeches/2010/0317_at.shtml> (accessed June 2014).

Turner, A., Haldane, A.G., and Wooley, P. (eds) (2010) *The Future of Finance: The LSE Report*, London: London School of Economics and Political Science.

US Senate Permanent Subcommittee on Investigations (2011) *Wall Street and the Financial Crisis: Anatomy of a Financial Collapse*, 13 April. Available at: <http://www.levin.senate.gov/newsroom/press/release/us-senate-investigations-subcommittee-releases-levin-coburn-report-on-the-financial-crisis> (accessed June 2014).

US Treasury Department (2008a) 'Fact sheet: Proposed Treasury authority to purchase troubled assets', 20 September. Available at: <http://www.treasury.gov/press-center/press-releases/Pages/hp1150.aspx> (accessed June 2014).

US Treasury Department (2009a) 'Fact sheet: Public-Private Investment Program', 23 March. Available at: <http://www.treasury.gov/press-center/press-releases/Pages/tg65.aspx> (accessed June 2014).

US Treasury Department (2008c) 'Joint Statement by Treasury, Federal Reserve and the FDIC', November 23. Available at: <http://www.treasury.gov/press-center/press-releases/Pages/hp1287.aspx> (accessed June 2014).

US Treasury Department (2009c) 'Joint statement by Treasury Secretary Timothy F. Geithner, Chairman of the Board of Governors of the Federal Reserve System Ben Bernanke, Chairman of the Federal Deposit Insurance Corporation Sheila Bair, Comptroller of the Currency John C. Dugan, and Director of the Office of Thrift Supervision John M. Reich', 10 February. Available at: <http://www.treasury.gov/press-center/press-releases/Pages/tg21.aspx> (accessed June 2014).

US Treasury Department (2008b) 'Statement by Secretary Henry M. Paulson, Jr. on Treasury and Federal Housing Finance Agency action to protect financial markets and taxpayers', 7 September. Available at: <http://www.treasury.gov/press-center/press-releases/Pages/hp1129.aspx> (accessed June 2014).

US Treasury Department (2009b) 'Treasury, Federal Reserve and the FDIC provide assistance to Bank of America', 16 January. Available at: <http://www.treasury.gov/press-center/press-releases/Pages/hp1356.aspx> (accessed June 2014).

US Treasury Department (2008d) 'US Government actions to strengthen market stability', 14 October. Available at: <http://www.treasury.gov/press-center/press-releases/Pages/hp1209.aspx> (accessed June 2014).

Vogel, S. (2010) 'A socio-economic perspective on the financial crisis', *Socio-Economic Review*, 8, 3: 553–7.

Volcker, P. (2009) 'Experts' perspectives on systemic risk and resolution issues', Committee on Banking and Financial Services, House of Representatives, 24 September. Available at: <http://democrats.financialservices.house.gov/Hearings/hearingDetails.aspx?NewsID=1133> (accessed June 2014).

Volcker, P. (2010) 'Prohibiting certain high-risk investment activities by banks and bank holding companies', Committee on Banking, Housing, and Urban Affairs, US Senate, 2 February. Available at: <http://www.banking.senate.gov/public/index.cfm?FuseAction=Hearings.Testimony&Hearing_ID=54b42cc0-7ecd-4c0d-88c0-65f7d2002061&Witness_ID=091f5a89-dec4-4905-9fa1-678bfbec823a> (accessed June 2014).

Walker, J. and Cooper, M. (2011) 'Genealogies of resilience: From systems ecology to the political economy of crisis adaptation', *Security Dialogue*, 42, 2: 143–60.

Walters, W. (2006) 'Border/control', *European Journal of Social Theory*, 9, 2: 187–204.

Watson, M. (2009) '"Habitation vs. improvement": A Polanyian perspective on bank bail-outs', *Politics* 29, 3: 183–92.

Watt, N. (2011) 'David Cameron beats a hasty retreat over call for voters to pay down debts', *Guardian*, online edition, 5 October. Available at: <http://www.theguardian.com/politics/2011/oct/05/david-cameron-conference-speech-rewrite> (accessed June 2014).

Weber, M. (1978) *Economy and Society*, Berkeley, CA: University of California Press.

Weitzman, H. (2008) 'Volatility traders come into their own in turbulent times', *Financial Times*, 14 October, 43.

Widmaier, W.W. (2010) 'Emotions before paradigms: Elite anxiety and populist resentment from the Asian to subprime crises', *Millennium: Journal of International Studies*, 39, 1: 127–44.

Wigan, D. (2009) 'Financialisation and derivatives: Constructing an artifice of indifference', *Competition & Change*, 13, 2: 157–72.

Winters, B. (2012) *Review of the Bank of England's Framework for Providing Liquidity to the Banking System*, presented to the Court of the Bank of England, October. Available at: <http://www.bankofengland.co.uk/about/Pages/courtreviews/default.aspx> (accessed June 2014).

Wolf, M. (2008a) *Fixing Global Finance*, Baltimore, MD: Johns Hopkins University Press.

Wolf, M. (2008b) 'Why Paulson's plan is not a true solution to the crisis', *Financial Times*, 24 September, 19.

Wolin, N. (2010) 'Prohibiting certain high-risk investment activities by banks and bank holding companies', Committee on Banking, Housing, and Urban Affairs, US Senate, 2 February. Available at: <http://banking.senate.gov/public/index.cfm?FuseAction=Hearings.Hearing&Hearing_ID=54b42cc0-7ecd-4c0d-88c0-65f7d2002061> (accessed June 2014).

Woolgar, S., Coopmans, C., and Neyland, D. (2009) 'Does STS mean business?', *Organization*, 16, 1: 5–30.

Bibliography

Zaloom, C. (2008) 'How to read the future: The yield curve, affect, and financial prediction', *Public Culture*, 21, 2: 245–68.

Žižek, S. (2011) 'Žižek in Wall Street—Transcript', *Critical Legal Thinking*, 11 October. Available at: <http://criticallegalthinking.com/2011/10/11/zizek-in-wall-street-transcript/#more-4415> (accessed June 2014).

Index

Index

Printed and bound by CPI Group (UK) Ltd, Croydon, CR0 4YY